IBM Cognos 8 Planning

A practical guide to developing and deploying planning models for your enterprise

Ned Riaz

Jason Edwards

Rich Babaran

PUBLISHING

BIRMINGHAM - MUMBAI

IBM Cognos 8 Planning

First published: July 2009

Production Reference: 1240709

Published by Packt Publishing Ltd.
32 Lincoln Road
Olton
Birmingham, B27 6PA, UK.

ISBN 978-1-847196-84-2

www.packtpub.com

Cover Image by Filippo Sarti (filosarti@tiscali.it)

Credits

Authors
Ned Riaz

Jason Edwards

Rich Babaran

Reviewers
Steve Ladd

Sascha Mertens

Acquisition Editor
James Lumsden

Development Editor
Siddharth Mangarole

Technical Editors
Aanchal Kumar

Akshara Aware

Bhupali Khule

Editorial Team Leader
Akshara Aware

Project Team Leader
Lata Basantani

Project Coordinator
Joel Goveya

Indexer
Monica Ajmera

Proofreader
Dirk Manuel

Production Coordinator
Adline Swetha Jesuthas

Cover Work
Adline Swetha Jesuthas

About the Authors

Ned Riaz Ned Riaz is a Certified IBM Cognos Planning expert and principal partner at Agile Strategic Business Consulting, a consulting company that specializes in IBM Cognos Planning and Business Intelligence implementations.

Ned has obtained a B.S. degree in Accounting and Management Information Systems, and he passed the CPA (Certified Public Accountant) exam after finishing his degree. After finishing his education, Ned worked as an auditor, accountant, and finance director in many industries, such as banks, software reselling, and entertainment. He became involved in system development work in the late nineties, and deployed various medium-sized accounting and general ledger systems.

Ned joined Adaytum Software, the original manufacturer of Planning products, in late 1999 when Adaytum had less than 50 employees. He has been working with Planning products since Contributor 1.1 and Analyst 2.2 were released in early 2000. While working with Adaytum, Ned designed and built many Planning models for a wide range of customers.

During his days in Adaytum and Cognos, Ned designed and deployed models and systems for many large fortune 500 companies in various industries, such as pharmaceutical, hospital, aircraft operations, and retailers.

As a partner/employee of Agile Strategic Business Consulting, Ned has been involved in designing and deploying various models and systems at a large information delivery corporation since 2006.

Ned and his wife live in Central Minnesota. He enjoys cycling, badminton, and volunteering with rescued rabbits. He can be contacted at ned.riaz@ agilestrategic.com and on the Web at www.agilestrategic.com.

For their collaboration and insight, I would like to thank co-authors Jason Edwards and Rich Babaran. Having open communication between all co-authors greatly facilitated the writing of this book. In addition, I would like to thank the staff at Packt for providing the opportunity to write this book, as well as for their editors' guidance in editing and streamlining core concepts.

I would also like to thank my wife for her support during the writing of this book, and for helping me proof read and edit the book's contents.

Jason Edwards is a Certified IBM Cognos Planning expert and founding partner at Agile Strategic Business Consulting, a consulting company that specializes in IBM Cognos Planning and Business Intelligence implementations.

Jason has ten years of experience in application design and development by using corporate performance planning software in a broad range of industries, such as telecommunications, retail, pharmaceutical, and entertainment. He specializes in all phases of the development life cycle including requirements gathering, design, development, and deployment. With efficiency and resourcefulness, Jason has effectively led and managed highly successful IBM Cognos Planning implementations for clients in Europe and the United States.

Jason holds a Bachelor's degree in accounting and finance from Kingston Business School in the U.K. He started his career by modeling complex financial systems in spreadsheets. It was while working as an International Business Analyst for a global interactive games publisher a decade ago that he acquired his experience of the dynamic and powerful corporate performance planning software Adaytum (IBM Cognos Planning). From then on, Jason's passion for modeling sophisticated forecasting systems led him into a career of consultancy devoted to helping clients utilize the power of IBM Cognos Planning to achieve their organizational goals.

Jason believes that his dual expertise and experience in finance and information technology and his ability in building strong client relationships has helped him develop highly successful user accepted software solutions using IBM Cognos Planning.

Jason lives with his wife and daughter in Philadelphia. He enjoys recreational sports, such as cycling, soccer, and tennis and takes pleasure in exploring the great restaurants and parks of Philadelphia with his family and friends.

Jason is continually looking for new opportunities and challenges and can be contacted at jason.edwards@agilestrategic.com and on the Web at www.agilestrategic.com.

I would like to thank my highly talented co-authors and extend my sincere gratitude to the production team at Packt. I would especially like to thank my wife, family, and friends for their patience and their continued support and encouragement.

It was a pleasure to have co-authored this book with Ned Riaz and Rich Babaran. I am certain that this book will be of great help to anyone who is interested in understanding the techniques of application development using IBM Cognos Planning.

Rich Babaran has over 20 years of experience in financial modeling and analysis, corporate planning, performance measurement development, workflow modeling, and process improvement. He has spent the last 9 years helping Fortune 500 companies improve their planning processes using IBM Cognos Planning. In addition to architecting complete end-to-end planning solutions, Rich has helped clients turnaround critical implementations by applying innovative techniques learned from years of working in challenging environments. Rich has a degree in Management Economics at the Ateneo de Manila University and an MBA at the University of Illinois at Chicago. Rich can be contacted at rich.babaran@gmail.com.

My gratitude goes to Packt Publishing for giving us the opportunity to write this book and to my co-authors from whom I have learned a great deal. Also, I would like to thank the editors, reviewers, and the rest of the Packt crew who made our work better than we could have done alone. Most of all, I am grateful to my wife, who patiently endured my absence as I poured my time into this book. Her encouragements got me through the long hard days. If I stand tall, it's only because of the rock that I stand on.

Acknowledgment

The authors would like to extend their thanks to Janosys Inc. for their gracious support in the development of this book. Janosys Inc. is an authorized re-seller and services provider of IBM (Cognos Software), and would like to thank IBM for allowing us to use the product to build examples in this book. Amar Chabra is the president of Janosys Inc.

During his 15+ years of tenure at Cognos (now owned by IBM) and as a founder of Janosys, Inc. he has successfully deployed numerous Enterprise Planning (EP) and Business Intelligence (BI) Solutions in various industries across the USA.

Amar can be reached at achabra@janosys.com or at the web site www.janosys.com

About the Reviewers

Steve Ladd is a Certified Cognos Planning Solution Designer, and a Senior Consultant with a performance management consulting firm. He has 10 years of technology experience, with a focus on performance management systems.

Steve is a seasoned (PMP certified) project manager who has led the development of a diverse set of software solutions including financial planning, financial reporting, and business intelligence systems. His experience includes working with accounting, finance, operations, and IT in multiple industries, including retail, insurance, and healthcare. His technical proficiencies include web development, ETL design, and OLAP data modeling.

Steve lives in Austin, Texas with his wife Marisa and son Tyson. He is available for consulting work and may be contacted at `Steve.Ladd@Gmail.com`.

Sascha Mertens graduated from German University for Applied Sciences (HS Niederrhein) in 2001 as an engineer of Economics. Focusing on the business part of his degree, he began to work with Corporate Performance Management (CPM) topics in his thesis on 'Redesign of a controlling system by means of a Management Information System (MIS).'

When he started working at Deloitte in 2001, he was trained and certified in Analyst and Contributor by Adaytum—the original software producer—before they were acquired by Cognos and subsequently by IBM. With his gained knowledge, Sascha started working for the first German planning project with Volkswagen Financial Services AG, which was brought up to a status that is still live today. While this project was realized on a nearly full Analyst model with several thousand Analyst objects storing actual and plan data, he proceeded to grow himself with Cognos Planning and its development in the direction of web technology.

Once Sascha encountered the magic and the fun of translating the business requirements of CFOs and CIOs into powerful, full-blown, and integrated information systems, he continued to contribute his knowledge to many different projects. Through the modeling of system designs and architectural concepts, as well as their implementations into CPM systems, Sascha developed all kinds of planning models, such as sales planning, cost planning, personnel planning, and so on, up to the resulting financial plans.

Working closely with Cognos, Sascha became a beta tester for several upcoming Planning releases, and a community leader in one of the leading Cognos Planning forums on the Internet. With a deep knowledge of the system internals, he developed his own documentation tool for Cognos Planning systems which connects an interactive online documentation of an IBM Cognos Analyst to IBM Cognos Connection, and this is now used by a wide variety of his clients. With a strong focus on the conceptual and business side, he conducted a study for the 'State of planning within German companies' (*Standortbestimmung zur Planung in deutschen Unternehmen*) and offered various public webcasts, such as 'planning scenarios and simulations on board level', 'business planning for health insurance companies', 'decentralized sales planning within the franchise industry', and 'driver-based planning within a fleet management company'.

During his time with Deloitte, Sascha progressed his way to a senior managing level and designed and implemented Cognos Planning on a full-time basis in over 15 Cognos Planning and BI projects nationally, in Europe, and overseas, in the last six years. These covered nearly all kinds of industries with a concentration in the financial, biotech, and manufacturing industry and the public sector, spanning IT systems from a single server environment to huge service infrastructures holding more than 30 Planning servers that deliver services to more than 100 financial institutes. In 2006 and 2007, he designed and modeled Cognos Planning for the Austrian ministry of finance and implemented a planning system that was capable of planning the national budget of the whole country.

Since 2008, Sascha has worked for Conunit, a consulting firm specializing in CPM and BI solutions and the 'Cognos Partner of the year 2008 for Germany and Europe'. Within Conunit, Sascha and his team continue the Cognos Planning story with an offering of all kind of services around the IBM Cognos CPM and BI products, including full-scope projects (concept, design and implementation), version upgrades and their migrations, as well as performance enhancements and system improvement checks.

It was a great pleasure reviewing this book. I am sure that it will essentially help you to set up a planning system in your company.

I would also like to thank some great people from Deloitte and Cognos whom I worked with in collaborative projects, and who helped me gain experience with the product and all of the topics around CPM.

Table of Contents

Preface

In this book we provide you with a comprehensive introduction to the design and development of planning models using IBM Cognos Planning. We have divided the book into four parts. The first part (Chapters 1-3) provides a compelling argument for improving your enterprise planning process, and introduces you to the IBM Cognos Planning suite and the model development process. The second part (Chapters 4-7) discusses model building in detail. The third part discusses the web development process (Chapters 8-13). The fourth part (Chapters 14-16) covers maintenance and automation of the planning models.

What this book covers

Chapter 1 states the objective of this book and its intended audience. We uncover the most common issues that organizations face with their planning processes, including the difficulties of a spreadsheet-based planning environment. We introduce you to IBM Cognos Planning and how it addresses some of the most pervasive problems in today's business organizations. We talk about the benefits of IBM Cognos Planning in its role in Corporate Performance Management (CPM).

Chapter 2 gives an overview of the various IBM Cognos tools and their practical application. We provide a brief overview of each tool, and then illustrate the application of each tool by using the example of a regional restaurant chain.

Chapter 3 gives an overview of the model development process. We explain some of the important considerations before embarking on IBM Cognos Planning project. We discuss three important principles of model building and walk you through the main phases in building a planning model, including designing the model in Analyst, deploying the model using Contributor, and automating and maintaining some of the administrative tasks.

Chapter 4 describes the Analyst interface and teach you how to navigate and work with objects within Analyst. We explain in detail how you can use libraries to organize objects. Finally, we discuss various administration functions that can help you to manage libraries, optimize Analyst, search for BIFs and ODBC connections, and fix corrupt index files and references.

Chapter 5 covers the D-List in detail. We show you how to create and update a D-List from many different sources. We demonstrate how to add formulas into items in the D-List and resolve calculation conflicts and circular references. We show you how to format D-List items as numeric, text, and date data types. We explain the different categories of D-Lists and how they should be ordered in a D-Cube.

Chapter 6 demonstrates how data is stored in IBM Cognos Planning. We discuss the importance of the order of dimensions in enforcing calculation and format priorities. We teach you how to view multiple slices of the cube and how to save a selection of the cube as a separate object. We teach you how to restructure the dimensions of the cube by adding, deleting, substituting, and reordering dimensions. We cover some of the important functions available for the D-Cube, including global formatting, exporting, and other options that can make it easier for you to work with the program. We illustrate how to use data entry commands that will enable you to enter data, execute mathematical operations, or set restrictions on a cell, a range of cells, or the entire cube. Finally we introduce Breakback, a powerful feature that allows you to cascade changes throughout the cube by simply making a change to a calculated item.

Chapter 7 explains how to move data by using D-Links. We discuss the basic steps of creating a D-Link and the things that you need to think about when you move data. We show you how to connect to sources outside of Analyst in order to bring data into the D-Cube. We go through two special types of D-Links: Lookup D-Links and Accumulation D-Links. We demonstrate how we can use a virtual dimension to move data effectively and efficiently. We introduce you to the A-Table, an object that allows you to map dimension items between a data source and a D-Cube, using a variety of tools. Finally, we show you the various D-Link options that enable you to perform advanced tasks when using the D-Link.

Chapter 8 explains the purpose and capabilities of the Web-based and Windows-based components of IBM Cognos Planning. We also discuss the 3-tier architecture of IBM Cognos Planning, namely the Web Server, the Application, and the Data Tier. Lastly, we list and describe the functions of the Contributor Administration Console, toolbars, menu items, and the Tree.

Chapter 9 discusses the process of creating and configuring a Contributor application before deploying it on the Web for budgeting and forecasting. We also describe the need for application synchronization after changing the Analyst model. Finally, we look at the Contributor extensions that are available for extending the Contributor administrative and client functionality.

Chapter 10 covers various features of IBM Cognos Planning that pertain to securing and controlling the Contributor web client templates. First, we discuss the role of the e.List and rights configuration in securing a planning application. We show how to create and import the e.List and rights information. Then, we cover data and content security. We talk about the importance of access tables in securing Contributor web client template contents. We also demonstrate the purpose of the saved selections in defining access tables. Next, we discuss data validation and how to set up this important feature. Lastly, we briefly cover how the cut-down function can improve the performance of Contributor web client templates.

Chapter 11 describes various methods for importing data into a Contributor application from external sources.

Chapter 12 demonstrates the Contributor workflow process and how to use the Contributor Web Client and the Contributor Excel Add-in to enter budget and forecast data.

Chapter 13 teaches you how to create publish containers; how the two different publish layouts—the Table-only Layout and the View Layout—work; and the impact of the changing e.List, models, and dimension for publish, on publishing and reporting. We demonstrate how to produce real-time reporting by publishing the application as a package, and how to use IBM Cognos Planning Contributor as a data source in Framework Manager. Lastly, we describe the process of creating a Framework Manager model using the Contributor's Framework Manager Extension.

Chapter 14 shows you how to completely automate common tasks in Analyst, such as importing and exporting data from the model by using Analyst macros. We teach you how to give users rights to Analyst libraries and also to the objects contained in these libraries. Finally, we take a look at how Planning Manager can be used to illustrate the Analyst model data flow and to build custom menu screens so that users can easily navigate around the model.

Chapter 15 shows you how Contributor macros can be created and scheduled to automate administrative tasks such as the import and publishing of data. We demonstrate how to schedule these macros to run in IBM Cognos Connection or from a batch file. We also look at how to set up rights so that Contributor Administrators can perform specific administrative functions. Finally, we look at jobs, job clusters, and job servers.

Chapter 16 discusses the topic of IBM Cognos security, explaining the concepts of authentication, authorization, and the IBM Cognos 8 namespace. We also recapitulate how security is configured in Analyst and Contributor.

What you need for this book

To realize the full benefit of this book, you must be familiar with spreadsheets and must have done some modeling using this tool. Much of the subject of this book makes a distinction between IBM Cognos Planning and the spreadsheet-based planning process. It also helps to have basic understanding of data structures and some working knowledge of the standard query language, SQL. This book does not cover installation and configuration of the software. Please refer to the IBM support web site for instructions on installation this software, as well as the other software pre-requisites necessary for this IBM Cognos Planning to run.

Who this book is for

This book is written for first-time developers wanting an introduction to IBM Cognos Planning. It gives clear and easy-to-understand instructions on how to design, build, and deploy Planning models focusing only on the essential tools that you need to know. It is for anyone who wants to understand IBM Cognos Planning and make a transition to this tool from elsewhere.

Conventions

In this book, you will find a number of styles of text that distinguish between different kinds of information. Here are some examples of these styles, and an explanation of their meaning.

Code words in text are shown as follows: "So if the file is called `products.txt`, it would be appropriate to name the File Map as Products."

New terms and **important words** are shown in bold. Words that you see on the screen, in menus or dialog boxes for example, appear in our text like this: "Open the **Contributor Administration Console** from Windows **Start** button".

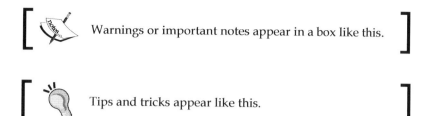

Warnings or important notes appear in a box like this.

Tips and tricks appear like this.

Reader feedback

Feedback from our readers is always welcome. Let us know what you think about this book—what you liked or may have disliked. Reader feedback is important for us to develop titles that you really get the most out of.

To send us general feedback, simply drop an email to feedback@packtpub.com, and mention the book title in the subject of your message.

If there is a book that you need and would like to see us publish, please send us a note in the **SUGGEST A TITLE** form on www.packtpub.com or email suggest@packtpub.com.

If there is a topic that you have expertise in and you are interested in either writing or contributing to a book, see our author guide on www.packtpub.com/authors.

Customer support

Now that you are the proud owner of a Packt book, we have a number of things to help you to get the most from your purchase.

Downloading the example code for the book

Visit http://www.packtpub.com/files/code/6842_Code.zip to directly download the example code.

The downloadable files contain instructions on how to use them.

Errata

Although we have taken every care to ensure the accuracy of our contents, mistakes do happen. If you find a mistake in one of our books—maybe a mistake in text or code—we would be grateful if you would report this to us. By doing so, you can save other readers from frustration and help us to improve subsequent versions of this book. If you find any errata, please report them by visiting `http://www.packtpub.com/support`, selecting your book, clicking on the **let us know** link, and entering the details of your errata. Once your errata are verified, your submission will be accepted and the errata added to any list of existing errata. Any existing errata can be viewed by selecting your title from `http://www.packtpub.com/support`.

Piracy

Piracy of copyright material on the Internet is an ongoing problem across all media. At Packt, we take the protection of our copyright and licenses very seriously. If you come across any illegal copies of our works in any form on the Internet, please provide us with the location address or web site name immediately so that we can pursue a remedy.

Please contact us at `copyright@packtpub.com` with a link to the suspected pirated material.

We appreciate your help in protecting our authors, and our ability to bring you valuable content.

Questions

You can contact us at `questions@packtpub.com` if you are having a problem with any aspect of the book, and we will do our best to address it.

1
Planning with IBM Cognos

The objective of this book is to introduce you to IBM Cognos Planning and provide you with a guide to help you get started. If you are a beginner seeking to expand your basic knowledge about IBM Cognos Planning, or perhaps a power-user who would like to start developing a model, then this book is for you. We provide you with a conceptual framework and cut to the heart of the subject without the technical clutter. We have structured this book in a way that focuses on the key aspects of IBM Cognos Planning while at the same time giving you step-by-step instructions on how to build simple models from the ground up. Like any software, IBM Cognos gives you tools that enable you to create solutions to problems. Tools by themselves do not solve problems; *you* do through the use of these tools. A lot has to do with the understanding of how to leverage the features of IBM Cognos in order to create new capabilities within your enterprise. That is what we hope you will learn from this book.

Throughout this book, we will offer our advice on building effective and efficient models and will provide tips on overcoming or avoiding some of the pitfalls of modeling. As with any skill, the aspiration for mastery of IBM Cognos Planning must begin with the fundamentals. We hope that after you have gone through the book, you will have gained the fundamentals that will prepare you to take on the challenge of building more complex models and, by harnessing the power of this software, improve on how your enterprise plans and manages performance.

Planning in a dynamic business environment

Today's dynamic business environment demands more accurate projection about the future. Forces such as intense competition, changing regulatory requirements, disruptive technologies, demands for financial transparency, and more sophisticated customers and investors compel companies to develop a clearer picture of the future so that they can react faster, while at the same time lower the level of uncertainty with their business. We have seen over time how markets have responded to companies that fail to deliver expected results. Those that fail have seen their stock value diminish. On the other hand, companies that consistently deliver are rewarded with higher market capitalization. The key to gaining the confidence of the market is in reducing the level of uncertainty by setting the right expectations. To do this, companies must be in tune with the realities of their business so that they can project the future more accurately and manage performance towards their goals. Yet, despite advancements in technology, a great number of companies operate their business using inadequate planning systems, effectively hampering their ability to execute their strategy. No matter how great its products are, a company cannot realize its full potential with a flawed planning system.

Enterprise planning solutions enable a company to plan accurately so that it can allocate its most precious resources effectively and respond to a dynamic business environment. The goal of enterprise planning must be achieved through a comprehensive performance management framework consisting of planning, scorecarding, and business intelligence. By establishing the company's future state, enterprise planning provides the basis by which performance is measured. From the plan, the company generates its key metrics to monitor performance. Through business intelligence and analytics, it attempts to understand deviations from plan so that it can respond appropriately. Enterprise planning engages people, process, and technology to anticipate the future. It is a multi-faceted discipline that spans the whole enterprise, and not just the Finance department. When everyone is aligned in a unified forward-looking motion, in touch with every vital aspect of the business, the company becomes more proactive and adaptive to changes in its environment.

Common problems with the planning process

Problems with traditional planning processes are commonplace. The process can be time consuming, involving countless hours of activities that add little value. Changes in the business environment are seldom reflected in the plan. The integrity of data is questionable. The process of collecting and consolidating plans creates a lag that makes information obsolete by the time it reaches the decision maker. For non-financial managers, the task of preparing the budget seems to be more of an invasion of their time rather than a rather a meaningful, productive exercise. They feel overwhelmed by the demands for financial projections that have little connection to the realities of their business. Many of these problems are evident in companies that have inadequate planning systems.

Disconnect between operating reality and financial plan

Ideally, operational targets are linked to financial measures. When the link is severed, decisions by people on the ground are not reflected in the financial plan, and high-level corporate strategies do not translate into discrete operational plans.

Confrontational versus collaborative

Many financial plans are developed in silos by individuals whose perspectives do not go outside of departmental boundaries. In many cases, even individuals within the same department work in isolation, unaware of how their work affects others. In such a fragmented enterprise, planning likely becomes a win-lose proposition and managers tend to view planning as an opportunity to protect existing resources rather than a purposeful endeavor.

Cycle times

Planning cycles must be in sync with major milestones in the business so that the company can reposition itself in anticipation of change. When the time it takes to develop the plan is too long, the plan becomes obsolete before it is finalized. Because of the tremendous effort involved in starting and completing a planning cycle, traditional planning cannot keep up with the business dynamics and is often relegated to an annual or semi-annual ritual.

Ownership and accountability

When plans are imposed from the top down, or from the finance area, they will likely fail to receive buy-in if there is a lack of common understanding of the basis for the plan. The planning process must engage all lines of business managers in a collaborative approach in order to ensure ownership and accountability, and the plan must reflect the contributions of both upper and lower layers of management.

Spreadsheet-based planning

While today's business literature has placed considerable focus on sophisticated enterprise-wide planning systems, most companies still plan using spreadsheets, sending planning templates back and forth, and spending an inordinate amount of time collecting and consolidating plans. A survey by CFO Research Services asked finance executives about their efforts to transform their planning, budgeting, and forecasting processes. Of those who responded, 73% rely primarily on spreadsheets and manual processes. Only 16% use analytical applications, and only 11% extract the necessary numerical information from their accounting modules. Spreadsheet-based planning is littered with problems and is often a chaotic, frustrating, and ineffective process, causing managers to submit unrealistic budgets and senior executives to fudge the numbers at the top. This drives a wedge between senior executives and lower-level managers, and alienates people who are accountable for the plan but feel a certain distrust of the numbers by which they are now measured. Other problems are familiar.

Lack of control

Developing a model in a spreadsheet appeals to many users because of its flexibility. You can develop a model without the need for a preliminary blueprint or prototype, because the spreadsheet imposes no rules or structure for designing or laying out your model. While this is all well and good for a simple model, you will soon realize that a spreadsheet-based planning process can quickly degenerate into "spreadsheet hell". A simple insertion of a row or column can be a daunting task when numerous worksheets are involved. Macros that execute routines must be recoded, retested, and redeployed to account for the change. The fact is that the spreadsheet, while a powerful personal tool, lacks the structure that is so vital in enforcing the discipline necessary to support and maintain any process on an enterprise scale.

Spreadsheet error

Even the most carefully-crafted spreadsheet carries the risk of formula errors. In a spreadsheet, formulas are embedded in cells and then copied across many rows, columns, worksheets, and workbooks. This method may not seem initially onerous, but when you have to make a change in formula to multiple spreadsheets, it is easy to make a mistake, especially when there is no central place where calculations reside. Errors come in many forms, from a simple typographical mistake to completely overlooking a critical component. Because the calculations are scattered and mixed with data, finding a formula error is like searching for a needle in a haystack.

Lack of transparency

All too often, spreadsheets are developed by individuals in finance and so are designed to be user-friendly to the designer. To a non-financial person, it could be the opposite. A spreadsheet that contains complex formulas that refer to multiple cells across several worksheets can be intimidating. When users do not understand how their numbers are arrived at, the planning process loses its integrity.

Consolidation and version control

When spreadsheets are distributed across the organization, the task of collecting and consolidating them can be extremely time-consuming. No wonder that in some companies the task of consolidating is a full-time job. Not only must the plan be submitted on time, it must be the correct version, and it must roll-up the latest organizational hierarchy.

How technology enables planning best practices

In recent years, many companies have migrated from spreadsheet-based processes toward more sophisticated enterprise planning tools. These tools promise a greater level of operational detail for analytical purposes, more robust financial reporting, real-time aggregation of data, and higher participation from users. The tools also liberate finance departments from the demands of collecting and consolidating data so that they can focus on analysis, and understand real business drivers. As software technology improves, companies are tasked with enabling planning best practices by adopting new tools. Some of the new capabilities but these tools provide can have far-reaching effects on the accuracy and timeliness of the plans, and have an almost immediate impact on the productivity of the users.

- **Real-time updates**: The business environment is so dynamic that relying on annual or quarterly financial updates may no longer be sufficient. A company's forecast must be based on events and conditions that can change over time. Because information is updated instantaneously, it maintains its relevance when it reaches the decision maker.

- **Ability to integrate with enterprise data**: Companies need to be able to tap into various ERP systems to extract data that impacts their planning and budgeting. Data such as labor rates, material costs, interest rates, and currency rates can directly affect profitability. The planning system must provide interfaces to disparate data sources so that the changes to the operational data can cascade into the financial plans when conditions change.

- **Hierarchical aggregation and granularity**: Planning takes place at many levels, so the ability to provide consolidated information as well as drill-down capabilities to a granular level of information in order to discover underlying issues, is critical to a planning system. Advances in technology have allowed data to be linked across all organizational levels, creating a unified platform for information.

- **Ability to translate between financial and non-financial metrics**: Planning engages multitudes of planners who think in terms of non-financial metrics. Planning templates must be customized to the planners' view using terms that are familiar to them. Because many planners deal with non-financial operational measures, the planning system must be able to translate operational measures into financial information.

- **Collaborative**: The Web enables the interactive participation of planners anytime, anywhere. New technologies enable people to work in real-time across geographies so that decisions can be made faster, with all of the decision makers interacting simultaneously.

Finance organizations that adopt dedicated planning tools are better able to support strategic Performance Management initiatives. Ventana Research believes that planning and budgeting will be transformed over the next five years by nearly universal use of software tools dedicated to this purpose.

Ventana Research

Introducing IBM Cognos Planning

IBM Cognos, a leading performance management software company brings together technology, analytical applications, and best practices to give companies an open, adaptive, and complete performance management platform. It offers solutions that deliver the integrated planning, consolidation, querying and reporting, analysis, and metrics management capabilities that enable better decision-making across the enterprise. IBM Cognos Planning is the cornerstone of the corporate performance management platform. It is developed for companies that possess even the most complex business planning models. It is a state-of-the-art, scalable planning and forecasting solution that gives managers real-time visibility into operational and financial plans. Its also gives financial analysts powerful modeling tools that enable the design of complex models, and allows the financial analysts to perform what-ifs and scenario planning using latest version of the plan. Its distributed administration architecture provides localized ownership and responsibility for the preparation, control, and maintenance of plans across functional, geographic, and organizational boundaries while still keeping a unified and secure planning environment.

Corporate Performance Management

Corporate Performance Management (CPM) is a term that describes the practices, processes, technologies, and metrics that are used to measure and manage a company's performance. There are a host of similar terms in business literature, such as **Business Performance Management (BPM)**, **Enterprise Performance Management (EPM)**, and **Financial Performance Management (FPM)**. Notwithstanding the differences in terminologies, the concept is the same: companies need a way to manage performance within a complete and comprehensive framework. CPM provides answers to three fundamental questions: "How are we doing?", "Why?", and "What should we be doing?" Leading organizations are succeeding through an integrated CPM approach that encompasses planning, scorecarding, and business intelligence. This approach enables companies to define strategic goals and then measure and manage performance against these goals. Such organizations establish performance expectations through planning, monitor performance by using scorecards, and understand what drives performance by reporting and analyzing information.

The following figure shows the various steps in the CPM approach:

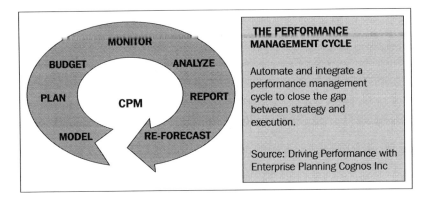

Benefits of IBM Cognos Planning

IBM Cognos Planning helps to improve financial and operational planning by giving companies the ability to transform a high-level strategy into discrete plans. It encompasses the entire company yet it enables the finance department to own and manage the process. It supports dynamic planning and provides the cornerstone for enterprise-scale performance management. Some of the benefits are:

- Centrally managed system to be used to produce budget, estimates, and forecasting reports
- Generation of reports through an iterative process that ensures data integrity
- Ability to support the generation of bottom-up budgets while enabling top-down adjustments
- Ability to capture commentary at all levels
- Ability to generate and retain "what-if" scenarios
- Drill-down capability
- Ease of use of the system with little requirement for technical proficiency
- Ability to deliver reports electronically
- User access security defined within the system
- Ability to provide user audit trail
- Model documentation and maintenance
- Ability to effectively store multiple time periods and iterations
- Ease of access to the system for management, accounting staff, and business users
- Ability to perform allocations within the system
- Ability to integrate with underlying data sources

Summary

The goal of this book is to give you the fundamentals of model building using IBM Cognos Planning. In today's competitive and dynamic business environment, companies need to manage performance effectively by setting accurate plans and monitoring performance against the plan. However, many companies still plan using traditional spreadsheet-based planning systems which are littered with problems. To address these problems they need a planning system that produces plans that reflect business realities, fosters collaboration, provides greater control, minimizes errors, and promotes ownership and accountability. IBM Cognos Planning, a cornerstone of Corporate Performance Management, offers a solution that engages all levels in the enterprise in a controlled, reliable, collaborative, and real-time planning process. Some of the new capabilities that IBM Cognos provides can improve the accuracy and timeliness of the plans and have an almost immediate impact on the productivity of the users.

2
Getting to know IBM Cognos Tools

IBM Cognos offers many products, and covering these products in depth requires dedicated books. In this chapter, we will just skim the surface and take a brief look at the major products frequently used by IBM Cognos Planning modelers and administrators. After reading this chapter, you will be able to:

- Explain how various tools are used in IBM Cognos to develop and deploy planning models, reports, and metrics
- Understand the application of each tool, by using the example of a regional restaurant chain

Scenario

Before introducing various IBM Cognos tools, let's sketch out a scenario to explain how IBM Cognos is used in corporate planning processes.

Panda Garden Inc., a regional restaurant chain, is headquartered in Minneapolis, Minnesota. Panda Garden has 20 restaurants throughout the metropolitan St. Paul/Minneapolis area. Each restaurant offers the same menu and operates under strict corporate guidelines.

As the Corporate Planning Manager, you are responsible for planning, analyzing, and reporting for each restaurant's financial activities, as well as consolidating the results of financial operations.

To fulfill your job responsibilities, you would like to do the following tasks:

- Send out a standard template, as illustrated in the following screenshot, to all of the twenty restaurants, to collect planning data

Operations	Week 1	Week 2	Week 3	Week 4	Week 5	Week 6	Week 7	so on
Entrée Sold:								
General Tso's Chicken								
Sesame Chicken								
Chow Mein								
Total Entrée Sold								
Payroll								
No. of Employees								

- Consolidate the collected information and then analyze the details to understand the profitability of each of the stores
- Inform senior management of *how are we doing* via metrics and scorecards
- Provide analytical and reporting tools to each restaurant manager so that they can analyze their operations and make financial decisions about their restaurants
- Be alerted immediately once a restaurant performs below its target and goals so that the restaurant manager can take immediate action

You can always use a spreadsheet program such as Microsoft Excel to complete the above tasks. However, you would find that a spreadsheet program, although flexible, is not scalable for your needs. Specialized, scalable planning software such as IBM Cognos Planning can ease your job and help you to accomplish your planning and forecasting tasks.

We will provide an overview of the following IBM Cognos tools in this chapter:

- IBM Cognos Planning – Analyst
- IBM Cognos Planning – Contributor (admin and client)
- IBM Cognos Excel Add-in for Analyst and Contributor
- IBM Cognos Metric Designer and Metric Studio
- IBM Cognos Reporting Studios
- IBM Cognos Framework Manager
- IBM Cognos Event Studio
- IBM Cognos Connection Web Portal

We will also relate the functionality of each tool to Panda Garden's planning and reporting needs. Note that the first three tools are traditionally described as the **Planning** tools, while the remaining are considered IBM Cognos **Business Intelligent (BI)** tools.

IBM Cognos Planning – Analyst

IBM Cognos Planning – Analyst is a business planning modeling tool that some people call *Excel on Steroids*. Analyst provides a multi-dimensional view, similar to an Excel Pivot table, of your planning data. It is a client tool and will typically require installation on a PC-based desktop.

Panda Garden Scenario

To collect data from each restaurant, you, as a Planning Modeler, can create the budget/forecasting template in Analyst, as illustrated in the following screenshot:

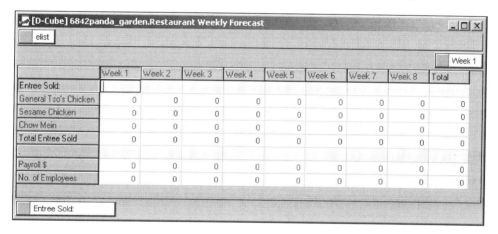

IBM Cognos Planning – Contributor

By design, IBM Cognos Planning – Contributor is a data collection tool. This program has two components: administration and client.

Contributor administration

The Contributor administration component is called **Contributor Administration Console (CAC)**. The CAC provides the functionality to publish the template created in Analyst over the Web after customizing its look and feel and applying any necessary security. It is a server-based tool and can be installed on a PC desktop or a server machine.

Panda Garden scenario

Using the CAC, you, as a Planning Administrator:

- Publish the Analyst template over the Web for restaurant managers, so that they can submit their plan numbers

- Customize the user interface of the template

- Apply security to each template so that each restaurant manager can see only their own data

The following screenshot demonstrates the CAC interface, in which planning administration tasks are performed:

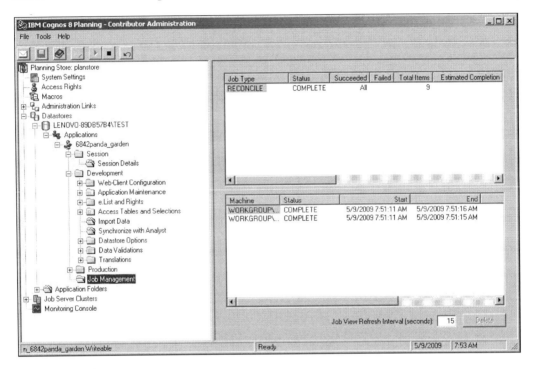

Contributor client

The Contributor client component is referred to as Contributor Web Client, or Contributor Grid, and it is a web site programmed using Java technology. IBM Cognos Planning software provides all necessary web site files and programs to load on a web server.

Panda Garden scenario

You, as a Planning Administrator, provide the URL of the Contributor web site to your users. Users are generally referred to as Planners or Contributors. A restaurant manager, essentially a Planner, opens the template for his/her restaurant on the Contributor web site. He/she enters his/her plan numbers and saves his/her data, which is stored in a planning database. The following screenshot shows an example of such a template:

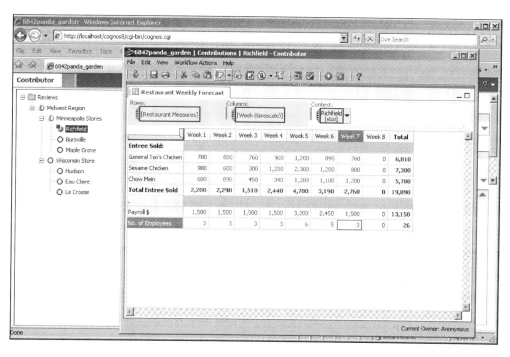

 IBM Cognos Analyst is a designer tool in which a modeler designs the model template, whereas IBM Cognos Contributor is a deployment tool used to deploy the planning templates to organizational units for plan submissions. Analogously, a modeler creates a cookie cutter in the Analyst program and then makes cookies from the cookie cutter in the CAC program, before distributing the cookies to organizational unit managers. These managers are responsible for submitting their budget and forecast using the Contributor web site.

IBM Cognos Excel add-in for Analyst and Contributor

IBM Cognos Planning also offers Excel add-in programs for the Analyst and Contributor Web Client. There is no add-in program for the CAC. By using these add-in programs, we can utilize MS Excel to complete common Analyst or Contributor Web Client tasks.

IBM Cognos Metric Designer and Metric Studio

Originated by Drs. Robert Kaplan and David Norton as a performance measurement framework, the Balanced Scorecard is a management system that enables your organization to set, track, and achieve its key business strategies and objectives. For example, your organization could have a Customer scorecard, a Financial scorecard, a Business Process scorecard, and a Learning and Growth scorecard.

Scorecards present performance metrics. A performance metric for a web site may be *Cost per Visitor*, which is the dollar amount spent to drive one unique visitor to a web site. For example, if you spent $100 to drive 1,000 unique visitors to your web site, then your cost per visitor is $0.10. IBM Cognos Metric Designer and Metric Studio tools help organizations to build metrics and scorecards.

Metric Designer

You can use Metric Designer to gather metrics from import sources and prepare them for use in Metric Studio. It is a client tool and is installed on a PC desktop.

Metric Studio

Users monitor the performance of metrics in Metric Studio. Scorecards and metrics are linked to reports created with Report Studio.

Panda Garden scenario

You, as a Metric Designer, create various revenue metrics for restaurant managers, so they can monitor their revenue performance daily. For example, you could create the metric *Quantity of Sesame Chicken entrées sold* by linking/importing data from the Sales System. Each store manager can use Metric Studio to view the daily status of this metric. This metric could help them understand the performance of this entrée.

IBM Cognos Reporting Studios

IBM Cognos offers three main report studios for report consumers: Report Studio, Analysis Studio, and Query Studio.

- Report Studio — use this tool to create structured and formal reports
- Analysis Studio — use this tool to analyze and drill-up/down through data
- Query Studio — use this tool to create self-serving ad hoc queries on your data

Panda Garden scenario

You, as a Report Writer, create and customize reports using these tools for your store managers. As report consumers, store managers access these tools to view reports and analyze data. An illustration from the Query Studio is shown in the following screenshot; illustrations from the Report or Analysis Studios are not shown here.

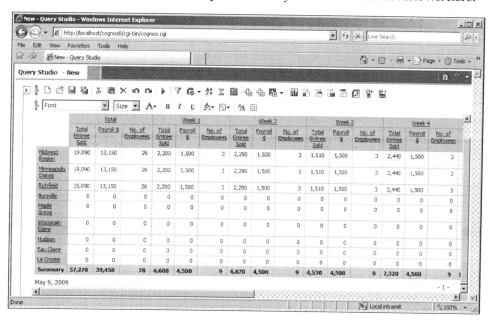

IBM Cognos Framework Manager

Organizations collect and store a lot of *raw* data. Business users need to analyze and report on collected data to understand the business and steer the business in the right direction. A data model is needed to bridge between the needs of business users and the raw data collected by various data points/systems. Framework Manager is a data modeling tool. A Modeler creates the **Framework Manager (FM)** model so that the users or report writers can use the model for reporting and analysis. It is a client tool and is installed on the Modelers' desktop.

Panda Garden scenario

You, as an FM Modeler, create and publish the FM model, so users and report writers in your organization can access and use it to report data using IBM Cognos Reporting Studios. The user interface of the Framework Manager program is demonstrated in the following screenshot:

IBM Cognos Event Studio

Decision makers in an organization need up-to-date notification of data changes in order to drive business decisions. Data changes take place as business events occur. For example, monthly sales are 20% below target on the 29th day of the month, or hard disk space in ten servers reaches maximum capacity. In the above examples of business events, decision makers would like to be notified immediately, so that they can rectify the situation.

IBM Cognos Event Studio is a notification tool. You define a condition or criteria on business data, and the Event Studio notifies you when the condition is met. The notification may take place through an email, a report, or a news alert.

Panda Garden Scenario

Assume that you want store managers to be notified when total employee hours exceed a specific threshold in a week. By using the Event Studio tool, you can create a condition on your payroll data. When this condition is met, the Event Studio alerts the store managers via emails.

IBM Cognos Connection web portal

IBM Cognos Connection, a web portal, is the place where all actions take place. It is the single and central point for accessing all of the IBM Cognos Studios and application-specific data that we have described in the earlier sections. Users use this portal to access their planning model, reports, analysis, metrics, events, and so on. System administrators use this portal to administer the IBM Cognos environment, including security, configuration, and status checks. The following screenshot shows the main IBM Cognos Connection page. The customizable task icons are available to users based on their job roles, for example, Report Authors and Content Administrator.

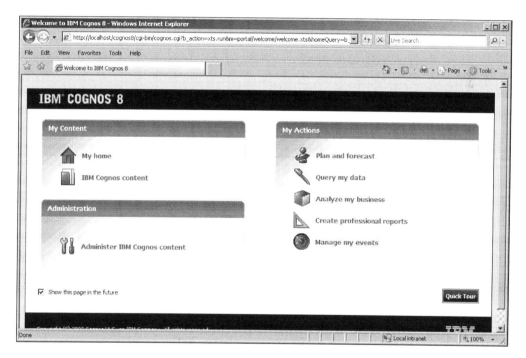

Summary

In this chapter, we saw an overview of various IBM Cognos tools and their application. The application of each tool was illustrated by using an example of a regional restaurant chain.

3
Understanding the Model Development Process

This chapter summarizes the key steps of the Model Development Process. The remaining chapters have been organized around these steps and we will refer to them throughout this book. Over the course of this chapter, the content across various upcoming chapters will be discussed, and you will learn how to:

- Design the model template in Analyst
- Build the Contributor application
- Enter and review plans in the Contributor Web user interface
- Publish and report on planning data
- Maintain the planning models

The process

The Model Development Process is a proven step-by-step approach for designing and deploying planning models in an organization. This process enables us to chart various activities involved in identifying the organization's planning requirements in order to devise functional and efficient modeling solutions.

The following diagram illustrates the Model Development Process and shows the typical stakeholders and IBM Cognos tools involved in the process:

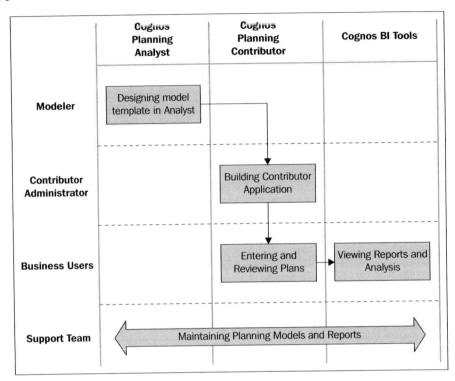

In the previous diagram, we saw four typical roles in organizations that are currently using the IBM Cognos Planning model and applications. They are described briefly as:

- **Analyst Modeler**: Responsible for gathering business requirements—designing, building, and testing Analyst models, and managing the data workflow within the model.

- **System** or **Contributor Administrator**: Responsible for creating, maintaining, and securing Contributor applications translated from Analyst models.

- **Business Users**: Responsible for entering, submitting, and reviewing planning data. Users will be referred to as the *Business Users* or *Planners*.

- **Support Team**: Responsible for maintaining models and applications, during or after the initial roll-out.

Considerations for building an Analyst planning model

When purchasing a vehicle, you may consider many attributes before finalizing your decision. For example, you may determine the type of vehicle to buy (sedan, minivan, and so on) or may evaluate the commuting needs. Likewise, before beginning to build the planning model, you must consider some key factors about our planning processes. To build and deploy the correct planning models in an organization, Project Managers, Business Users, Modelers, and other project stakeholders should consider the following factors at the initial stage of the planning project:

- Planning functional models
- Planning cycles and horizons
- Planning approaches

Planning functional models

Every business organization uses a variety of planning models to produce its business plans. A number of planning models are common in most of the organizations. For example, many business organizations have some form of revenue, cost of sales, payroll, capital, and operating expense models. On the other hand, some models are unique to a particular industry and trade. For example, a pharmaceutical company may have a Clinical trial or R&D model, or an international shipping company may need an aircraft fleet cost-control model.

Other models may reflect an organization's business focus. The organization may develop a model to project and control a particular cost that is critical to its business strategy. For instance, a beverage company that places a heavy emphasis on brand recognition may have a separate marketing model, or a consulting company that routinely rotates its employees to offices around the world may have a separate travel model. Whatever purpose the models serve, it is important that you understand the rationale underlying the organization's use of them, so that you can build models that are more closely aligned to the organization's business needs.

Planning cycles and horizons

You also need to be aware of the organization's planning cycle and horizon. The **planning cycle** refers to the frequency by which an organization develops or updates its business plans. The planning horizon refers to how far into the future the organization plans. An organization may have multiple planning cycles, but may only plan for a single time horizon. The frequency with which an organization plans depends on many factors. For instance, organizations that operate in highly dynamic and competitive environments, such as technology companies, tend to have more frequent planning cycles. Companies in more stable environments, such as an alkaline batteries manufacturing company, tend to have less frequent cycles.

Planning horizons may be driven by the organization's strategic focus or the nature of the business. For instance, the planning horizon of a pharmaceutical company's R&D plan may span up to 20 years, which is the amount of time that a clinical drug may take to get from inception to testing and eventually to marketability. A construction company may require multi-year plans to coincide with the time it takes to construct a building. More commonly, organizations develop a plan once a year in the form of an annual budget. The organization then revisits and calibrates the plan mid-year, after several months of actual data has been gathered. Actual data is used to measure year-to-date performance against the plan, so that the organization can forecast for the remainder of the year. The typical planning horizon is twelve months, usually the organization's fiscal year. If a long-range plan exists, the long-range plan is updated with changes to the annual plan or forecast.

Planning cycle refers to the frequency at which an organization develops or updates its business plans. Planning horizon refers to how far into the future the organization plans.

Knowing an organization's planning cycle and horizon is important when building a model. Many organizations use cycle-specific models because the business assumptions and calculations tend to differ between planning cycles. For instance, an organization can have a P&L model for the annual budget and another for the mid-year forecast because an annual budget and mid-year forecast usually require different data and calculation requirements.

Knowing an organization's planning cycle can give you an insight into how you may want to build your models. The organization may start with detailed plans once or twice a year. If rolling forecasts are prepared, the forecasts may be done at a higher level, for instance, at an account or organizational summary level. This means that you may have to create a detailed model and a summary model.

Knowing the planning horizon enables you to construct the appropriate timescale that can be used by other models. An organization that plans its revenue every quarter may also plan its expenses in the same way. An efficient planning model is built on standard data structures, such as timescale. Thus, timescales are an important consideration because they can be shared across several of the organization's planning models.

Planning approaches

Business organizations can use different approaches to plan their budgets and forecasts. You need to consider these approaches when building the model, as these approaches dictate how the model will be designed and deployed. Examples of common approaches are as follows:

- **Zero-based budgeting**: Each planner prepares estimates of their proposed revenue or expenses for a specific period of time as if they were planning for the first time. By starting from scratch at each budget cycle, for example, managers are required to take a closer look at all of their revenues and expenses.

- **Driver based**: Driver based planning models typically calculate plan numbers by adding, subtracting, or multiplying various drivers or metrics. Examples of drivers: number of units sold, price of a product, and so on.

- **Top-down**: Top Upper-level management sets the targets and pushes them to lower management who then pushes them further down the organization. Then the plans for achieving the targets are submitted up the chain of command for review and approval.

- **Bottom-up**: Lower-level management prepares the plans and then submits them up the chain of command for review and approval. The approval and rejection process follows until the plan and finalized.

Designing the model template in Analyst

A planning model is a set of Analyst objects whose purpose is to generate specific plans using a variety of data inputs, assumptions, and calculations. We will discuss the Analyst objects in greater detail in Chapters 4 through 7. In practice, a model is named after the output it produces. An output can be a specific budget for product lines or it can be a category of expenses consisting of several general ledger accounts, such as payroll.

Once you have identified the model output, break it down into its inputs, assumptions, and calculations. For example, a salary plan may be the outcome of the inputs of employees and positions, their current salary, earned merit increases, and bonuses. The salary for newly-hired staff may be assumed based on their position. To produce the salary plan, the model would calculate the merit increases and bonuses for each employee by multiplying the salary by the merit and bonus percentages and then by adding the results to the salary. Then it would pull the appropriate salary for each new hire depending on position. Finally, the model would aggregate all of the employees' and new hires' salaries to come up with the salary plan. In this simplified example, four model functions are apparent: inputs, assumptions, calculations, and outputs. In fact, you can say that a model is a collection of these four functions. The IBM Cognos Planning Analyst tool allows you to build objects that collect inputs from users, designate assumed values, and perform calculations on them in order to produce the expected output.

Flowcharting the model structure

Before building an effective planning model, it is important to develop a detailed flowchart that logically illustrates all of the model's structural components. Just as an architect develops a building's blueprints before even breaking the ground, you must begin with the model's blueprints. Often, many modelers skip this important step and begin constructing the objects, without a clear path to the final outcome. Unfortunately, such haste results in a disorganized and inefficient model. A poorly-designed model can adversely impact an application's performance and cause a downstream effect on user productivity. The consequence can be severe. When the model is deployed to hundreds or thousands of users, a single instance of inefficiency will multiply at an equivalent scale.

Flowcharting helps you to avoid these problems. It gives you a glimpse of the final product and forces you to think through the various factors and issues that must be addressed before starting to build the model. A disciplined and methodical approach can steer you away from many of model building's hidden pitfalls. Indeed, a well thought out flowchart can cut the build time significantly by minimizing rework and trial and error.

Flowcharting can lead you to uncovering the important design elements, such as the dimensions, datastore, and data flow. A good flowchart should show the sources of data inputs, and whether they are entered by the planner or originate from other data sources such as an ERP system or a general ledger system. The flowchart should also illustrate the way that data will be stored and used, how it enters the model, and how it flows from source to target. Finally, the flowchart should describe the different ways in which data can be viewed so that you can gather the various dimensions that need to be included in the model. For instance, data can be viewed by cost center, departments, or profit centers. Alternatively, it can be viewed across time (days, weeks, months, years) or by versions (this year, last year, plan, scenarios).

 Some developers may refer to model flowcharts as model schematics or **Data Flow Diagrams** (DFD).

You, the Modeler, typically initiate this design step in the model development process after learning and understanding the key business planning requirements. You then 'white-board' the design of the model template, and then document the design specification in a document called a **Detailed Design Specification** (DDS). Finally, you take the design specification and implement it in IBM Cognos Planning Analyst using the Analyst's features and functionality. The Analyst environment, interface, and objects are covered in Chapter 4.

The concept of multi dimensionality

IBM Cognos Planning is based on a multi-dimensional data structure in which data is organized around specific attributes, or dimensions. In the following table, data is organized around **Account, Year, Version, Cost Center**, and **Month**. Each record in the table contains data by account, year, version, cost center, and month.

```
Untitled - Notepad
File Edit Format View Help
Account Year    Version Cost Center    Month    Amount
74058   2005    Actual  0341           Aug      54.60
74058   2005    Actual  0622           Sep      218.45
74058   2005    Actual  0325           Oct      65.59
74058   2005    Actual  0600           Nov      261.96
74058   2005    Actual  0361           Jan      217.54
74058   2005    Actual  0425           Feb      1,021.41
74058   2005    Actual  0026           Mar      309.50
74058   2005    Actual  0763           Apr      464.86
74058   2005    Actual  0421           May      511.62
74058   2005    Actual  0043           Jun      75.19
74058   2005    Actual  0025           Jul      367.04
74058   2005    Actual  0766           Aug      16.36
74058   2005    Actual  0232           Sep      102.50
74058   2005    Actual  0526           Oct      41.03
74058   2005    Actual  0225           Dec      447.54
74109   2006    Plan    0010           Jan      147.00
74109   2006    Plan    0012           Feb      94.00
74109   2006    Plan    0626           Mar      449.00
74109   2006    Plan    0429           Apr      582.00
74109   2006    Plan    0731           May      124.00
74109   2006    Plan    0004           Jul      318.00
74109   2006    Plan    0762           Aug      141.00
74109   2006    Plan    0321           Sep      83.00
74109   2006    Plan    0381           Oct      95.00
74109   2006    Plan    0226           Nov      23.00
774109  2006    Plan    0423           Feb      47.0074109
```

One of the most common ways of presenting multi-dimensional data is in the form of a cube. In a multi-dimensional cube, data is displayed as one slice at a time along two or more dimensions. Each slice represents a subset of the population. Those familiar with Excel pivot tables should have little problem grasping this concept. However, those who are only familiar with spreadsheets can still find some similarities. In a spreadsheet, the rows and columns are actually two separate dimensions. A third dimension, the worksheet, gives you a three-dimensional view of data. If you enter data into the first cell in a spreadsheet, you are actually entering the data along three dimensions—Sheet 1, Column A, and Row 1. Hence, when you reference that cell, Excel denotes it as **Sheet1!A1**.

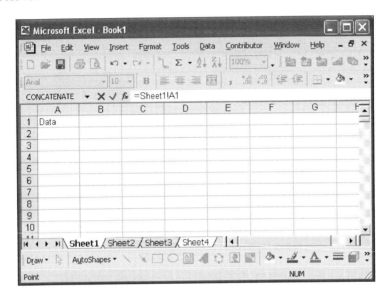

A multi-dimensional cube lets you view data the same way. But a cube can have several dimensions. Each dimension contains a list of related data such as accounts, version, cost center, or time period. When two or more dimensions intersect, the intersection represents a record or view of the data. For instance, a cost center dimension may list all the cost centers in the organization. A second dimension lists a group of expense accounts, a third lists 12 months, and a fourth lists the version (Plan or Actual). The intersection of these dimensions gives you data by cost center, by account, by month, and by version. The following Excel pivot table is an example of a multi-dimensional cube. Here you see a slice of the cube with the following dimensions: **Account, Cost Center, Month,** and **Version.**

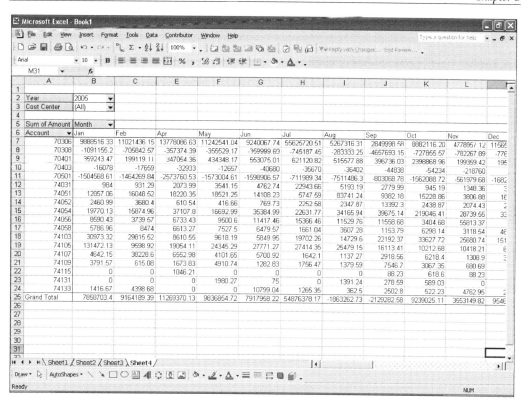

In a multi-dimensional cube, you can arrange data in a variety of ways by swapping rows, columns, and pages. This is a powerful feature that facilitates in-depth data analysis. Those who have worked with multi-dimensional cubes understand their benefits. Multi-dimensional cubes can help you sift through masses of data to find valuable information. IBM Cognos Planning takes multi dimensionality a step further by leveraging its features to enforce rules and standards in order to make model maintenance easier.

Analyst is the tool that lets you create the planning template that the users will use to enter their plans, while Contributor is the tool that lets you replicate the templates and deploy them to a number of users based on a defined hierarchy. The plans are stored in a central database, and users connect to it through the Web. In a spreadsheet environment, similarities exist. You have a master template that you can use to build the worksheets. The worksheets are stored in a central folder, within sub-folders that are organized according to a hierarchy. Users connect to the shared folder to access their worksheets.

Understanding dimensions, datastore, and data flow

Analyst objects are the building blocks of the planning model. These objects enable you to define the data structure, store and calculate the data, and move data from source to targets. There are a host of objects in Analyst, each offering useful capabilities. However, the key objects are the D-List, D-Cube, and D-Link. These objects are indispensable to a model and thus deserve special attention. The key objects, as well as some important ancillary objects, will be discussed later in this book.

Determining dimensions: D-List

The D-List is the basic building block of the model. In Analyst, dimensions are referred to as D-Lists. Each item in a D-List represents an attribute of the data. In a D-List, we decide what data to include in the model and how the data will behave. The data could be something that will be entered by the planner; it could be pre-populated, or it could be calculated. For example, to build a model of your personal expenses, you may have a list of expense categories (travel, food, and entertainment), you may want to track your spending over time (month, quarter, and year), and you may want to compare different versions of spending (actual and planned). Each of these lists of items could be a D-List. In the Spending Category D-List, you might include a **Total** that sums up **Travel**, **Food**, and **Entertainment** (see the following screenshot). In the Versions D-List, you may want a "Variance" between actual and planned values. There is virtually no restriction to the type of data that you can include. However there are certain principles to adhere to when creating D-Lists. Chapter 4 discusses the D-List in greater detail.

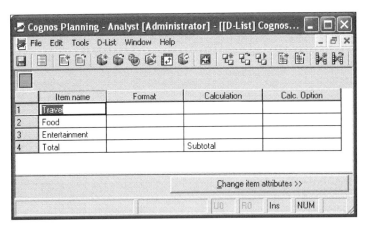

The first step in constructing a model is to identify the dimensions that will be used. There are many sources of information that will give you an idea of the dimensions that you need. Data entry templates from the organization's existing planning systems or Excel spreadsheets can suggest many ways in which data is gathered. The spreadsheet can also reveal the calculations used. Performance reports can be used to determine what the model outputs will be. Often, simply inquiring about the business can be a good start. Consider that you're working on a project that requires you to design and build a revenue forecasting model for a Fortune 100 global consumer electronics retailer. One approach to determining the dimensions of this forecasting model is to ask the following questions:

- What does the company sell? The dimensions could contain a list of consumer electronics products, such as MP3 players and laptops, product categories such as audio and computers, or even brands.

- Who is the company selling to? The retailer's customer list could be a dimension.

- Where does the company operate? Dimensions may contain a list stores, states, cities, countries, global regions, or market segments.

- What is the forecasting timeline? The timeline dimensions may be weeks, months, quarters, or years.

 The words "D-List" and "dimension" are often used interchangeably. When used in the context of a cube, "dimension" is often more appropriate.

Building the datastore: D-Cubes

Whereas the D-List is where the data is defined, the D-Cube is where the data is stored. After you have decided what data will be included in the model, you determine how the data will be stored. The D-Cube is formed by two or more D-Lists. A typical planning model consists of several cubes. The cubes store a particular set of data and perform a specific function. For example, an Employee cube may store data about employees. A P&L cube may contain revenue and expense data. D-Cubes can be functionally classified as either an *input* cube that allows data entry, a *calculation* cube that processes data, or an *output* cube that displays the result. The Employee cube can be broken into an Employee Input cube (see the following example), Employee Calculation cube, and Employee Summary cube. Chapter 5 covers D-Cubes in greater detail.

The words "D-Cube" and "cube" are often used interchangeably. Except for the terminology, there is no distinction between the two. "D-Cubes" are usually used in an Analyst setting, but "cubes" can work as well

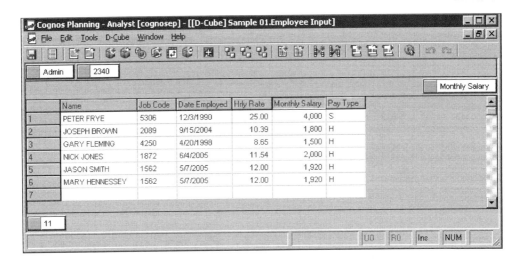

The key to building D-Cubes is to understand their primary function. Is the cube a place where planners will enter data? Will it be used simply to stage data? Will it be used to calculate inputs and feed the result somewhere else? Will it be used to present data in a report format for reviewers? These important questions must be answered before building the cube.

Another factor to think about is data. Data is stored in a cube. Consequently, the cube structure needs to follow the format of the data source that will be feeding it. As a modeler, you need to understand what type of data will be going into the model. For instance, planners need data to compare and analyze planning and actual information. They would like to see actual year-to-date sales compared to next-year projections. During the initial design process, you may decide to work with the data provider to review the source data and develop a process to extract, load, and validate data in planning models.

Perhaps the most important consideration is size. In a multi-dimensional data structure, size is always a constraint. Size has a direct impact on performance; the greater the size, the more time it will take to process data and transmit it over the web. In fact, performance can be such a tremendous constraint that it affects the way the model is designed. Chapter 7 discusses the D-Cube is greater detail, including some of the common issues with size, and also provides a few tips and tricks for optimizing the model's performance.

Controlling data flow: D-Links

In a model that shares data among several cubes, data must flow from one cube to another. The D-link is an object that moves data. Similar to a data transformation or ETL tool, the D-Link maps dimension items in the source to dimension items in the target, enabling you to control the flow of data within the model. For multi-dimensional cubes where data sparseness can be a problem, the D-Link has a practical purpose. The D-Link allows you to break a large cube into smaller, specialized cubes while still making the same data available. Most models use function-specific cubes, where outputs from one cube are inputs to another. The D-Link connects input, calculation, and output cubes, bringing them together to allow the seamless movement of data. Any cube that requires data in order to perform its function can retrieve data without going outside of the model. Because data can be reused, it only needs to enter the model once, thereby simplifying the data import process. The D-Link's ability to transport data is not limited to cubes. D-links can import data from a database, an ASCII file, an Excel spreadsheet, or a Contributor application. Chapter 7 discusses D-Links in detail.

 The words "D-Link" and "link" are often used interchangeably. Except for the terminology, there is no distinction between the two. "D-Link" is usually used in the context of Analyst.

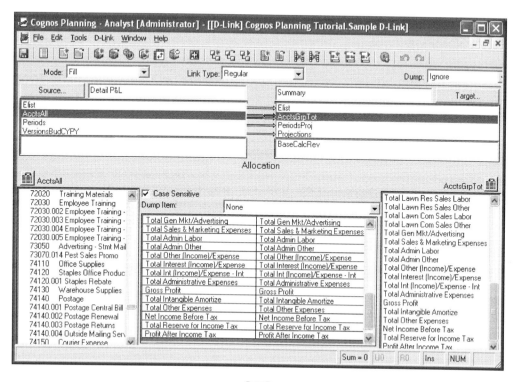

What makes an optimal model?

The saying goes: "There is more than one way to skin a cat." The same can be said about model building. There are myriad ways to create the same output by using a combination of inputs, assumptions, and calculations. IBM Cognos Planning allows you to create highly complex models using its advanced forecasting algorithms and scenario planning facilities. With this capability at your disposal, you may be tempted to build a model that "does everything at the push of the button". While such automation can appear impressive, it is often accompanied with many problems. Complex models make ownership and maintenance difficult. A highly-customized model can become so inflexible that when it's time to enhance it, starting from scratch is an easier option, rather than building on its current form. Support and maintenance can also become a nightmare when you need to go through a laundry list of tasks to prepare for the next cycle. The tendency towards over-automation and over-customization, must be tempered with caution. More often than not, the model that "does everything" also requires everything to support and maintain it.

So what is an optimal model? The answer is one that delivers planning information in a timely manner at the lowest possible cost. Although delivering better information has always been at the forefront of every planning project, the cost of delivering it tends to be elusive. To be sure, the financial cost of the system is closely monitored, but there are costs hidden within the system's inner workings that cannot be quantified and are often left to persist. The cost can take many forms: What is the cost of a poorly designed model? What is the cost of a Contributor application taking twice as long to process? What is the cost of thousands of users waiting an extra 10 seconds each time they can download a planning model? These costs must be taken into consideration when building the model. You, as a Modeler, must not only build a model that does its job, you must do so without placing an undue burden on these cost factors.

Principles of model building

If you ask ten people what makes an optimal model, you are likely to get ten different answers. This is not surprising. The quest for the one-size-fits-all formula has been a long one, owing mostly to the differences in the ways that organizations plan, but also to the openness of the tool and the absence of a shared body of knowledge. Although there are no hard and fast rules, there are three guiding principles that can help lead you down the correct path.

- Efficiency
- Performance
- Maintenance

Efficiency

An optimal model must be built with an eye towards efficiency. An efficient model is one that takes the shortest path to performing its task. Usually this means fewer objects in the model. But it could mean other things: Data flows in one direction, D-Cubes perform clear and specific functions, calculations are more intuitive and easy to understand, D-Lists contain as few dimension items as possible, redundancies are non-existent, and data is organized in a logical fashion. Efficiency and simplicity go hand-in-hand. Simplicity eliminates clutter. It begs the question: Is this absolutely necessary? To a savvy Modeler, the concept of simplicity may be counter-intuitive and run contrary to his nature. Yet the ability to take complex processes and re-engineer them down to a few moving parts is indispensable to model building. Indeed, it is a higher skill, one that compels you to abandon conventional wisdom, think out of the box, and explore unfamiliar territories.

Performance

An optimal model is one that performs its task faster using the same resources. Performance combines effectiveness with timeliness. This means delivering the right information at the right time. The model must be able to process data and respond to user requests within reasonable time and without unnecessary delays. Although not everyone will agree on what "reasonable time" means, everyone can agree on what constitutes "unnecessary delays". It is the difference between how the model performs and how it *should* perform. A model that is built on a weak foundation almost always bears extra processing overhead that takes additional time. There are essentially three areas where performance is most visible:

- Application processing
- Web client access
- Web client processing

Application processing refers to the server batch process that implements changes to the model, or loads data. Web client access is the point where users connect to the database to retrieve or save their plans. Web client processing is where users actually work with their planning templates, entering data and switching from cube to cube. All of these areas have a direct impact on user productivity, so that any lag in performance creates cost in some form.

Maintenance

An optimal model is one that requires the least amount of effort to set up and maintain. In a constantly-changing business landscape, organizations must be able to adapt to new environments quickly. Competitive pressures may push organizations to shorten their planning cycles or drive them to a new strategic direction. Planning models must reflect new realities in order to accurately project the future. They must therefore be flexible and easy to maintain. An optimal model is built on the premise that change is constant. The model must allow for its assumptions and calculations to change without a complete overhaul. It must use standards and share objects so that changes can cascade rapidly throughout its various parts. The model should enable a non-developer to easily take ownership of it without the need for advanced training.

These principles can be self-reinforcing. For instance, an efficient model usually performs faster and is easier to maintain. However, they are not exclusive and trade-offs can occur. When two good approaches contradict, you must weigh the benefit of one over the other and accept the trade-off. In a way, modeling is an art. No strict rules govern how a model should be built, lending the entire exercise to one's own creativity. As a modeler, you should look to these principles for guidance, while keeping a close watch on other factors. In the final analysis, the planning system, like any other system, must be viewed in the light of its benefits, as well as its cost.

Building the Contributor application

The second step in the model development process is to build the Contributor application by using the Analyst template model. You, as a Contributor administrator, build the Contributor application using the New Application Wizard.

 An Analyst model becomes an application in the Contributor program.

The terms "model" and "application" are used interchangeably in practice. In many organizations, a modeler can perform the role of a Contributor administrator, while in other organizations these two roles are separate.

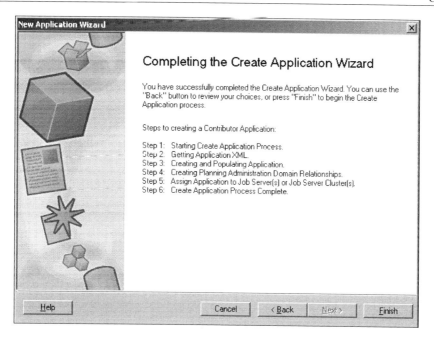

There is a special dimension called e.List. This plays an important role in designing the planning model. Although the e.List is simply a dimension in an Analyst planning model, such as sales territory, region, or sales person, this dimension plays a critical role when deploying the Analyst model to business users in Contributor. This special dimension controls the distribution of the Analyst template to business users, referred as Contributors, and also secures business users' access to an application.

Analogously, let's say you want to send an HR newsletter to all of the department heads in your organization. Carry out the following steps:

1. Create a newsletter (Analyst model template).

2. Print out copies of the newsletter (copying templates in Contributor application).

3. Determine who will be the recipients of the newsletter.

In this example, the e.List becomes the list of recipients. Thus, once the Analyst planning model template is ready and the Contributor application is built, the e.List controls who the recipients of the model template are. An e.List typically represents the organization hierarchy, for example, regions, cost centers, profit centers, and departments. In the following screenshot, Contributors represented by countries will log on to the Contributor web site and access the Analyst template model for planning and forecasting. The following e.List screen shows an organizational hierarchy in a tree format:

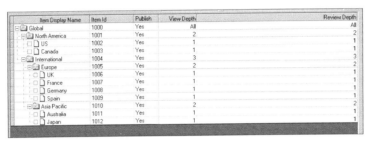

After the Contributor application has been built by using the **Create New Application Wizard** in the Contributor Administrator Console, you (as a Contributor administrator) can now configure the application. Typically, the Contributor configuration options increase the Contributor web site usability and access controls. You may also secure your planning data to ensure that only authorized users can see the planning web site and planning data. Chapter 9 discusses the topic of building the Contributor application.

 The Contributor administrator configures and controls the Contributor application in the Contributor Administrator Console program.

It is common to find multiple planning models or applications in an organization. For example, there may be an application for sales and another for cost of sales, and it is not uncommon for a business user to analyze the impact of sales changes on the cost of sales application. The IBM Cognos Planning tool provides linking similar to a copy-and-paste function that can be used to transfer data from one application to another application. Therefore, in our example above, various linking techniques can be used to transfer data from the Sales application to the Cost of Sales application. Two Contributor data transfer or linking features are an admin link and a system link. The admin link is initiated by the Contributor administrator while the system link is run by users. You, as a Contributor administrator, can run the admin link manually or schedule it to run automatically. In the recent versions of IBM Cognos Planning program, a user can run an admin link indirectly, if permitted to do so by an administrator. Users manually execute System links. We will cover importing and linking data in Chapter 11.

Entering and reviewing plans in the Contributor Web user interface

Once the Contributor application or web site is ready, business users can then enter the budget or forecast for their respective organizational units. The entry and review process ties to an organization's planning cycle. An organization, for example, may require their business users to plan monthly, yearly, or within some other timeframe.

In Contributor, two business users' roles exist: the planner and the reviewer. The planner enters data in the Contributor application in the Contributor web client. The reviewer reviews the submissions of reviewers or planners. For example, a Minnesota sales manager (planner) is responsible for submitting their budget to the mid-western sales region manager (reviewer). The Contributor Web interface topic is covered in detail in Chapter 12.

The following screenshot gives a brief overview of the Contributor web site user interface:

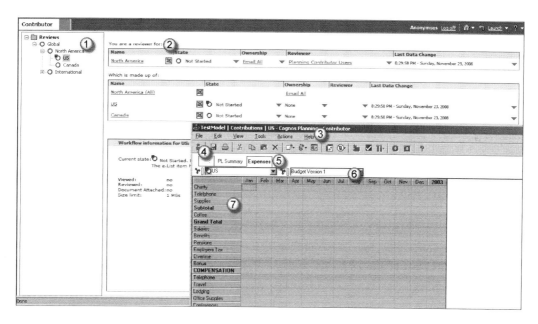

- Tree and e.List: The tree on the leftmost side of the screen shows the areas for which business users are responsible for contributing (Contributions) and reviewing (Reviews), in a hierarchical form.

- The table on the rightmost side of the screen provides information, such as the workflow state of the item, the current owner, the reviewer, and when the item last changed.

- Menus provide access to common functions, such as copy and paste, print, and submit budget.

- The toolbar provides shortcuts to the same functionality as the menus.

- Tabs contain information organized by subjects, for example, in a sales application, you may have tabs for sales assumptions, sales input, and sales summary. A tab on the Contributor web site corresponds to a D-Cube in the Analyst program.

- Dimensions are lists of related items such as Profit and Loss items, months, products, customers, and cost centers. Dimensions also contain necessary calculations, such as total sales or gross profit.

- Data Entry and View cells: Business users enter or view planning information in this area. This area can be available for input (white cells) and read-only (gray cells).

Publishing and reporting planning data

Contributor, by design, is a planning data collection tool and though it creates, aggregates, and summarizes the data well, business planners will still need a robust reporting solution for querying and reporting planning data. IBM Cognos, as a BI leader, provides various tools, such as Analysis Studio, Report Studios, and Query Studios, to meet business users' reporting and analysis needs. The following paragraphs highlight the processes of integrating the planning data with the BI tools.

In the initial stage of a IBM Cognos multi-tools implementation, both the **Business Intelligence (BI)** modeler and you, as a planning modeler, work together to understand the users' reporting and analysis requirements. After learning the reporting requirements, both you and the BI modeler determine the Contributor data delivery options and work together to create the planning model and BI reports/analysis.

Once the planning model is ready, business users submit their plans and forecasts on the Contributor web site. The Contributor program stores users' submissions in one of the following types of supported database: MS SQL server, Oracle, and IBM DB2.

The Contributor submissions are stored in a proprietary XML format that cannot easily be accessed for reporting purposes. The data is held in a complicated format that cannot easily be read. There is a method for accessing this data using the Planning Data Service (formally the Contributor Data Server), but it is a slow process and is more suitable for ad hoc querying rather than for a full-scale BI reporting solution. For a more flexible BI reporting solution, the data can be published to a separate star schema database. The techniques for accessing live data or published data are explained in detail in Chapter 13, and are summarized as follows:

- **Live data**: This method allows you to read live Contributor data through the Planning Data Service, and does not need to be published. A package can be created that contains the connection to the live Contributor data in two ways.

- **Published data**: The Contributor data can be published to a separate star schema database. The publish process collects the data stored in XML format and moves it to a star schema database for more flexible reporting.

The publish process and the different techniques for accessing Contributor data for reporting purposes are explained in greater detail in Chapter 13.

Maintaining the planning models

The planning models periodically require minor to major modifications and maintenance. Most of the modifications are completed to accommodate changing business needs. Unlike ERP systems, which are used for transactional activities, planning models are generally used for a specific period of time. For example, a typical budget cycle could last only three to four weeks in a year. Most of the model modifications are needed before the planning cycle starts, and these modifications could affect both Analyst models and Contributor application configurations. Modelers, Contributor administrators, or a specialized support team, typically maintain or update planning models.

Maintaining the planning models and application may require many administrative activities, which will vary depending on the complexity of the models and the business needs. However, the following maintenance activities are common in many organizations using the IBM Cognos Planning tools:

- **Updating the model template**: As business requirements grow or diminish, the current model design may no longer satisfy business needs. Hence, the design of the model may require modifications and revisions. BI models will also require downstream changes.

- **Updating business assumptions**: Even if there is no change in the model design, typical business cycles will require some assumption updates, for example, changes in the tax rates, days to calculate depreciation, and so on.

- **e.List/users or data security changes**: Organizations often change their organizational chart and structure, and the planning model should immediately adapt to these changes. As an e.List stores the organization's hierarchy, this dimension requires constant updates to meet the business's needs. Users often move and transfer their jobs, and so their security access and privileges would need to be updated frequently.

IBM Cognos Planning offers automation features for scheduling various administrative tasks to facilitate maintenance of the applications. You, as a Contributor administrator, or the support team, can work with their IT department to automate various routine tasks, for example, publishing or transferring data between applications using admin links. Chapters 14 through 16 cover the maintenance topics.

Example: ABC Company

To illustrate the concepts discussed in this book, we will use a simple Profit and Loss model of our fictitious company, ABC Company. This model makes use of the common Analyst objects and functions that are important in the subsequent chapters. It will also be the template upon which we will build the Contributor web application. You can download this model from Packt Publishing's web site, `http://www.packtpub.com/files/code/6842_Code.zip`. The following are details of the company.

- Employees: 4,000

- Expense Departments: 1,100

- Products: 350

- Planning Cycle: Yearly budget

- Planning approach: Bottom up

- Number of Planners: 35 planners across the United States

- Fiscal Period: Calendar

- **Model Requirements**: In May 2009, the Director of ABC Company's Financial Planning Department has selected the IBM Cognos Planning tool to create the budget template for their 35 users. He/she asked you to work with the business users and design, and deploy the revenue and expense planning models for 2010 fiscal year. Some specific requirements are explained in the following section:

- **Revenue planning**:
    ◦ Plan next year (2010) revenue by products
    ◦ Apply current year (2009) drivers and price information
    ◦ Provide 'what if' capability to users
    ◦ Assume inflation of 4.5%
    ◦ Number of revenue planners = 15

- **Expense planning**:
  - ○ Plan next year (2010) expenses by accounts
  - ○ Apply current year (2009) actuals to drive next year expenses
  - ○ Provide 'what if' capability to users
  - ○ Number of expense planners = 20

- **Consolidate P&L**:
  - ○ Summarize next year (2010) revenue and expense plan
  - ○ Compare next year (2010) plan against the current year (2009) and actuals

- **Reports**:
  - ○ One canned P&L by departments and organization for the President and VPs
  - ○ One Analysis report to analyze revenue plan for revenue planners

Summary

In this chapter, we discussed the Model Development Process. Initially, we talked about the key factors that you need to watch out for, before designing and building the IBM Cognos Planning model.

We devoted the rest of the chapter to discussing the key Model Development Process, and the following steps were carried out:

- We explained the designing of the Analyst model, the importance of model flowcharting, the concepts of dimensions, datastores, data flow, and the principles of good Analyst model design
- We described the steps needed to create the Contributor application from the Analyst model
- We saw how the business users will enter and review the Contributor application
- We talked about the publishing process, and how to use Contributor planning data for analysis and reporting using IBM Cognos BI tools
- We discussed the maintenance of planning models and reports

In the next chapter, we will discuss the Analyst user interface and the key Analyst model building objects: D-Lists, D-Cubes, D-Links, A-tables, and File Maps.

4
Understanding the Analyst Environment

This chapter discusses the Analyst environment. Here we introduce you to the Analyst interface and discuss the various menus and toolbars that you need to know to work with the program. We show you how to access objects and navigate around the interface. We touch briefly on the various Analyst objects, and discuss the ways that you can organize the objects by using libraries. Finally, we cover some of the important administrative functions that enable you to validate your model and check for errors.

Getting familiar with Analyst

Analyst uses a **Graphical User Interface** (**GUI**) to allow you to access objects, enter data, and execute commands. There are three parts to the interface: menu toolbar, icon bar, and the display panel. The menu toolbar lets you access objects, execute routines, and perform administrative functions. The icons are shortcuts to the most commonly-used commands—commands such as opening an object or creating a new one. The display panel displays the objects, and allows you work with them. When you click on an object, the menu toolbar will display the actions that you can perform on the object. You can skip the toolbar and perform some of the more common actions by clicking the icons immediately below the toolbar. In this section, we will cover the basic navigation and administrative menus. The menus relating to specific objects will be covered in their respective chapters.

The following image shows the Analyst interface:

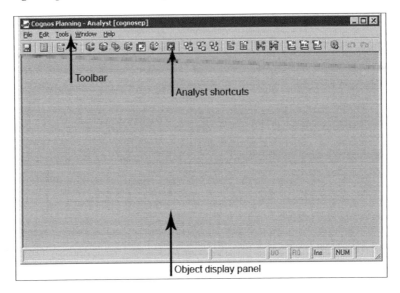

Using Analyst shortcuts

The icons along the toolbar allow you to open, create, or run objects at the single click of a mouse. The following is a list of Analyst icons and their functions:

Saves the active object.

Opens object Summary Info. Available only when object is open.

Create new D-List.

Open a D-List.

Create new D-Cube.

Open a D-Cube.

Reselect a D-Cube.

Open a new view of the active D-Cube.

Transpose a D-Cube.

Update a D-Cube.

Drills down to the data source.

Create a new D-Link.

Open a D-Link

Execute a D-Link.

Create a new File Map.

Open a File Map.

Create a new A-Table.

Open an A-Table.

Create a new Macro.

Open a Macro.

Execute Macro.

Publish.

Undo the last action.

Redo the last action.

Accessing Analyst objects

You can open a single object or multiple objects at the same time, but can only work with one object at a time.

To access a single object:

1. Click on **File | Open.**
2. Select the object type.
3. Click on the library containing the object.
4. Select the object.
5. Click on **OK** to open the object.

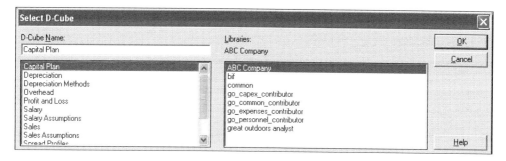

To open multiple objects:

1. Click on **File | Library | Objects.**

2. *Ctrl*-click on the objects in the upper pane of the **Library Functions** box. You can narrow down the list of objects by selecting the object type from the upper-right drop-down box.

3. Move the selected objects down to the lower pane by clicking on the down arrow on the middle toolbar.

4. Click on the **Open** 📂 icon to open the objects that you selected. Click on **OK**, when prompted.

In the following example, the **Profit and Loss**, **Capital Plan**, and **Overhead** cubes can be opened at the same time if you click on the **Open objects** icon.

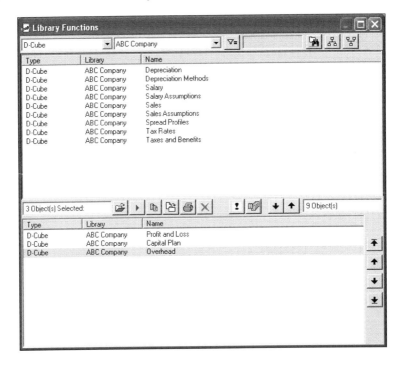

 The **Library Functions** box gives you a host of capabilities that allow you to work with multiple objects at the same time. This is particularly useful when you are building models and constantly making changes. You can open, rename, copy, print, or delete a group of objects by using this function. You can filter on objects, check object references, preview the objects, and perform a number of other actions.

Navigating within Analyst

Analyst uses standard GUI functionalities. You can maximize and minimize objects, cascade or tile multiple objects, copy and paste, and find text or numeric values. You can move objects or resize them to fit the screen. You can sort data, or dimensions, or mapped items. You can transpose cube dimensions, and swap rows, columns, or pages by dragging and dropping them.

Some of the useful navigational commands include:

To copy:

- Click on **Edit | Copy** (or press *Ctrl+C*).

To cut:

- Click on **Edit | Cut** (or press *Ctrl+X*).

To paste:

- Click on **Edit | Paste** (or press *Ctrl+V*).

To find values:

- Click on **Edit | Find** (or press *Ctrl+F*)
- Type the value in the **Find** box. Select **Match case** if necessary.
- Click on **Edit | Find Next** (or press *F3*) to find the next occurrence of the value.

To tile cascade objects:

- Click on **Window | Cascade**.

To tile multiple objects vertically:

- Click on **Window | Tile Vertically**.

To tile multiple objects horizontally:

- Click on **Window | Tile Horizontally**.

The building blocks of an Analyst model

The Analyst objects are the building blocks of planning model. An Analyst object is a sub-program, or a tool that performs a specific function, such as defining data structure, storing data, moving data, connecting to data sources, or automating tasks. An Analyst model consists of objects that are built upon each other. Each object serves a function that enables other objects to perform theirs. For example, a D-Cube will require at least two D-Lists to form its dimensions. A D-List might need a Saved Format, or another D-List to define its data attributes. An Allocation Table can use a D-List or data in a D-Cube as its source or target. Some objects are multi-functional. For example, a D-List can be a dimension of a cube, a source of an A-Table, and the source of dimension items for another D-List.

Virtually every object can be shared. For instance, a D-List can form the dimension of several D-Cubes. The ability to share objects is an important feature that can make maintenance so much easier. When a shared object is updated, its dependent objects are updated as well. With this collection of tools, you can create planning models that can be used as a Contributor web template that can be deployed to hundreds or thousands of planners, or be used strictly as an Analyst model for rigorous analysis.

Analyst objects

In Chapter 3, we briefly discussed the primary objects of an Analyst model: D-List, D-Cube, and D-Link. This section introduces you to the remaining objects that we need to be familiar with.

D-List

The D-List is a list of data attributes that define what data will be included in the model, how it is displayed, what values it can take, and what operation can be performed on these values.

D-Cube

The D-Cube is a multi-dimensional cube formed by two or more D-Lists. The D-Cube stores data. We can enter data into a D-Cube or transfer data from another D-Cube or an external data source. We can view the data in a variety of ways by dragging and dropping rows, columns, or pages.

D-Link

The D-Link transfers data into a D-Cube. In the D-Link, we define the data source and target D-Cube. The source of data in the D-Link can be another D-Cube, an ASCII file, or a database. When we create a D-Link, we determine how source dimensions and their dimension items correspond to target dimensions and their dimension items. We can map multiple sources to a single target and a single source to multiple targets.

Allocation Table (A-Table)

The A-Table maps source dimension items to target dimension items. It is used in conjunction with a D-Link. The A-Table is useful for complex or dynamic mapping, or when you are mapping a large set of data. The A-Table can be used by multiple D-Links, so that when we update the A-Table, all D-Links that use it will be updated as well. You can update A-Tables manually, or even import them from an external source such as an ODBC connection that points to your database.

File Map

File Map allows us to connect to an ASCII file so that we can transfer the data into a D-Cube. In the File Map, we define what fields in the ASCII file are dimensions in the target D-Cube, and what fields are data or dimension items. We also format the ASCII data to correspond to the data format of the target.

Saved Format

Saved Formats are mainly used in conjunction with a D-List. In a D-List, we format dimension items as Text, Numeric, or Date. By saving this format, we create a Saved Format object that can be reused by other D-Lists, or that can be applied to a full D-Cube. When we update the Saved Format, all D-Lists that use it will be updated as well.

Saved Selection

Saved Selections are used in conjunction with a D-Cube. A Saved Selection is a slice of the cube that you have saved. They can be compared to a view in a relational database. When we open a Saved Selection, we open only that slice of the cube. This is useful when we have a large cube with many dimensions.

Macro

A Macro consists of commands that automate certain activities that we perform in Analyst. We can record our tasks in a macro, and then schedule the macro to perform the task any time.

Organizing objects by using libraries

A library is a container that stores objects. It provides a way to group and organize objects. An entire planning system can easily involve hundreds or even thousands of objects. So organizing them in a logical manner helps you and other users to easily find objects. Objects that are stored in a library can reference objects outside of the library. This allows you to store objects in any library and still make them accessible to other objects. You can store an entire model in one library, or spread parts of the model between two or more libraries. You can store different versions of the same model is separate libraries. In addition to providing a way to organize objects, libraries offer a way to secure objects. When there are multiple Analyst users, you may want to restrict certain users from having access to your models. Analyst provides library-level security. Because you can set security on a library, you can give users write, read, or no access to objects in the library. By securing access to objects, you can control how models can be built. Any user that uses an object in a library where the user only has read access will not be able to alter the object.

 An Analyst model that will be used as a Contributor template can have no more than two libraries, one containing the model itself and the other containing shared objects. You will not be able to create the Contributor application if the objects reside in more than two libraries.

Creating a library

Underlying the library is a Windows folder. When you create a library, Analyst will prompt you to enter the path to the folder, or will create the folder, if none exists. Once the library is created, you can store your objects in it. These objects will reside in the folder.

To create a library:

1. Click on **File | Administration | Maintain Libraries and Users**.
2. In the **Maintain Libraries and Users** box, click on **Add**.

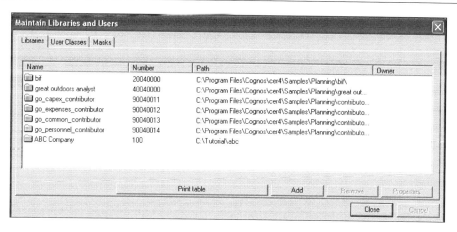

3. In the **Add New Library** dialog, enter the following:

   ○ **Library No.** — Enter a unique number. This number will be permanently attached to a Contributor application, so it is a good practice to establish a numbering system that is logical and sensible.

   ○ **Name** — Enter the name of the library. The name must be representative of the objects that will be stored in the library. You might want to use the words "common", "staging", and "archive" to indicate the type of library.

   ○ **Description** — Enter a description of the library.

   ○ **Path** — Enter the path to the library folder. The folder is typically named in the same way as the library, but if you expect to be changing the library name later, you may consider using something more permanent, such as the library number, so that you do not have to change the folder name if the library name changes.

 If multiple users will be using Analyst, it is best to use **Universal Naming Convention (UNC)** paths to the library folder so that the users will be able to share objects, and you, as an administrator, can have access to all objects.

4. Click on **OK** to create the library.

Deleting a library

When you delete a library, you only remove the connection between Analyst and the Windows folder. You must delete the Windows folder after you remove the library.

To delete a library:

1. Click on **File | Administration | Maintain Libraries and Users**.

2. In the **Maintain Libraries and Users** box, click on **Remove**.

3. Delete the library folder in Windows Explorer.

 When you create an object in Analyst, Analyst creates a new file under the Windows folder that has been configured for the Analyst library, where the object resides. The files are given the suffixes .h0, .d1, and .d2, representing the type of object. You should not tamper with these files, or you will run the risk of severing the object references and corrupting your models' index files. If you want to create, delete, move, or copy objects, you should do it from within Analyst.

Considerations for creating libraries

There are several things to think about before you create your library structure. Some of the questions you should ask are:

- How many models will be built?
- How is ownership of the models distributed within the organization?
- Will there be multiple users using Analyst?
- Will users be building and maintaining their own models?
- Will there be multiple levels of ownership of the models?
- What objects will be shared?
- Will data be staged in Analyst?
- Do you need to archive models?
- Do you need to duplicate models for versioning purposes?

A library structure can be a simple one, or it can be complex, depending on your answers to these questions. If you expect that many models will be created, you may want to create separate libraries for each model, and establish a naming and numbering convention. You may decide to create a global common library for all models, and a regionalized common library for a particular group of models. For instance, you can have a common library for all of the Analyst models and another for expense models. If many users will be using Analyst, you will have to decide on how you will secure the objects so that users will only have access to their own models as shared objects.

Shared objects are usually maintained and controlled by the Analyst administrator, but model-specific shared objects can be owned by the model owner. These objects will have to be stored in a central library that is available to the users. You also have to decide how to organize libraries for data. Data usually enters the models through a staging area and is distributed to various models. The staging could be a library, containing cubes specifically built to stage data. In a situation where model ownership involves many users, data many need to move from one central staging library to a regionalized staging library. Finally, you may decide to archive your models for future reference. Thus you may need to create a library solely to archive objects.

Types of libraries

There are no restrictions to how you can organize your libraries. A great deal has to do with a variety of factors, including those described earlier. However, there are certain categories of libraries that have been used in practice. These are the common, model, data or staging, and archive libraries.

Common library

Common libraries store shared objects. The common library must be accessible to users that use the shared objects. For instance, if a D-Cube in another library uses a D-List in the common library, the user must have read access to the common library in order to be able to open the D-Cube. Any object can be stored in the common library, but to keep the libraries consistent, you must store only those objects that you plan to share with others. A rule of thumb to use when deciding whether or not to share objects is to ask the question: Does the object hold data that is used by several models. There are many types of data that can be used globally. For instance, timescales (days, months, years), versions (budget, forecast, actual), and accounts.

Another question to ask is: What data do you want to control and impose upon other models? Examples of such data are exchange rates, tax rates, corporate assumptions, pay scales, and so on. In addition to controlling data, you may want to control the way that models are built, by storing their structural sources in a common library. For instance, if you want to standardize the accounts used in the Analyst models, you can create a master accounts D-List that supplies the accounts D-Lists to the various models. By storing common objects in a central location and sharing them, you can keep models from deviating from your organization's policies, and gain better control over how plans are developed.

Model library

Model libraries contain the primary objects that make up the Analyst model. When you deploy a planning model to the users, you deploy the objects in the model library. In general, the model library should contain the calculation D-Lists, D-Cubes, and D-Links, as well as other model-specific objects. You may use objects in the common library, but you should avoid going outside of the model and common libraries if you plan to deploy the model using Contributor. As a rule, you should store those objects in the model library that are used exclusively by the model. You should not store objects that you plan to share. Likewise, you should not store objects that do not play a part in the model's primary function. For instance, macros, reports, saved selections, and saved formats are ignored by Contributor. Thus, they do not need to be in the model library. As we shall discuss in later chapters, what you store in the model library will determine whether or not the model can be deployed in Contributor.

Staging library

The staging library contains objects that are used to stage data. In most of the cases, data from external sources does not conform to conventions used in the planning models. Thus, data must be staged, and all of the necessary data conversions must be done in Analyst. The staging library contains objects that *cleanse* data so that they can be linked to the Contributor models or to Analyst models. These objects are usually distinct from the ones used in the models because they perform a completely different function.

Although you can stage data in Analyst, it is better to have the staging handled elsewhere, such as in a database or ETL tool. By using these tools, you can make the necessary data conversions and import clean data into a data mart that can easily be fed directly into the Contributor import tables or Analyst models. By doing this you eliminate the need for *staging* objects that you will have to maintain all of the time.

Archive library

Archive libraries contain copies of objects and data. Occasionally, you may want to preserve a previously-used model for back-up or audit purposes. You may also want to preserve data in order to use them to create historical baselines for the next planning cycle. When you archive objects, you create a copy of them at a point in time. The objects stored in an archive library should be static copies only, and should have no references to objects outside of their library. If the archived object is dependent on an active object outside the library, any change to the active object will alter the archived object and everything that references that object. Thus, it is important that when you archive an object, you include all possible object references to the archived objects.

Basic administration tools

Analyst provides some functions to enable you to administer the models. With these functions you can manage libraries, search for BiFs and ODBC connections, change your Analyst configurations, and refresh broken references and index files.

Maintain Libraries and Users

The **Maintain Libraries and Users** menu allows you to create, delete, and rename libraries. It also allows you to grant users access to libraries. Earlier in this chapter, we went through the steps of creating and deleting a library. Chapter 16 will discuss in detail the steps required to add roles and groups and assign them to libraries.

To enable the **Maintain Libraries and Users** option:

* Click on **File | Administration | Maintain Libraries and Users**.

Rebuild the index file

The index file is a system-generated table that lists all of the objects in the library. On rare occasions, the index file becomes corrupt. This is known to happen when you frequently copy or move the object files or library folders by using Windows Explorer, instead of doing it in Analyst.

To rebuild the index file:

1. Click on **File | Administration | Rebuild Index**.
2. Select the library whose index file you want to rebuild.
3. Click on **OK**.

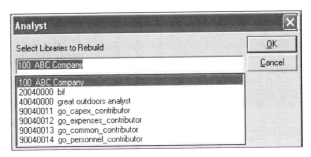

Refresh references

Occasionally, references can become corrupt, especially when models are large and the relationships between objects are very complex, or when objects are constantly copied, moved, or deleted. By refreshing references, you restore the relevant connections between objects, and remove invalid references.

To refresh references:

1. Click on **File | Administration | Refresh References**.
2. Select the library to refresh.
3. Click on **OK**.

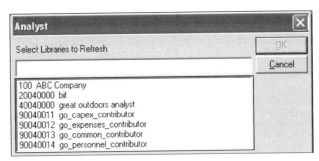

Validate D-Lists

You can validate the D-Lists in your library, and check for syntax or calculation errors in all of your formulas.

To validate D-Lists:

1. Click on **File | Administration | Validate D-Lists**.
2. Select the library that contains the D-List. *Ctrl*-click to select multiple libraries.
3. Click on **OK**.

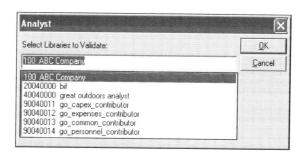

Locate ODBC sources

When you connect to a variety of data sources using ODBC, you can track the objects that use ODBC sources.

To locate ODBC Sources:

1. Click on **File | Administration | Locate ODBC Sources**.
2. In the **Select ODBC source** box, select the name of the ODBC connection, or select all ODBC connections.
3. In the **Select library** box, select the library where the ODBC connection is use, or select all of the libraries.
4. Under **Look for objects of type**, select **D-List**, or **D-Link**, or both.
5. Click on **Search Now** to begin the search. The object that is using the ODBC connection will appear in the rightmost pane.
6. You can use the **Filter** to filter on an object by typing the object name, or you can filter on the table name by entering the table name.

7.   In the rightmost pane, you can open, print, or preview an object by right-clicking on it, and then selecting the appropriate option from the context menu.

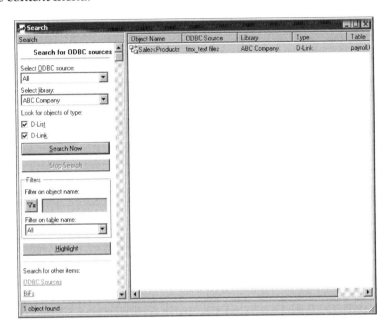

Locate Built-in Functions

You can locate Built-in Functions in the library. A **Built-in Function (BiF)** is a pre-built calculation used in a D-List to perform complex algorithms. You can locate a certain type of BiF, or a specific one, by using this feature. You can locate the BiF in one library or in all libraries. You can also filter on or highlight a particular BiF.

To locate Built-in Functions:

1.   Click on **File | Administration | Locate Built-in Functions**.
2.   In the **Select Built-in Function** box, select the name of the BiF, or select **All**.
3.   In the **Select library box**, select the library where the BiF is used, or select all of the libraries.
4.   Click on **Search Now** to begin the search. The BiF that is being used in the library appears in the rightmost pane.
5.   You can filter on a BiF by typing the BiF name. Click on **Highlight** to highlight the BiF that you want to view.
6.   You can open, print, or preview the object by right-clicking on it, and then selecting the appropriate option from the context menu.

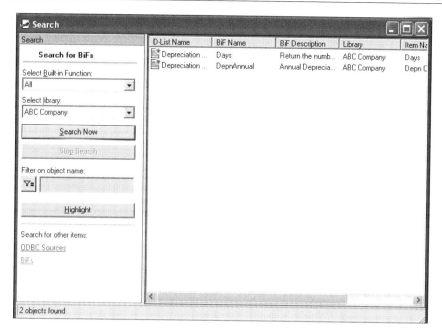

Configuring Analyst

The following section discusses some of the important configurations that you can do in Analyst. In most of the cases, these configurations will have already been completed during installation, but it is good to know where to find them in case you want to change them.

Changing the path to the Filesys.ini

This is important if you are installing or configuring Analyst. This option allows you to change the path to the `Filesys.ini` file. The `Filesys.ini` file is the control file that contains the location of the various files required by Analyst in order to function. When Analyst restarts, it looks to this file to find the paths to the `Libs.tab`, `Users.tab`, and `Groups.tab`. These TAB files contain information on your specific library and users. `Filesys.ini` also contains the path to the locks and login files, files that track user logins and locks objects, so that no two users can have edit rights on the same object. The paths to these files must make use of universal naming conventions, so that when you have multiple installations of Analyst, you can point to the same files and have users work on the same system, sharing objects, and models.

To change the `Filesys.ini` path:

1. Click on **Tools | Options**.
2. Click on the **General** tab.
3. In the **Active Filesys.ini file** box, enter the path to the `Filesys.ini` file.

Changing the maximum workspace

The **maximum workspace** is the amount of memory that you reserve for Analyst when the program is active.

To change the maximum workspace:

1. Click on **Tools | Options**.
2. Click on the **General** tab.
3. In the **Maximum Workspace Size** box, enter the amount of the workspace that should be reserved. A rule of thumb is to use approximately half of your PC's RAM.

Changing keyboard layout

To change the keyboard layout:

1. Click on **Tools | Options**.
2. Click on the **Language** tab.
3. In the **Keyboard Layout** box, select the language that you want to use.
4. Click on **OK**.

Changing the number of undos and redos

You can undo or redo actions in Analyst by enabling this feature. But you should use this only if it is absolutely necessary. This feature requires a great deal of memory and impairs performance so much that it is often left disabled. If you are working with large cubes, you may be limited in the number of Undo/Redo steps that you can perform, or you may not be able to use this feature at all, depending on the workspace that you reserve.

 Instead of enabling the Undo/Redo feature, use the **File | Reset** action to restore the cube to its last saved state.

To enable the Undo/Redo feature, carry out the following steps:

1. Click on **Tools | Options**.
2. Click on the **Undo** tab.
3. Enable **Undo/Redo** (by default this feature is disabled).
4. Under **Undo Limits**, enter the following:
   - **Undo Stack Size (excluding D-Cube data)**
   - **D-Cube Data Undo Stack Size**
   - **Maximum Undoable View Size**

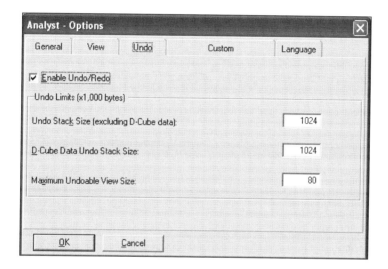

Summary

In this chapter, we introduced you to the Analyst interface and showed you how you can navigate within and work with objects in Analyst. We touched on the important Analyst objects and their functions. We discussed, in detail, how you can use libraries to organize objects, and offered you our approach to creating a solid library structure. We showed you how you can configure Analyst and enable additional program features. Finally, we discussed the various administration functions that let you manage libraries, optimize Analyst, search for BiFs and ODBC connections, and fix corrupt index files and references.

5

Defining Data Structures: D-List

In the previous chapter, we introduced you to D-List. In this chapter, we will cover the characteristics of D-List in greater detail. We will show you how to create and update a D-List from many different sources. We will demonstrate how to embed formulas, and how to resolve calculation conflicts and circular references. We will also show you how you can format D-List items to numeric, text, and date datatypes. We will explain the different categories of D-Lists and how they should be ordered in a D-Cube. Finally, we will explain the e.List and the important role it plays in the model.

Overview of D-List

In the previous chapter, we defined D-List as a list of data attributes that define what data will be included in the model, how this data is displayed, what values it can take, and what operations can be performed on these values. Think of D-List as the items on the rows and columns of a spreadsheet, or the fields in a table. When you create the field, you start by defining its attributes. With the D-list, you do the same thing. You determine what data will be entered by the user, what will be pre-populated from other data sources, and what will be calculated.

The following is an example of a Profit and Loss D-List:

	Item name	Format	Calculation	Calc. Option
	[D-List] ABC Company.Profit and Loss Summary			
1	Gross Revenue			
2	Allowances			
3	Net Revenue		=	
4	Cost of Sales			
5	Gross Profit		=	
6	Salary			
7	Benefits			
8	Occupancy			
9	Depreciation			
10	Advertising			
11	Travel			
12	Miscellaneous			
13	Total Operating		Subtotal	
14	Operating Profit		=	
15	Profit		Subtotal	
16	Taxes			
17	Profit after Taxes		=	

Change item attributes >>

Creating the D-List

There are several ways in which you can create a D-List. You can create it manually by typing the D-List items or copying and pasting the items from another source such as Excel. Or you can import the items from a data source, such as a database, text file, D-Cube, or another D-List. You can connect to any ODBC data source and update the D-List with new items from the source automatically.

Manually typing the D-List Items

You can type text, numbers, and special characters directly into the D-List. Analyst is case-sensitive. You can type the words "Profit", "PROFIT", and "profit" as distinct items in the D-List. However, you should avoid doing this so as not to confuse the user. Also, most reporting systems are not case-sensitive and this will become a problem if you are publishing data for reporting purposes. When typing the item name, keep the number of characters as few as possible so that when used as a row dimension or column, the D-List does not take up so much width space that it leaves little room for viewable data.

To manually create the D-List:

1. Click on **File | New | D-List**.

2. Type the list of items in the **Input New Items** box. See the following illustration:

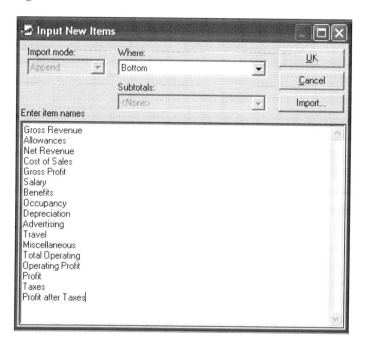

3. Click on **OK**.

4. Save the D-List.

You can build your list in Excel and copy it into the **New Input Items** box. For instance, instead of typing a sequence of unique numbers, you can write a formula in Excel and then copy the results.

Importing D-List items from an ASCII file

You can import D-List items directly from an ASCII delimited file. This is the most basic way of importing items. When using this approach, you will be prompted to select the field that contains the items that you want to import. You will not have the option to pick and choose items in the file. So use this method only if all of the data in the field you have selected are relevant D-List items.

To import items from an ASCII delimited file:

1. Click on **File | New | D-List**.

2. In the **Input New Items** box, click on the **Import** button.

3. Select **Import from ASCII File**.

4. Browse for the source file, and then click on **OK**.

5. In the **Apply Structure** box, click on **Use Delimiter** and select the type of delimiter used by the ASCII file.

6. Under **View of raw imports columns**, click on the column that contains the items that you wish to import. Then, under **Select attribute**, select **Item Name**. If the ASCII file contains parent-child hierarchy information, click on the parent column and select **Parent, Parent 2, Parent 3**, and so on. See the following illustration:

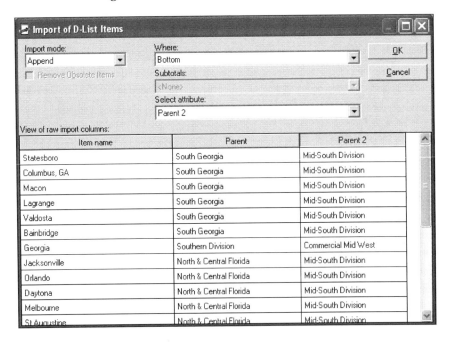

7. Click on **OK**.

8. A message will appear: **Do you want to turn this import into an import link for this D-List**. By clicking on **Yes**, you will create a connection to the source ASCII file so that you can import new items from the same file using the same configuration. Click on **No** if you do not want to save the parameters.

Importing the D-List items from a File Map

A File Map is an object that lets you connect to an ASCII delimited file. Used in conjunction with a D-Link, a File Map lets you define the dimension and data items so that you can link data from the text file into a cube. However, you can use a File Map as your source for D-List items, just as you can with a text file. There is essentially little difference between the two, as neither method provides the ability to select specific data sets.

To import D-List items from a File Map:

1. Click on **File | New | D-List**.
2. In the **Input New Items** box, select the **Import** button.
3. Select **Import from Mapped ASCII File**.
4. Click on **File Map**.
5. In the **Apply Structure** box, click on **Use Delimiter** and select the type of delimiter used by the file.
6. Under **View of raw imports columns**, click on the column that contains the items that you wish to import. Then, under **Select Attribute**, select **Item Name**. If the File Map contains child-parent hierarchy information, click on the parent column and select **Parent**, **Parent 2**, **Parent 3**, and so on.
7. Click on **OK**.
8. A message will appear: **Do you want to turn this import into an import link for this D-List**. By clicking on **Yes**, you will create a connection to the File Map so that you can import new items from the same object using the same configuration. Click on **No** if you do not want to save the parameters.

Importing the D-List items from an ODBC source

If your source is a database, a spreadsheet, or a text file, you can connect to it by using the Windows ODBC connection tool. You must configure the ODBC connection in Windows before using this option. See Chapter 7, for instructions on configuring the ODBC connection. Once the ODBC connection is configured in Windows, it becomes an option that you can use to import D-List items. The most important advantage of using this method is that you have the ability to manipulate data before importing it. However, this method requires some knowledge of SQL in order to manipulate the data.

To import items from an ODBC source:

1. Click on **File | New | D-List**.

2. In the **Input New Items** box, select the **Import** button.

3. Select **Import from ODBC (SQL database)**.

4. In the **ODBC logon** box, click on the ODBC source and enter your user ID and password. Click on **OK** to connect.

5. In the **Active ODBC-source: Text Files** box, under **Available tables**, click on the table containing the D-List items.

6. In the **SQL Statement** box, write the SQL statements to extract the required data from the appropriate table. The results will appear under the **Preview of columns** box when you click on **Fetch**. Click on **OK** to connect to the data source.

7. Under **View of raw imports columns**, click on the column that contains the items that you wish to import. Then, under **Select Attribute**, select **Item Name**. If the table contains child-parent hierarchy information, click on the parent column and select **Parent**, **Parent 2**, **Parent 3**, and so on.

8. Click on **OK**.

9. A message will appear: **Do you want to turn this import into an import link for this D-List**. By clicking on **Yes**, you will create a connection to the ODBC data source so that you can import new items from the same source using the same configuration. Click on **No** if you do not want to save the parameters.

Importing the D-List items from data in a D-Cube

You can import D-List items from a D-Cube. To do this, you must select a slice of the source cube that consists of rows and columns, and only one item on each page. Think of the source data as a table that represents the rows and columns that are visible to you when you open the cube. You can see several rows and columns in a slice, but only one page at a time.

To import items from D-Cube data:

1. Click on **File | New | D-List**.

2. In the **Input New Items** box, select the **Import** button.

3. Select **Import from D-Cube Data**.

4. Select **D-Cube**, and then click on **OK**.

5. In the **Select page to import** box, select the rows, columns, and page that contain the data you want to import, and move them from the **Items available** to the **Items included pane**.

6. Click on **Slice**.

7. In the **Select Row and Column** box, select which dimensions will be the rows and columns of the cube.

8. Click on **OK**.

9. Under **View of raw imports columns**, click on the column that contains the items that you wish to import.

10. Under **Select Attributes**, select **Item Name**.

11. Click on **OK**.

12. A message will appear: **Do you want to turn this import into an import link for this D-List**. By clicking on **Yes**, you will create a connection to the D-Cube so that you can import new items from the same object using the same configuration. Click on **No** if you do not want to save the parameters.

Importing the D-List Items from another D-List

You can import items into a D-List from another D-List. If you use this method, you can choose which items in the source D-List you want to import, or you can opt to import all of them. This is most useful when you have items such as a chart of accounts, a cost center list, or a department list, and you need to construct separate D-Lists that contain subsets of the complete list. A good practice is to import the complete list into a master D-List and then import the subset from the master D-List. This will ensure a consistent naming convention across all of the models.

To import items from another D-List:

1. Click on **File | New | D-List**.

2. In the **Input New Items** box, select the **Import** button.

3. Select **Import from another D-List**.

4. Select the D-List, and then click on **OK**.

5. Select the items you want to import from the **Items available** pane and move them to the **Items included** pane. Click on **OK**.

6. In the **Specify Import** box, select the following:

   i. Import Mode:

      Append—add new items to the existing list.

      Update—add new items, and modify existing items according to the items in the data source.

   ii. In the **Where** box, select how you want to arrange the items that you are importing.

iii. In the **Subtotals** box, specify the subtotal that you want the all of the items to roll into, or choose either of the following:

None — Do not roll new items to any subtotal.

Allocate — Allocate each of the items to one or more subtotals.

iv. Under **Import Options**, select the following options as described. If none of these options is selected then all of the items will be imported unformatted, and their calculations will be ignored.

a. **Import Detail Items** — select this option if you want to import only detail items from the source D-List.

b. **Import Calculated Items** — select this option if you want to import only calculated items from the source D-List.

c. **Import Format attribute** — select this option if you want to import the format of the D-List items you are importing.

d. **Import Formulae** — Select this option if you want to import the formula of the D-List items that you are importing.

7. Click on **OK**.

8. A message will appear: **Do you want to turn this import into an import link for this D-List**. By clicking on **Yes**, you will create a connection to the source D-List and save your selected parameters, enabling you to import new items later. Click on **No** if you do not want to save the parameters.

Setting the import parameters

You can control the way you import data into a D-List when you are using the import methods (discussed in previous section). If you are adding new items to an existing D-List, you can append the new items, or you can replace any existing list with the new items. You can arrange the items manually or by using a predefined order. You can also add new items to an existing subtotal, or to several subtotals, automatically.

To set the import parameters:

1. Under **Import Mode** select the following:

i. **Append** — Add new items to any existing list.

ii. **Update** — Add new items, and modify existing items according to items in the data source.

2. In the **Where** box, select how you want to arrange the items you are importing.

3. In the **Subtotals** box, specify the subtotal that you want all of the items to roll into, or choose either of the following:

    i. **None**—Do not add new items to any subtotal.

    ii. **Allocate**—Allocate the items to more than one subtotals.

Modifying the import parameters

When you create a D-List using any one of the import methods, you have the option to save the import parameters. If you decide to change the parameters later, you can still do so using this step. You can also disconnect the import link if the source is no longer valid.

To modify the import parameters:

1. Click on **File | Open | D-List**.
2. Select the D-List, and then click on **OK**.
3. Click on **D-List | Options**.
4. Click on the **Import** tab.
5. In the **Import from** box, select the method used to import the items. Select **No Import Link** if you want to disable the link to the source.
6. Enter the import parameters as required.
7. Click on **OK**.
8. Save the D-List.

Updating the D-List

When you import data from a data source using any of the import options above, you can update the D-List with new items from the data source.

To update the D-List:

1. Click on **File | Open | D-List**.
2. Select the D-List, and then click on **OK**.
3. Click on **D-List | Update**.

Updating D-List item names from a data source

When item names change in the data source, you want your D-List item names to change accordingly without having to delete and recreate the D-List item. For instance, suppose you had an account called "51000 Travel" and that account was renamed to "51000 Travel and Entertainment". You want the D-List item to be renamed to the new account description. The problem is that when you import the new description, Analyst will see this as a new item instead of a revision of an existing item. If you have your import link configured to delete items that do not exist in the source, Analyst will delete "51000 Travel" and all of its data, and create "51000 Travel and Entertainment". That is not what you want. What you want is for Analyst to rename the account and preserve the data it contains. You can do this through the **Unique names** function of the D-List. The Unique names function allows you to define a string of characters in the item name that is unique. When you update the D-List, the program compares the unique string to the source and if the string exists, the program modifies the existing item name with the names from the source.

To enable the Unique names function:

1. Click on **File | Open | D-List**.
2. Select the D-List, and then click on **OK**.
3. Click on **D-List | Options**.
4. Click on the **Unique names** tab.
5. Click on the space after the last character of the unique string.
6. Click on **OK**.
7. Save the D-List.

In the following illustration, the first four characters represent the unique string. Anything to the right of the unique string will be renamed to the new description in the source.

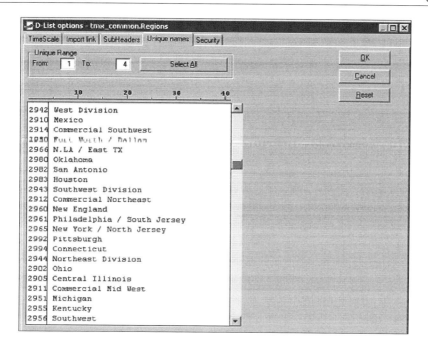

Adding new items to a D-List

You can add new items to an existing D-List. You can do this manually by typing the items directly into the input box, or by importing the items using one of the import methods that were discussed previously.

To add new items to a D-List:

1. Click on **File | Open | D-List**.
2. Select the D-List, and then click **OK**.
3. Click on **D-List | Add Items**.
4. Select how you want to add the items. Then follow the same steps described previously for creating a new D-list (manual or import).

Deleting D-List items

You can manually delete an item. If you are using the import link, the item will be deleted when the **Remove Obsolete Items** option is checked. Once removed, the item and its data will be deleted permanently.

To delete new D-List items:

1. Click on **File | Open | D-List**.
2. Select the D-List, and then click **OK**.
3. Click on **D-List | Delete Items**.
4. Select the items that you want to delete in the **Items available** pane, and move them to the **Items included** pane. Click on **OK**.
5. Click on **Yes**, when prompted to delete the item.
6. Save the D-List.

Reordering D-List Items

You can reorder items in a D-List. Reordering items will not delete data. You can choose to reorder manually or by using a predefined method. The reorder option provides a number of ways of organizing the items. Typically, you should use the manual method if the positions of the items need to remain in a certain way. This is usually the case with calculation D-Lists. You should use the predefined method if the items in the D-List items can follow a logical order (such as alphabetical or numerical), and if you are using the import link to update the D-List. Most aggregation D-Lists can be reordered in this way.

To reorder D-List items:

1. Click on **File | Open | D-List**.
2. Select the D-List, and then click on **OK**.
3. Click on **D-List | Reorder**.
4. Select how you want to reorder the items. If you select **Manual**, the **Reorder items** box will appear. In the **Items included** pane, move the items to their new positions by using the arrow buttons. If you do not opt for the manual method, select the order from the list of predefined methods.
5. Click on **OK**.
6. Save the D-List.

Implementing D-List changes

If you change a formula in a D-List, you can view the effect that this change will have on the data in the D-Cube by using the **Implement** option. Implementing a change will not save the D-List, so you can reset the D-List to its previously-saved state if you decide to cancel the change. If, after implementing the change, you accept the formula change, you can save the D-List. You will not be able to save the D-Cube if your changes to the D-List have not been saved.

To implement changes to a D-List without saving:

1. Click on **File | Open | D-List**.
2. Select the D-List, and then click on **OK**.
3. Make your changes to the D-List.
4. Click on **D-List | Implement** to view the effect of the changes.
5. Click on **File | Reset** to revert to the original D-List.

Before implementing a change, make sure that all acceptable changes to the D-List have been saved. If you are forced to reset the D-List, Analyst will restore the last saved version and all of your changes, including the ones that are acceptable, will be lost.

Non-permissible characters in a D-List

Each D-List item can take up to 50 characters. You can use letters, numbers, spaces, or special keyboard characters. However, there are certain characters that you should avoid. These characters are reserved for use in the Analyst program when executing certain built-in functions or calculations. They are:

- Semi-colon (;)
- Brackets ([ ])
- At signs (@)
- Braces ({ })

Sometimes you need to create a blank D-List item as a way of creating a break between rows or columns. You can do this by typing a pipe (|). The pipe character becomes a space when viewed in a D-Cube in Analyst or Contributor.

Item ID (IID) in a D-List

When you create a D-List item, you do so by typing the display name. Upon saving the D-List, the Analyst program assigns an **Item ID (IID)**, starting with 1, to the item. This IID is permanently associated with the item. If you delete the item, you delete the IID forever. If you recreate the item, the program assigns a new IID, even if the new item is exactly the same as the old one. The IID identifies the D-List item. If you change the display name, the IID stays the same. The IID is used in calculations and D-Links. It allows you to change the display name without affecting the references to the D-List item.

In Excel, when you use text in a formula, you have to revise the formula each time that the text changes. This is not the case in IBM Cognos Planning. Text is not used in formulas. Instead, IIDs that refer to text are used. This enables you to change the text without having to update the formula.

To view the IID of a D-List item:

1. Click on **File | Open | D-List**.
2. Select the D-List, and then click on **OK**.
3. Click on **File | Summary Info**.
4. Click on the **Item Details** tab.

The following illustration displays the Item ID of the Profit and Loss Summary D-List:

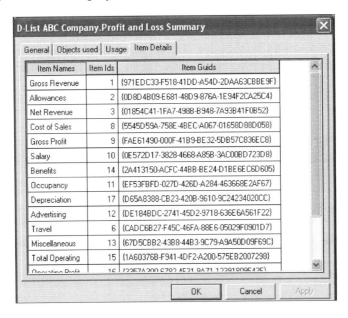

Entering formulas in a D-List

After you have created the D-List, you can start writing formulas. Each D-List item provides a calculation box into which you can directly type your formulas. There are important rules that must be adhered to when writing calculations. This section discusses the rules and techniques for writing formulas. It also covers some of the conventions for writing conditional statements, and explains how to use BiFs to perform complex time-based calculations.

To enter a formula in a D-List:

1. Click on **File | Open | D-List**.
2. Select the D-List, and then click on **OK**.
3. Find the D-List item into which you want to enter a formula, and then click on the cell directly under the **Calculation** column. Next, click on **Change item attributes** at the lower-right corner of the D-List to open the Calculation box.
4. Type the formula into the **Calculation** box.
5. Click on the **Apply** button.
6. Save the D-List.

How formulas are written

Analyst works with the basic mathematical operators: addition (+), subtraction (-), multiplication (*), division (/), percentage (%), and power (^).

When writing a formula, you use the D-List item name to refer to the item. For instance, in the illustration below, the formula for Net Revenue is Gross Revenue – Allowances.

To embed this formula into Net Revenue, type the following in the Net Revenue calculation box:

+{Gross Revenue}

-Allowances

See the following illustration:

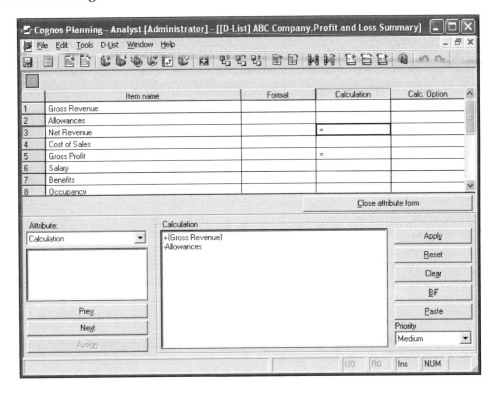

Note that **Gross Revenue** is enclosed in braces (**{ }**). In Analyst, any D-List item name that contains spaces must be enclosed in braces. Analyst ignores spaces, tabs, and line returns outside of the D-List item name. So you can arrange the formula in any manner. For instance, you can rearrange the previous formula to:

-Allowances+{Gross Revenue}

Or

{Gross Revenue}   -   Allowances

Even though Analyst requires that you type the *item name* in a formula, it actually refers to the item by its IID. So if you change the name, the formula will automatically change to reflect the new name. Moreover, formulas are case-sensitive. GROSS REVENUE will not work if the item name is Gross Revenue.

The IID ensures that when you change the display name, calculations do not need updating. When you change the display name, the formula will pick up the change, so you do not need to rewrite it.

Using the Paste function when writing formulas

You can import the item name into your calculations by using the Paste function. When you click on the **Paste** button, Analyst displays all of the D-List items, and you can select the items that you want to include in the formula. Once imported, the items appear in the calculation box, and you can rearrange them accordingly.

Use the following steps to use the **Paste** function:

1. Open the D-List.
2. Find the D-List item into which you want to enter a formula, and then click on the cell directly under the **Calculation** column. Next, click on the **Change item attributes** at the lower right corner of the D-List to open the calculation box.
3. Click on the **Paste** button. The list of items will appear under the **Items available** pane.
4. Select the items that you want to include in the formula, and move them to the **Items included** pane.
5. Click on **OK**.

Writing conditional statements

You can write a conditional statement that checks whether a condition is true or false before applying the calculation. The conditional operators are IF, THEN, ELSE, AND, and OR. All conditional operators must be in upper case. Relational operators are: equal to (=) greater than (>), less that (<), greater than or equal to (>=), less than or equal to (<=), and not equal to (<>).

Here are the most common conditional statements.

*   Basic syntax:

    IF

    THEN

    Where IF establishes the criteria. If the data meets the criteria, then Analyst executes the calculation defined in THEN. Otherwise, Analyst produces zero.

- Syntax for using an alternative expression:

```
IF
THEN
ELSE
```

  Where IF establishes the criterion. If the data meets the criterion, then Analyst executes the calculation defined in THEN. If the data does not meet the criterion, Analyst executes the calculation defined in ELSE.

- Syntax for two or more conditions using AND:

```
IF (Condition 1 AND Condition 2)
THEN
ELSE
```

  Where IF establishes the criteria that requires all of the conditions should be met. If the data meets all of the criteria, then Analyst executes the calculation defined in THEN. If the data does not meet all of the criteria, then Analyst executes the calculation defined in ELSE.

- Syntax for two or more conditions using OR:

```
IF (Condition 1 OR Condition 2)
THEN
ELSE
```

  Where IF establishes the criteria that requires any one of the conditions to be met. If the data meets any of the criteria, then Analyst executes the calculation defined in THEN. If the data does not meet any of the criteria, then Analyst executes the calculation defined in ELSE.

- Syntax for nested criteria:

```
IF (Criteria 1)
THEN
IF (Criteria 2)
THEN
ELSE
```

  Where IF establishes the criteria that requires any one of the conditions to be met. If the data meets the criteria, then Analyst executes the calculation defined in THEN. If the data does not meet the criteria, Analyst proceeds with the next criteria and repeats the logic.

Conflicts in calculation

In a multi-dimensional cube, conflicts in calculation can occur. Suppose you have a D-Cube that uses two D-Lists that both have calculations. The first D-List has a subtotal that aggregates its items (Product1 + Product2 + Product3). The second D-List multiplies Unit by Price (Unit * Price). In this example, you have two possible calculations:

Calculation 1:

```
(Product1(Units*Price)+ Product2(Units*Price)+ Product3(Units*Price)
```

Calculation 2:

```
(Product1(Units)+ Product2(Units)+Product3(Units)) *
(Product1(Units*Price)+ Product2(Units*Price)+ Product3(Units*Price)
```

Depending on the priority of the calculations, Analyst will produce entirely different results. Analyst will add all the units and add all the cost per unit, then multiply the results by each other or (the correct way) Analyst will multiply the units by cost for each product, then add the results.

Using the D-List priority option

Analyst enforces priorities in two ways. The first is through the order of the dimensions of the cube. This is the primary way where the conflicts in calculations need to be resolved. We will discuss the order of the D-List later in Chapter 6. The second way that Analyst resolves conflicts in calculations is through the D-List priority option. As a rule, use this option only if the order of the dimensions of the cube does not succeed in resolving the conflict. Usually this happens when you have two calculation D-Lists and certain intersections need to be calculated in a way that is different from that enforced by the order of the dimensions. This method must be used sparingly, and only in exceptional situations. Too many instances of D-List priorities may mean that your cube will function better as two separate calculation cubes.

To set the D-List priority function:

1. Click on **File | Open | D-List**.
2. Select the D-List, and then click on **OK**.
3. Find the D-List item into which you want to enter a formula, and then click on the cell directly under the **Calculation** column. Next, click on **Change item attributes** at the lower right corner of the D-List to open the **Calculation** box.
4. In the **Priority** box, select **High** to raise the priority of the calculation. Select **Low** to lower the priority of the calculation.

 You can avoid conflicts in calculation by keeping only one calculation D-List in a D-Cube. A calculation D-List is one that has a calculation beyond simple addition or subtraction. A D-Cube that has more than one calculation D-List is likely to encounter calculation conflicts that are difficult to resolve.

Built-in functions

Analyst provides **built-in functions (BiF)** that perform calculations beyond basic arithmetic. BiFs are pre-built calculations that have been developed specially to perform complex mathematical algorithms — particularly those that span across time. Many forecasting calculations require a time horizon to function properly. For instance, in a multi-dimensional data structure, a year-to-date calculation will require at least two dimensions to produce the correct result: the dimension containing the value to accumulate and the dimension containing the timescale. This is not possible when your calculations can only be entered in one D-List. The BiF overcomes this limitation by taking the time dimension into account when performing the calculation. Thus, for the BiF to work, it must always be accompanied by a timescale D-List.

Another characteristic of the BiF is that it is self-contained. You cannot type additional formulas in an item that contains the BiF, although you can use the item in a formula elsewhere. You cannot have a BiF in the same D-List as the timescale. The timescale must be a separate dimension. You can have more than one BiF in a D-List, but a BiF can exist in only one D-List for the same cube. Not all BiFs will work in Contributor, so you must consider this limitation if you plan to deploy the model using Contributor. New BiFs are enabled in Contributor with each new release of IBM Cognos Planning. So you should check your version to determine which BiFs can be used for your Contributor model.

There are a host of BiFs that can do a variety of calculations. The following table lists some of the more commonly-used BiFs:

BiF	Description
Cumul	Cumulates a series of data
Day	Returns the number of days in each period based on the start and end dates in the timescale D-List
DCF	Discounted Cash Flow
Decum	Decumulates a series of data
Deytd	Calculates the original series from year-to-date figures
DepnAnnual	Annual Depreciation: Straight Line, Sum of Year Digits, Diminishing Balance
DepnDB	Diminishing balance depreciation
DepnSLN	Straight-Line depreciation
DepnSYD	Sum-of-Year-Digits depreciation
Differ	Calculates the difference between the current and previous periods
Drive	Forecast based on one or more drivers
Feed	Feeds the closing balance of one period into the opening balance of the next

BiF	Description
Forecast	Combine actual and budget into a rolling forecast
Grow	Compound or linear growth
Linavg	Linear average
Mix	Mix actuals and forecasts into one series
Movavg	N-period moving average
Movmed	Finds the median
Movsum	N-period moving sum
NPer	Number of periods for future value with constant payments and interest rate
NPV	Net Present Value
Outlook	Year-end outlook calculation, revises forecast to meet the plan
PMT	Constant payment to give the future value with a constant per period % interest rate
PV	Finds the present value of a stream of future payments and the percentage interest rate
Rate	Constant per period percentage interest rate to give the future value with constant payments
Repeat	Repeat data in the first few periods throughout the time scale.
Round	Calculates rounded values for a given input item
Time	Time information about your cube
TimeSum	Accumulate an expense over several periods
TMax	Finds the maximum value in a list of items
TMin	Finds the minimum value in a list of items
YTD	Accumulates the values along a timescale for each month up to the year-end

Inserting a BiF into a D-List Item

When you insert a BiF into a D-List item, you go through a couple of steps using a wizard. Some BiFs will require you to enter the values that represent a method to be used. Most of the BiFs will require you to designate another item in the D-List for at least one of the BiF's inputs, so make sure that the item exists before you start the wizard.

To insert a BiF into a D-List item:

1. Click on **File | Open | D-List**.

2. Select the D-List, and then click on **OK**.

3. Find the D-List item into which you want to enter a formula, and then click the cell directly under the **Calculation** column. Then click the **Change item attributes** at the lower-right corner of the D-List to open the **Calculation** box.

4. Click on the **BiF** button.

5. In the **BiF Function Wizard—Step 1 of 2** box, select **Function Category**. Then select the BiF under the **Function Name**.

6. Click on **Next**.

7. In the **BiF Function Wizard—Step 2 of 2** box, enter the information required by the BiF.

8. Click on **Finish**. The BiF calculation will appear in the **Calculation** box.

9. Click on **Apply**.

10. Save the D-List.

Configuring a Timescale D-List

A Timescale D-List is a D-List that is used as a time dimension. The D-List typically contains the months of the year, but it could be years, weeks, or days. As a rule, when you create a D-List that lists days, weeks, months, or years, you must configure it as a timescale, even if the D-List contains items other than time.

To configure a Timescale D-List:

1. Click on **File | Open | D-List**.

2. Select the D-List containing the time dimension items.

3. On the toolbar, click on **D-List | Options**.

4. In the **TimeScale** tab, select the **Use as TimeScale** checkbox. When you select this checkbox, Analyst automatically determines the number of days depending on the time. If the item is a month, it defaults to 30 days. If the item is a year, the program generates 365 days.

5. You can define the number of days more accurately by using the **Mode** function. In the **Mode** box, select the following:

   i. **Normal**—set the **From** and **To** dates. You must use only one date format. The program generates the number of days based on these dates.

ii. **Custom**—enter the number of days within each time D-List item, and then enter the beginning date of the timescale. The program generates the **From** and **To** dates for the rest of the timescale.

> A custom timescale is useful when you have a fiscal year that contains a mixed number of days in a month, or if the fiscal year does not follow the normal calendar. By the defining the number of days in the timescale D-List, you avoid having to require the number of days for your calculations.

6. Configure the other settings (optional):

   i. **Start of fiscal year**—enter the **Day** and **Month** of the start of the fiscal year.

   ii. **Use SwitchOver**—select this checkbox to activate the switchover feature. This feature is used in conjunction with the **SwitchOver date**.

   iii. **SwitchOver date**—enter the date that defines the transition from past to present. This information is used by some BiFs, including `Drive`, `Outlook`, `DCF`, `ICF`, `Grow`, `Mix`, and `Stockflow`.

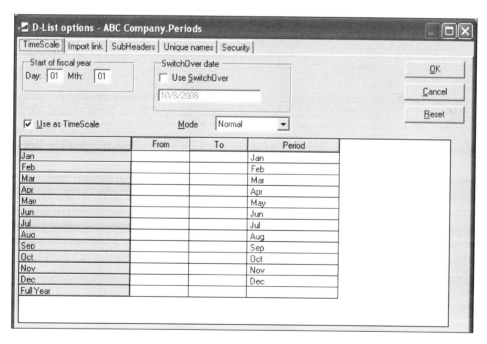

7. Click on **OK**.
8. Save the D-List.

A Timescale D-List will display a clock symbol in the upper-left corner of the D-List. See the following illustration:

	Item name	Format	Calculation	Calc. Option
	Jan			
	Feb			
	Mar			
	Apr			
	May			
	Jun			
	Jul			
	Aug			
	Sep			
0	Oct			
1	Nov			
2	Dec			
3	Full Year		Subtotal	

BiFs and Timescales should never be in the same D-List. In order for a BiF to work, a separate and distinct timescale D-List must exist alongside the BiF.

Formatting D-List items

The way that data is formatted affects how it is displayed and treated in Analyst. This is important because it determines what values can be accepted by the D-List item and whether or not calculations apply.

Numeric format

With a numeric format, you restrict the data that can be entered into the D-List item to numeric values. You also determine how the value is displayed. You can set decimal places, scale numbers up or down, use commas, currency signs, and percentages.

To apply the numeric format:

1. Click on **File | Open | D-List**.
2. Select the D-List, and then click on **OK**.
3. Find the item you want to format, and then click on the cell under the **Format** column. Next, click on **Change item attributes**.
4. In the **Attributes** drop-down list, select **Format**.

5. Select **Numeric**. Set the format as follows:

i. **Scaling Factor**—select the number that the data will be divided by. For instance 1,000 with a scaling factor of 1,000 will display 1. The number 1 with a scaling factor of .001 will display 1,000. This option affects only how the number is displayed, not the number value itself.

 When you enter data into a scaled item, you must enter the true value, and not the displayed value.

ii. **Use thousand delimiter**—select this checkbox if you want a thousands to be separated by commas.

iii. **Blank if zero**—select this checkbox if you want zeros to be displayed as blanks.

iv. **Decimal Places**—select the number of decimal places that the value will be displayed in.

v. **Negative**—enter the prefix and suffix for negative values. For instance, entering the open parenthesis "(" into the prefix and the closed parenthesis ")" into the suffix will display negative values enclosed in parenthesis such as (100) will display -100.

 When you place a percentage sign (%) in the suffix box, any value will have the percentage sign attached to it. For instance, the value 5 becomes 5%. However, even though you see 5%, the underlying value is still 5, not .05. In Analyst, the suffix is not a mathematical representation, but rather a symbol attached to the value.

6. Click on **Apply**.
7. Save the D-List.

Date format

A date format lets you enter data in a variety of date and time formats. You can perform calculations on the dates. Analyst reads the date you enter according to its stored number and displays the stored number in date or time format.

To apply the date format:

1. Click on **File | Open | D-List**.
2. Select the D-List, and then click on **OK**.

3. Find the item you want to format, and then click on the cell under the **Format** column. Next, click on **Change item attributes**.

4. In the **Attributes** drop-down list, select **Format**.

5. Select the following formats:

    i. **Date** — select this checkbox, and then select the date format.

    ii. **Time** — select this checkbox, and then select the time format.

    iii. **Date/Time** — select this checkbox to display the date and time format.

    iv. **Start/End** — by default, **Start** is enabled. Select **End** if you want the stored number to start a day earlier. Analyst generates 0 for 1/1/1900. By clicking on **End**, 1/1/1900 is stored as 1, 1/2/1900 is stored as 2, and so on.

6. Click on **Apply**.

7. Save the D-List.

Dates in formulas

You can use dates in calculating the number of days. Analyst uses the stored value of the dates in the calculation.

For instance: January 1, 2008 has a stored value of 39448. February 1, 2008 has a stored value of 39479. Thus the equation:

    {End Date} – {Beg Date} = 31

Where End Date is February 1, 2008 and the Beg Date is January 1, 2008.

Text format

Text formats allow the entry of alpha-numeric data including special characters. When you format data as text, Analyst automatically forces the calculation to zero.

Use the following steps to apply the numeric format:

1. Click on **File | Open | D-List**.

2. Select the D-List, and then click on **OK**.

3. Find the item you want to format, and then click on the cell under the **Format** column. Next, click on **Change item attributes**.

4. In the **Attributes** drop-down list, select **Format**.

5. Select **Text**.

6. Click on **Apply**.

7. Save the D-List.

D-List format

A D-List format is a special format that restricts data to only the list of items in another D-List. When you enter data in a D-List item that is formatted on another D-List, a drop-down list will display the values that can be entered. You will not be able to enter any other value.

To apply a D-List format:

1. Click on **File | Open | D-List**.
2. Select the D-List, and then click on **OK**.
3. Find the item you want to format, and then click on the cell under the **Format** column. Next, click on **Change item attributes**.
4. In the **Attributes** drop-down list, select **Format**.
5. Select D-List.
6. In the **Libraries** box, click on the library containing the D-List that will be used as the format.
7. In the **D-List** box, click on the D-List.
8. Check the **Show Items** box to display the item in the D-List.
9. Click on **Apply**.
10. Save the D-List.

 In a cube, you can open the list of items in a D-List formatted cell by typing any character. You can filter an item by typing the first few letters of the item name.

Using D-List formatted items in calculations

You use a D-List format when you want to use text in your formula. The following example illustrates how you can use a D-List formatted item in a calculation.

Suppose you have a D-List called Employee Calc. In this D-List, you have two items: Employee Type and FTE. Employee Type allows two types of entries: Full Time and Part Time. If you enter Full Time, FTE generates 1.0. If you enter Part Time, FTE generates 0.5. Otherwise, it generates 0.

Thus, FTE is calculated as follows:

```
IF Employee Type = "Full Time"
THEN FTE = 1.0
IF Employee Type = "Part Time"
THEN FTE = 0.5
ELSE 0
```

In Analyst, you cannot insert text in a formula. Instead, you use the IID within a D-List formatted item in the place of the text. To create the preceding formula in Analyst, you need to do the following steps:

1. Create a D-List containing the **Employee Type**: **Full Time** and **Part Time**.

2. In the Employee Calc D-List, format the **Employee Type** item on the Employee Type D-List. See the following illustration:

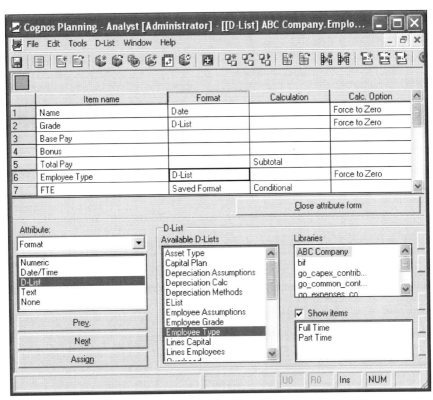

3. In the FTE D-List item, type the following formula:

```
IF Employee Type = 1
THEN FTE = 1.0
IF Employee Type = 2
THEN FTE = 0.5
ELSE 0
```

Where 1 is the IID for `Full Time` and 2 is the IID for `Part Time` in the Employee Type D-List

 In Analyst, instead of using text in formulas, you use the IID of D-List items. Using the IID instead of the display name means you can change the item display name without having to rewrite the formula.

Calc option

There are situations where data needs to be calculated differently when viewed in aggregate. Suppose you have two D-List items: units and cost per unit. At aggregate level, units are summed up, whereas, cost per unit is weighted. The D-List Calc Option gives you the ability to change the behavior of an item on other D-Lists' calculations.

To set the Calc Option:

1. Click on **File | Open | D-List**.
2. Select the D-List, and then click on **OK**.
3. Find the item you want to change and click on it. Then click on **Change item attributes**.
4. In the **Attributes** drop-down list, select **Calc Option**.
5. In the **Calc Option** box select one of the following:
   i. **None**—the D-List item aggregates when viewed at an aggregate level.
   ii. **Weighted Average**—the D-List item is weighted on another item when viewed at an aggregate level. You must select the item that is used as the weight, in the **Items to weight by** box.

   iii. **Time Average**—the D-List assumes the calculation below when viewed from a time aggregation such as a year total or quarter total. This setting should not be made on a timescale D-List, but rather on the calculation D-List.

       a. **Time Average**—the item displays the average of the data across time.

       b. **First Period**—the item displays the data at the start of the timescale, for example, for Feed BiFs.

       c. **Last Period**—the item displays the data at the end of the timescale.

       d. **Zero**—the item displays zero.

   iv. **Force to Zero**—all of the calculations are suppressed for this item and zero is displayed.

6. Click on **Apply**

7. Save the D-List.

Categorizing D-Lists

D-Lists are categorized into five different types: calculation, aggregation, non-calculating, timescale, and control. Knowing the type of D-List is important when building D-Cubes:

- A calculation D-List contains calculations other than subtotals and subtractions. When a D-List performs multiplication, division, conditionals, or any BiF, it is considered a calculation D-List.

- An aggregation D-List usually is a list of items with a subtotal. Examples of aggregation D-Lists are products, departments, cost centers, accounts, and so on.

- Non-calculating D-Lists are D-Lists that have no calculations. Often they contain headers, placeholders, flags, or a list of unrelated items that do not require a total.

- Timescale D-Lists are D-Lists that are configured as timescale. Timescale D-Lists are generally used with BiFs or calculations that span a period of time.

- A control D-List typically contains items that represent a version or iteration of the data. Examples of versions are budget, actual, or last year.

- Each type of D-List has a specific position in the order of D-Lists that make up the D-Cube. When you build a D-Cube, select the D-Lists that become the dimensions and then determine the order of the D-List. As a rule, the order of D-Lists should be as follows:

1. Calculation

2. Aggregation

3. Non-calculating

4. Timescale

5. Control

In the following illustration, an **Employee Calc D-Cube** is created from five D-Lists: **Employee Calc** (calculation), **Departments** (aggregation), **Value** (non-calculating), **Periods** (timescale), and **Versions** (control). The order of the items in the bottom pane is the order of the D-Lists in the D-Cube.

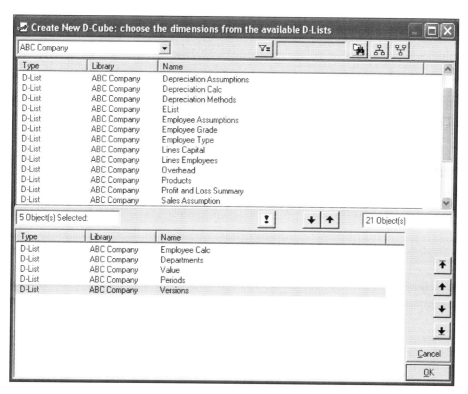

The order of dimensions is important because it determines the priority of calculations when calculations from two separate D-Lists intersect. The Analyst must select which calculation takes precedence. When conflicts between two formulas of equal priority occur, the calculation in the D-List that is positioned last gets precedence. Thus, the D-Lists with the more complex calculation, particularly those with logical operators (IF, THEN, ELSE), must be first, in the order to have the lower priority.

The e.List

So far we have defined the D-List as the place where the structure of the data in the model is defined. There is one other function that the D-List performs: to provide hierarchical structure for the Contributor application. This brings us to the e.List. e.List is an important component of a planning model. In Contributor, the e.List contains the hierarchy that determines how plans are distributed and aggregated. An example of an e.List is a list of departments, regions, and divisions, arranged hierarchically. The departments roll up to regions, which roll up to divisions, and eventually to the company total. Typically, the e.List represents the organizational structure, but it could be any hierarchy that is used for planning purposes.

As we will discuss in detail in Chapter 9, the Analyst model can be deployed to a large number of users via the Web by using Contributor. In order to create a Contributor application from an Analyst model, you must have an e.List as a separate D-List for a D-Cube that will be used to collect data. In the Analyst model, the e.List is simply a placeholder—a dimensional structure that enables the hierarchy information to be populated into the Contributor application. Because the e.List contains the hierarchy, it is considered an aggregation D-List, and should be positioned accordingly in the order of dimensions. The content of the e.List can be a simple hierarchy, for instance, Dept 1, Dept 2, and Total, or a single item. However, it is better to use the simple hierarchy because this approach allows you to view the results of your calculations when the e.List is rolled up. This is particularly important when you are building the model and you need to view aggregated data at various levels of the e.List hierarchy. When you create the Contributor application, the program uses the e.List to create a container into which the hierarchy can be loaded by using Contributor's e.List import utility.

The following illustration shows an **Analyst D-Cube** that uses a single item e.List:

[D-Cube] ABC Company.Profit and Loss		Feb	Mar	Apr	May	Jun	Jul	Aug	Sep
Gross Revenue	873	8,861,726	8,505,580	8,902,758	8,972,473	8,910,997	8,471,482	8,158,647	8,74
Allowances	730	255,656	254,256	265,351	266,949	261,089	252,920	237,139	25
Net Revenue	143	8,606,070	8,251,324	8,637,407	8,705,524	8,649,928	8,218,556	7,921,508	8,48
Cost of Sales	110	4,250,872	4,072,527	4,256,907	4,306,504	4,296,242	4,067,633	3,935,707	4,19
Gross Profit	033	4,355,198	4,178,797	4,380,500	4,399,020	4,353,686	4,150,924	3,985,801	4,29
Salary	000	10,000	10,000	10,000	10,000	11,167	11,167	11,167	1
Benefits	458	458	458	458	458	515	515	33	
Occupancy	192	345,205	382,192	369,863	382,192	369,863	382,192	382,192	36
Depreciation	111	173,333	187,500	209,167	300,833	317,500	489,167	489,167	48
Advertising	346,457	346,457	389,764	303,150	346,457	476,378	519,685	606,299	64
Travel	153,846	153,846	153,846	230,769	153,846	153,846	153,846	153,846	15
Miscellaneous	100,000	100,000	100,000	100,000	100,000	100,000	100,000	100,000	10
Total Operating	1,104,064	1,129,300	1,223,760	1,223,407	1,293,786	1,429,268	1,656,571	1,742,704	1,77
Operating Profit	3,324,969	3,225,898	2,955,037	3,157,093	3,105,234	2,924,418	2,494,353	2,243,097	2,51
Profit	3,436,080	3,399,232	3,142,537	3,366,260	3,406,068	3,241,918	2,983,520	2,732,264	3,00
Taxes	1,558	1,558	1,558	1,558	1,558	1,750	1,750	113	
Profit after Taxes	3,434,522	3,397,673	3,140,979	3,364,701	3,404,509	3,240,168	2,981,770	2,732,150	3,00

Summary

In this chapter, we discussed the D-List in detail. We showed you several ways of importing items into a D-List. You can update the D-List manually or automatically by using the D-List update function. When you update the D-List automatically, you can modify the item names by using the Unique names function. After you create the D-List, you can insert formulas, formats, and calculation options. The program provides BiFs that perform complex calculations that span a period of time. When writing formulas, you must take the priorities in calculation into consideration. You can overcome conflicts in calculations by enabling the calculation priority option in the D-List, or by using the order of dimensions in a D-Cube. Finally, we discussed the role of the e.List as a means of providing dimensional structure for the hierarchy that will be built in Contributor.

6
Storing Planning Data: D-Cube

In this chapter, we will discuss how data is stored in IBM Cognos Planning Analyst. We will begin by defining the D-Cube and explaining the things that you need to think about before creating the D-Cube. We will discuss the importance of the order of dimensions in enforcing calculation and format priorities. We will show you how you can view the multiple slices of the cube and how you can save a selection of the cube as a separate object. We will explain how you can restructure the dimensions of the cube by adding, deleting, substituting, and reordering dimensions. We will cover some of the important functions available with the D-Cube, including global formatting, exporting, and other options that can make it easier for you to work with the program. We will illustrate how you can use data entry commands that will enable you to enter data, execute mathematical operations, or set restrictions for a cell, a range of cells, or the entire cube. Finally, we will cover Breakback—a powerful feature that allows you to cascade changes throughout the cube simply by making the change to a calculated item.

Overview of the D-Cube

In Analyst, data is stored in a D-Cube. The D-Cube is a multi-dimensional data structure similar to an OLAP or Excel pivot table. Each of the dimensions contains a list of related data. For example, in a four dimensional cube, the first dimension may contain the items in P&L statement, the second may list the departments, the third show the timescale, and the fourth may show the version (Budget or Actual). In this example, you have the P&L statement by month, by department, and by version. The D-Cube must have at least two dimensions. If more than two dimensions exist, the other dimensions appear as pages.

The following screenshot depicts a four dimensional D-Cube. The first two dimensions form the rows and columns. The third and fourth dimensions are displayed as pages, in the upper-left corner of the D-Cube. You can switch to different pages in the cube by clicking the page drop-down list and selecting another page.

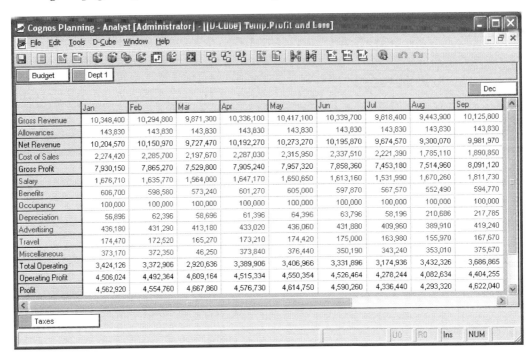

Creating a D-Cube

Creating a D-Cube takes a few simple steps but it requires a great deal of forethought. Before creating the D-Cube, you must think through the dimensions that will form the cube. You must know what data will populate the D-Cube. You must know what category of D-Lists your selection falls under so that you can prioritize the calculations appropriately. You must know what function the D-Cube performs. Is it an input cube, a calculation cube, a summary or reporting cube, or a staging cube? You must also know in which library the D-Cube will be stored, and whether the D-Cube will be shared or will be exclusive to a model. Finally, you must consider size and performance, especially if you plan to deploy the D-Cube in Contributor.

To create a D-Cube:

1. Click **File | New | D-Cube**.
2. In the **Create new D-Cube** box, select the D-List that makes up the D-Cube.
3. Drop the D-List onto the lower pane.
4. Order the D-List. Click on **OK**.
5. Enter the D-Cube name, and then click on **OK**.

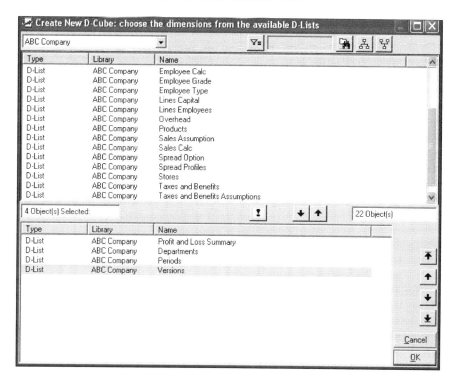

By default, the D-Cube opens with the longest D-List as the rows and the timescale as the columns. You can transpose the cube or swap the dimensions by dragging and dropping them. When you close and reopen the D-Cube, it will revert to the default view.

Order of dimensions

In the previous chapter, we explained the importance of having the proper order of dimensions in the D-Cube. The order of dimensions is important because it determines which calculation takes precedence when calculations from two separate D-Lists intersect. The order also determines the priority of formats when the cell has opposing formats. As a rule, the dimensions must follow this order:

1. **Calculation**: Calculation D-Lists contain mathematical operations over and above simple addition. Any use of operators, such as multiplication, subtraction, division, or the use of a BiF, make the D-List a calculation D-List.

2. **Aggregation**: Aggregation D-Lists usually contain a hierarchy of items, such as an organizational hierarchy, a list of products, customers, or cost centers, or a list of items with a simple subtotal.

3. **Non-Calculating**: Non-Calculating D-Lists contain no calculations.

4. **Timescale**: Timescale D-Lists contains items that span a period of time, such as months, weeks, or days.

5. **Versions**: Version D-Lists contain iterations of the data, such as Actual, Budget, Forecast, and Revised Budget.

 It is critical to set the proper order of dimensions before building the Contributor application. If you reorder the dimensions after the application is created, all of the data in the D-Cube will be deleted. In addition, reordering dimensions changes the structure of the import tables and, therefore, the way that you import data into Contributor.

Size considerations

The size of the D-Cube is measured by the number of cells in it. The number of cells you can have in a D-Cube is limited only by your computer's memory. When you build a D-Cube, you should keep in mind the amount of memory available on the computer on which the model will be used. You will not be able to open a large cube if your PC does not have enough memory to handle the data. If the model is deployed in Contributor, size is an even more important consideration. Even with a powerful computer, you will experience performance lag because a large model must pass through the organization's network. In a wide area network, the problem associated with a large model becomes more apparent.

To determine the number of cells, find the product of the number of items in all of the D-lists in the D-Cube. For instance, if a D-Cube has five D-Lists, which have the following number of items: 8, 1, 10, 5, and 12, the number of cells in the D-Cube will be 4,800. This is 8*1*10*5*12.

You can find the number of cells in the dimension selection box, as illustrated in the following screenshot:

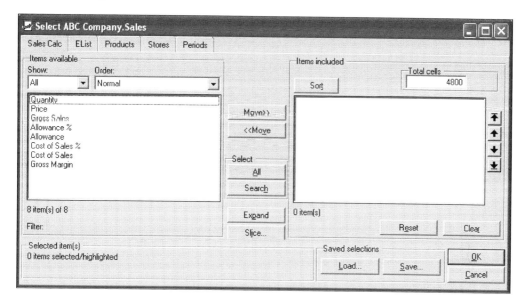

The number of items in a dimension has an inverse impact on the magnitude of size increases for additions to the cube. The fewer the items, the bigger the impact that an addition will have to the size of the cube. In the example of the cube above, if you add one item to a dimension that has only one item, you will double the size of the cube. However, if you add one item to a dimension that has 10 items, you will increase the size of the cube by only ten percent.

One clue that your D-Cube may have a problem with size is the number of dimensions. While there is no limitation on the number of dimensions that a cube can have, having too many of them can become a problem. With a D-Cube that has too many dimensions, any additional item in one of the D-Lists increases the size in an order of magnitude depending on the number of items in the D-List. If possible, keep the number of dimensions to not more than five. If you need to have a D-Cube that provides views of data beyond five dimensions, consider splitting the D-Cube. You are more likely to require less memory if you have several smaller cubes than with one super cube.

With Analyst, you can open a D-Cube that has several million cells on a PC that has 512MB of RAM. However, if you plan to deploy the model in Contributor, the threshold for the number of cells is much lower. An acceptable benchmark is roughly 500,000 cells per e.List. This benchmark is subject to many other factors, such as network latency, client PC memory, and CPU, all of which can contribute to model performance.

Working with the D-Cube

When working with the D-Cube, you have several functionalities that help you to hone in on the information that you want. By default, the D-Cube opens in full view, but you can open only a slice of the cube and save the slice for later viewing.

Opening a full view of the D-Cube

The most straightforward way to view the D-Cube is to open all dimensions. To open a full D-Cube:

1. Click on **File|Open|D-Cube**.

2. Select the D-Cube. Click on **OK**.

3. Select the **Full** option. Click on **OK**.

Opening a selection of the D-Cube

A selection is a subset of a D-Cube. You can only open the specific items of the dimensions that you want to view. Because the data in a selection is fewer than the full view, less memory is required and the D-Cube opens and recalculates faster. To open a selection of the D-Cube:

1. Click on **File|Open|D-Cube**.

2. Select the D-Cube. Click on **OK**.

3. Select the **Edit Selection** option. This option opens the dimension selection box, where you can select the items that you want to view in the D-Cube slice.

    As shown in the following illustration, the **item selection** box lets you select the items from a dimension that you want to include in your view. In the item selection box, each tab represents a D-List. To select the items, move the items from the **Items available** pane (on the left) to the **Items included** pane (on the right).

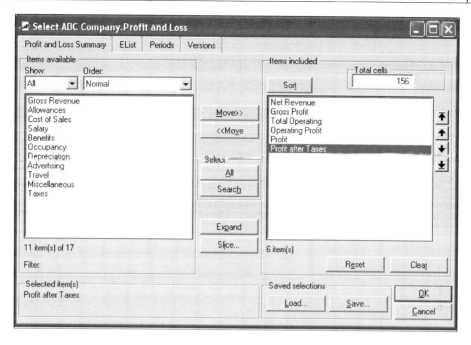

4. Click on **OK**.

Viewing different slices of the D-Cube

You can view the D-Cube in a variety of ways. You can open a selection of the D-Cube, or several selections at the same time. If you have a selection open, you can change it to another selection. The ability to switch views makes it easier to work with the D-Cube. For instance, suppose you have a D-Cube that has two versions: **Budget** and **Actual**. If you want to enter only budget data, you may want to open only the Budget dimension and keep the Actual dimension closed. You can have multiple selections of the D-Cube open at the same time in the same way that you open the D-Cube. This allows you to arrange the selections next to each other on the same screen.

To modify the views of the D-Cube:

1. With the D-Cube open, click on **D-Cube|Selections**:
    i. **New Slice**: This option allows you to create a new view of the same D-Cube, with the same selection.

ii. **Reselect**: Modify the current selection. Selecting this option allows you to add or remove dimensions in the current view.

iii. **Save**: Save the current selection as a saved selection. This option allows you to save the current view so that you can open it again later

2. If you select **Reselect**, move the items that you want to add to or remove from the current view from the **Items included** to the **Items available** pane, or vice versa, respectively. Click on **OK**.

Saving a selection

You can select a view of a D-Cube and then save this selection so that you do not have to reselect the same view the next time that you open the cube. When you save a selection, you create a "saved selection"—an object that is derived from the cube.

To save a selection:

1. Click **File | Open | D-Cube**.
2. Select the D-Cube.
3. Under **Mode**, select **Edit Selection**.
4. Select the D-List items that you want to view in the D-Cube, and move them from the **Items available** pane to the **Items included** pane. If you do not select anything in the **Items available** pane, then all of the items will be included in the selection, including any future additions to the D-List.
5. Under the **Save Selections** option on the lower-right corner of the dialog box, click on the **Save** button.
6. Enter the name of the saved selection. Click on **OK**.

 If you have a saved selection, you can load it into the item selection box. The dimension item selection box is used in many functions, including export, D-List imports, and D-Cube allocations (to be discussed later).

Opening the saved selection

Once saved, the selection becomes a separate object that can be copied and shared. However, because it is a subset of the cube, you have to go through the cube to access the saved selection.

To open the saved selection:

1.   Click on **File | Open | D-Cube**.
2.   Select the D-Cube.
3.   Under **Mode**, select **Saved Selection**.
4.   Select the **Saved Selection**. Click on **OK**.

Modifying the saved selection

You usually modify a saved selection when the cube has changed; for instance, when new items have been added or when dimensions have changed. Remember that if a saved selection is shared, any modification may affect all of the objects that use it. So be cautious when you do this.

To modify the saved selection:

1.   Click on **File | Open | D-Cube**.
2.   Select the D-Cube.
3.   Under **Mode**, select **Edit Selection**.

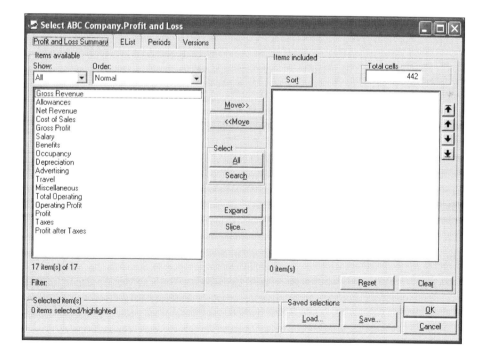

4. Click on the **Load** button in the lower-right corner of the dialog box, to open the list of saved selections.

5. Select the saved selection. Click on **OK**.

6. Modify the saved selection by adding to or removing D-List items from the Items included pane

7. Click on the **Save** button.

8. Select **Saved Selection**, and then click on **OK** to save your changes.

9. Click on **OK** to open the saved selection.

Restructuring dimensions of a D-Cube

You can add, delete, substitute, or reorder dimensions of a D-Cube. Before you do this, you must think about how your data will be impacted. In Analyst, when you make these changes, you can preserve the data in the cube. However, in Contributor, adding, deleting, substituting, or reordering dimensions will cause all of the data in the cube to be deleted. If you restructure a Contributor cube, you must publish your data so that you can reload it after the cube is restructured. Another thing to think about is how the new structure will affect the links. In almost all of the cases, the D-Link allocations will have to be updated in order for the links to work. As a rule, after you restructure your cube, you must review your links to make sure that the relationships are intact.

Adding a dimension

A cube consists of data viewed along two or more sets of related data attributes. When you add a dimension, you create a completely new set of data attributes. You must designate the item in the new dimension to which the current data will belong. For example, suppose you have a cube that lists expense items by department and by month. Here, you can view data along these three dimensions. If you add a fourth dimension, say a versions dimension that consists of actual and budget, you must designate the existing data as either actual or budget. Also, when you add a dimension, think about where in the order of dimensions you will position it. Sometimes, a new dimension can affect the existing calculation priorities so it's a good idea to check for this.

To add a dimension to a D-Cube:

1. With the D-Cube open, click on **D-Cube|Dimensions|Add**.

2. The following message will appear: **This operation cannot be undone. The D-Cube will be saved before the operation can be performed. Do you want to continue?** Click on **Yes**.

3. Select the D-List that you want to add to the D-Cube.

4. Select the position of the new dimensions in the order of dimension by clicking on the D-List that will be under the new dimension. Click on **OK**.

5. Select the D-List item in the new dimension to which the current data will belong, and move the item to the right-hand pane. Click on **OK**.

6. The following message will appear: **Do you want to open the entire cube?**

7. Click on **Yes** if you want the entire D-Cube to open. Click on **No** if you only want the item that you selected to open in the D-Cube.

Deleting a dimension

When you delete a dimension, you need to decide which items in this dimension you want to retain. If you select more than one item, Analyst will aggregate the data in the new cube. If you do not select any item, Analyst will aggregate all of the data. The example in the preceding section uses a four dimensional cube that lists expenses, by department by month by version. If you delete the version dimension, you must decide whether the remaining data will belong to actual or budget. If you select both or neither of them, Analyst will add together the actual and budget and put the result into the new cube.

To delete a dimension in a D-Cube:

1. With the D-Cube open, click on **D-Cube|Dimensions|Delete**.

2. The following message will appear: **This operation cannot be undone. The D-Cube will be saved before the operation can be performed. Do you want to continue?** Click on **Yes**.

3. Select the D-List that you want to delete from the D-Cube. Click on **OK**.

4. Select the D-List items containing the data that you want to be summed after the dimension is deleted. If no selection is made, all of the detail items are summed. Click on **OK**.

5. The following message will appear: **Do you want to open the entire cube?**

6. Click on **Yes** if you want the entire D-Cube to open. Click on **No** if you only want the item that you selected above to open in the D-Cube.

Substituting a dimension

You can substitute an existing dimension with another dimension. When you substitute dimensions, you have to decide, via an allocation table, how the items correspond in the new and old dimensions. Once you complete the allocation table, the data will simply transfer to the new dimension items accordingly.

To substitute a dimension in a D-Cube:

1. With the D-Cube open, click on **D-Cube | Dimensions | Substitute**.

2. The following message will appear: **This operation cannot be undone. The D-Cube will be saved before the operation can be performed. Do you want to continue?** Click on **Yes.**

3. Select the new D-List. Click on **OK**.

4. In the **Select dimension to substitute** box, select the D-List that you are replacing. Click on **OK**.

5. The program searches for objects that reference the old D-List and prompts you to substitute the new D-List in these objects. Click on **Yes** to substitute the new D-List and update the references. Click on **No** if you want to update the references manually, later.

6. In the **Old-New Match Item** box, map the items in the old D-List to the items in the New D-List. Click on **OK**.

Reordering D-Cube dimensions

You would typically reorder dimensions to enforce calculation priorities. In Analyst, reordering dimensions will not cause you to lose data, but your calculations may behave differently depending on the new order.

To reorder the dimension:

1. With the D-Cube open, click on **D-Cube | Dimensions | Reorder**.

2. The following message will appear: **This operation cannot be undone. The D-Cube will be saved before the operation can be performed. Do you want to continue?** Click on **Yes**.

3. In the **Reorder dimension** box, move the dimensions to their new positions using the arrows in the box. Click on **OK**.

Formatting data using the D-Cube Format

You can apply a global format to all of the data in the D-Cube. This D-Cube format will be overwritten by any format that is applied locally in a D-List.

To format the D-Cube:

1. Click on **File | Open | D-Cube**.

2. Select the D-Cube.

3.   On the toolbar, click on **D-Cube | Format**.

4.   Select the required format from the options shown in the following screenshot.

As shown in the following illustration, the steps to format a D-Cube are similar to those for formatting a D-List:

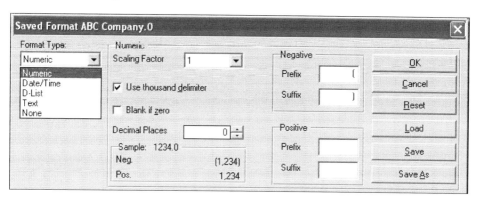

Numeric

You can apply the **Numeric** format by using the following steps:

1.   In the **Format Type** box, select **Numeric**. Set the format as follows:

   i.   **Scaling Factor**: Select the number that the data will be divided by. For instance 1,000 with a scaling factor of 1,000 will display 1. The number 1 with a scaling factor of .001 will display 1,000. This affects only how the number is displayed, not the value of the number.

   ii.   **Use thousand delimiter**: Select this checkbox if you want thousands to be separated by commas.

   iii.   **Blank if zero**: Select this checkbox if you want zeros to display as blanks.

   iv.   **Decimal Places**: Select the number of decimal places to which the value should be displayed.

   v.   **Negative**: Enter the prefix and suffix for negative values. For instance, the prefix '(' and suffix ')' will display negative values enclosed in parentheses. For example, (100). The prefix '-' will display -100.

2.   Click on **OK**.

Date format

You can apply the **Date** format by using the following steps:

1. In the **Format Type** box, select **Date/Time**.
2. Select one of the following formats:
    i. **Date**: Select this checkbox, and then select the date format.
    ii. **Time**: Select this checkbox, and then select the time format.
    iii. **Date/Time**: Select this checkbox, and to display date and time format.
    iv. **Start/End**: By default, **Start** is enabled. Select **End** if you want the stored number to start a day earlier. Analyst generates zero for 1/1/1900. By clicking on **End**, 1/1/1900 is stored as 1, 1/2/1900 is stored as 2, and so on.
3. Click on **OK**.

Text format

To apply the **Text** format, select **Text** in the **Format Type** box, and then click on **OK**. Text formatted items will accept letters, numbers, and special characters.

D-List format

Although a D-List is an option in a D-Cube format, it has no practical function. You cannot have a cube whose data consists of only D-List formatted data. In all cases, a D-List format is useful only when it is used locally.

Format priority

The format priority is determined by the order of the dimensions. When two or more D-Lists contain items that are formatted differently, the format in the first D-List takes precedence. It is more efficient to apply a D-Cube format and then format the D-List item when it requires a different format. Having a global format reduces the chance of conflicts in formatting. If possible, keep your local formats confined to the calculation D-List only.

Exporting data from the D-Cube

You can export data from the D-Cube into an ASCII file or to the clipboard. The export function gives you the ability to format how you want to export the data. You can set the delimiter, insert headers, and arrange the order of the dimensions.

You can also suppress zero values in calculated data so that the export function will not include records that have zero or null data.

To export from a D-Cube:

1. Open the D-Cube.
2. Click on **D-Cube|Export**.
3. The **Export** function displays four tabs:

    i. **Export**

    ii. **Header/Footer**

    iii. **Zeros**

    iv. **Show Det/Tot**

Export

Observe the following:

1. Under the **Export to** option, select whether you want to export to a file or to the clipboard. If you are exporting to a file, enter the path and name of the file that you want to export the data to. Alternatively, you can click on the **Browse** button to save the file.
2. Click the **Select** button to open the item selection box, and then select the dimension items containing the data you want to export.

 If you have a saved selection containing the data that you want to export, then you can load that selection into the dimension selection box.

Groups

Select how you want the dimensions to be displayed as columns:

- **Single Column**: Export each dimension as a single column.
- **Multiple Column**: Select one dimension whose items you want displayed as separate columns, and set the rest of the dimensions as single columns. The last dimension marked as **[data]** under the **Dimension Order** box contains the items that will used as multiple columns (see the following example):

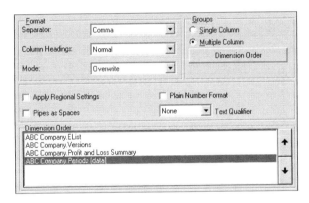

Single vs. multiple columns

The following table illustrates a single column file with each dimension laid out as a separate column:

e.List	Version	P&L Item	Month	Amount
Dept 1	Budget	Revenue	Jan	2,274,420
Dept 1	Budget	Revenue	Feb	2,285,700
Dept 1	Budget	Revenue	Mar	2,197,670
Dept 2	Budget	Revenue	Jan	2,287,030
Dept 2	Budget	Revenue	Feb	2,315,950
Dept 2	Budget	Revenue	Mar	2,337,510

The following table illustrates a multiple column file. In this example, the items in the Month dimension are displayed as separate columns.

e.List	Version	P&L Item	Jan	Feb	Mar
Dept 1	Budget	Revenue	2,274,420	2,285,700	2,197,670
Dept 2	Budget	Revenue	2,287,030	2,315,950	2,337,510

Format

In the **Format** section, select the following:

- **Separator**: Set the delimiter to be used in the export file. Select **Comma**, **Tab**, **Semicolon**, or **Aligned Columns**.

- **Column Headings**
    - ° **Normal**: This is the default setting. If you export in multiple columns, this option will include columns headers on each page but not for the rows and page dimensions. If you export in single columns, this no column headers will be included.
    - ° **At Top**: This option includes the D-List names and column headers at the top of first page only.
    - ° **Above Each Page**: This option includes the D-List names and column headers at the top of each page of the export.
    - ° **None**: This option does not include column headers at all.

- **Mode**
    - ° **Append**: Add the data to any previously-exported data in the same file.
    - ° **Overwrite**: Overwrite any previously-exported data in the same file.

- Data formats:
    - ° **Apply Regional Settings**: Select this checkbox to use the regional settings in your operating system as the format for the export.
    - ° **Pipes as Spaces**: Select this checkbox to replace any pipe symbols (|) with spaces.
    - ° **Plain Number Format**: Select this option to remove any numeric formats that you applied in the D-List. The values are exported in as many decimal places as is necessary in is basic format. All commas, currency signs, and percentages will be removed. Negative values enclosed in parenthesis will be prefixed with a minus sign. Non-numeric formats (Text, Date, and D-List) will be retained.
    - ° **Text Qualifier**: Choose whether you want the data exported with a single quote or double quote text qualifier.

- **Dimension Order:** Determine the order of the dimensions that will be exported as columns. Move the dimensions up or down using the arrows, or click the **Dimension Order** button to arrange the dimensions according to their order in the D-Cube.

Header/Footer

This option lets you enter a title and/or footer to the export file. Enter the title or footnote by typing directly into the text box.

Zeros

This option suppresses any record with zero values. This option is independent of the zero suppression in force when you are viewing the D-Cube. You can suppress zeros in rows or columns by highlighting the dimension labeled R or C respectively. You can deselect a selected dimension by pressing *Ctrl* and clicking on the highlighted item. To suppress zeros in pages, select **Suppress Zero Pages**. If you want to suppress zeros in all of the dimensions, highlight all of the dimensions and then select **Suppress Zero Pages**.

Show Det/Tot

This option lets you choose whether you want to export only detail items or calculated items by highlighting the dimensions containing the detail or subtotal items, as appropriate. There are separate selection boxes for detail and total items.

Breakback

Breakback is a powerful feature in IBM Cognos Planning. With Breakback, you can enter data into calculated cells and change the variables that make up the formula according to rules that you specify. Breakback is commonly used to propagate changes to a total across its detail items, in proportion to the value of the detail items.

Suppose you have five products, showing a total of 1500 units:

Product	Current
Product A	100
Product B	200
Product C	300
Product D	400
Product E	500
TOTAL	1500

With Breakback, if you enter 3000 in the total, the detail products will change as follows:

Product	With Breakback
Product A	200
Product B	400
Product C	600
Product D	800
Product E	1000
TOTAL	3000

Breakback distributes the changes in the TOTAL to Products A to E in proportion to their original share of the total. Breakback works on addition, subtraction, multiplication, and division. It can handle multiple calculations across multiple dimensions and hierarchies.

Breakback on hierarchies

You can apply Breakback on a grand total consisting of multiple subtotals across various hierarchical levels. In a simple hierarchy where you have only one subtotal, Breakback distributes the value across its children proportionately. In a multi-level hierarchy, Breakback cascades the changes one level at a time down through the hierarchy. If you enter a value into a total, Breakback will distribute the value proportionately to the subtotals immediately below the total, then to the subtotal the next level down, and so on.

Configuring D-Cube options

There are several options that you can use to improve the look of the D-Cube. You can set the width, add lines, enable data color conventions, and show the sum, count or average of highlighted numeric items. These options work only in Analyst. They will not work in Contributor. There is one option that gives you greater control over Breakback. This option will work in Contributor.

Widths

This option allows you to set the width of the rows and columns. You can set **Exact** or **Minimum** widths. The program does not wrap the labels, so you must know the width of the longest label in order to set the width properly.

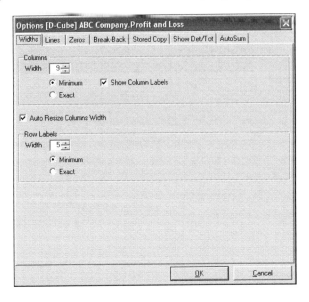

Lines

This option puts a line before or after a calculation. The lines can go horizontally or vertically. You can set the thickness and the style of the lines.

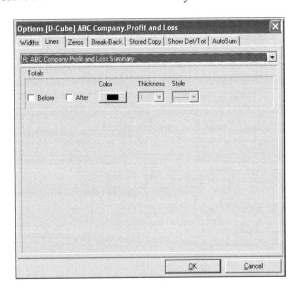

Zeros

This option allows you to hide rows, columns, or pages that have zero data. You can set this option on rows, columns, and pages. Or you can suppress specific dimensions by clicking on the dimension on the lower pane. You can select multiple items by pressing *Ctrl* key and clicking simultaneously on those items. *Ctrl+click* the items that you want to remove.

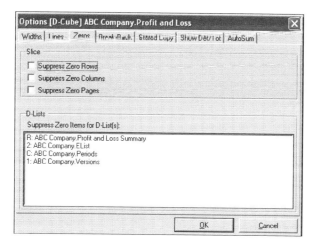

Breakback

This option lets you set Breakback to a decimal or integer. Select **Decimal** if you want the changes to Breakback to be made up to the decimal level. Select **Integer** if you want the Breakback to round to an integer.

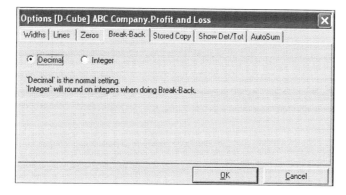

Stored Copy

When you enable this option, Analyst stores the saved copy of the cube in memory so that it can track changes to the data, and display the change in a variety of colors. Disabling this option can improve performance as your computer will not need to store the saved version, freeing up more memory to handle the working version.

This option is best disabled in staging cubes. Staging cubes are typically large and require a great deal of memory. Because they are not used for data input, there is no benefit in having this option turned on.

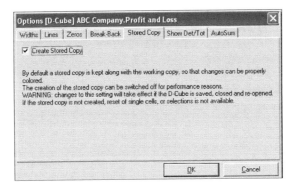

Show Det/Tot

This option lets you automatically hide detail or calculated dimensions. Highlight the dimensions that you want to be automatically hidden when you open the D-Cube.

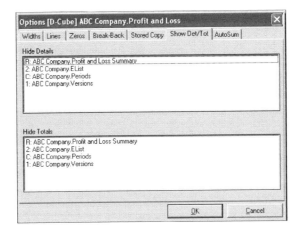

AutoSum

This option lets you apply an operation to highlighted cells in the D-Cube.
The result of the calculation is displayed in the lower-right corner of the D-Cube.

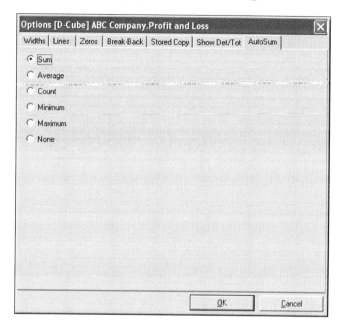

Entering data into D-Cubes

There are several ways of entering data into a D-Cube. The simplest way is to type
the data directly into the cell. But you can also enter data in several other ways: you
can copy and paste data from a spreadsheet, you can enter data into a range of cells
using the data-entry command function, or you can link data from a source outside
of the D-Cube.

Data color conventions

Analyst displays data in a variety of colors. Non-calculating data entry cells display
data in blue. Calculated cells display data in black. When you type into a data entry
cell, the data first appears in green. When you press *Enter*, the data turns purple
and any calculated data will turn red. When you save the D-Cube, the data that you
entered turns blue. These colors represent stages in the way the D-Cube processes
data. Green means that the data has been typed. Red means the data has been stored in
memory and the D-Cube recalculated. Blue means the data has been stored in the file.

Data entry commands

Analyst provides several commands that let you enter data or apply a mathematical operation on a cell, range of cells, or the entire D-Cube. You can apply restrictions such as hold, lock, and protect. These tools give you powerful scenario planning capabilities. For instance, you can set a baseline plan, increase or decrease sections of the plan, or hold several key numbers so that they do not change when your assumptions change.

Entering data using the keyboard characters

You can populated a range of cells by the typing certain keyboard characters. For instance, if you type 100 followed by the greater than sign, "100>", the program will populate all cells to the right of the current cell with 100. Typing 100 followed by the pipe symbol, "100 |" will populate the cells below with 100. The basic keyboard functions are as follows:

- Greater than sign (>): Copies data to the right
- Less than sign (<): Copies data to the left
- Pipe (|): Copies data downward
- Carat (^): Copies data upward
- Colon (:): Stops the cells from populating when used in conjunction with the other commands above

Applying mathematical operations

You can apply mathematical operations to a cell or range of cells. For instance if you type "add10" on a cell, the program will add 10 to the data currently in the cell. So if the data is 100, typing "add10" will change it to 110. The same method can be used for subtraction, multiplication, division, and a host of other operations. The following table lists the various operations that you can use in Analyst:

Command	Example	Description
Zero	zero	Sets the range to zero.
Set	set99	Sets the range to the value that you type after the operator.
Add	add10	Adds the amount that you enter to current values in the cell. You can use the plus sign (+) instead of Add.

Command	Example	Description
Multiply	multiply1.2	Multiplies the current values in the cell by the value that you enter. You can use the asterisk (*) instead of Multiply.
Divide	divide2	Divides the current values in the cell by the value that you enter. You can use the forward slash (/) instead of Divide.
Percent	percent10	Replaces the current values with the specified percentage of their current value. You can use the percent sign (%) instead of Percent.
Increase	increase10	Increases the current values by the amount that you enter.
Decrease	decrease10	Decreases the current values by the amount that you enter.
Reset	reset	Resets cell values to last saved version
Hold	hold	Holds the range of cells against Breakback. Cells can still be changed by entering or copying data or by D-Links.
Release	release	Removes the holds on a range.
Lock	lock	Write-protects the range. Cells can still be changed by breakback, but not by entering data or by D-Links.
Unlock	unlock	Removes the locks on a range.
Protect	protect	Protects cells from data entry. The cells can still be changed by breakback or by D-Links.
Unprotect	unprotect	Removes cell protection.
Power	Power2	Raises the underlying values by the power indicated by the number specified.
Random	random100	Creates random numbers between 1 and the number specified.
Round	Round10	Rounds the data to the magnitude specified. If you round a total, a breakback will be triggered, altering the details so that they add up exactly to the rounded number.
Thousands (K)	100K	Multiplies the number by 1,000.
Millions (K)	1M	Multiplies the number by 1,000,000.

To apply an operation to a range of cells:

1. Highlight the cells.
2. Right-click on the selection, and then select **Apply Commands** from the context menu.
3. Select the operator.
4. Type the required value next to the operator. Click on **OK**.

To apply a mathematical operation to a selection of a D-Cube:

1. With the D-Cube open, click on **D-Cube | Commands**.
2. Select the operator.
3. Type the value next to the operator (for example, **Add10**).
4. Click on either:
   i. **Select All**: Applies the command to all dimensions.
   ii. **Select**: Applies the command to a selection of the D-Cube. Select the items in the dimension selection box and click on **OK**.
5. Click on **OK** to apply the command.

Locking, protecting, and holding cells

By default, all of the cells are editable, including calculated cells. However, you can lock, protect, or hold a cell or a range of cells. Locked cells prevent you from typing data or linking data into the cell. Protected cells prevent you from entering data but allow you to link data from another D-Cube. Held cells prevent the data from being changed as a result of Breakback. To undo the **Lock**, **Protect**, and **Hold** functions, select **Unlock**, **Unprotect**, and **Release**, respectively.

To lock, protect, or hold a cell:

1. Right-click on the cell.
2. Select **Lock, Protect**, or **Hold**.
3. Click on **OK**.

To lock, protect, or hold a range of cells:

1. Highlight the cells.
2. Right-click on the selection, and then select **Apply Commands** from the context menu.
3. Select **Hold, Protect**, or **Lock**.
4. Click **OK**.

To lock, protect, or hold a selection of a D-Cube:

1. With the D-Cube open, click on **D-Cube | Commands**.
2. Select **Hold, Protect**, or **Lock**.
3. Click on either:

   i. **Select All**: Applies the command to all dimensions.

   ii. **Select**: Applies the command to a selection of the D-Cube.
   Select the items in the dimension selection box and click on **OK**.

4. Click on **OK** to apply the command.

Summary

In this chapter, we discussed the D-Cube in greater detail. We showed you how you can create a D-Cube, and stressed the importance of the order of dimensions and size. We walked through the different ways of viewing a cube, and demonstrated how you can slice the cube and save the selection for later viewing. We showed you how you can apply a D-Cube format and export data from the D-Cube. We discussed Breakback, a powerful feature that lets you enter data into calculated cells and propagate these changes across the variables that make up the formula. We discussed the various D-Cube options that you can use to improve the look of the cube, and additional functions that facilitate data entry. Finally, we discussed the various data entry commands that you can apply to a cell, a range of cells, or the entire cube.

7
Moving Planning Data: D-Links

In this chapter, we will explain how we can move the data by using D-Links. We will discuss the basic steps of creating a D-Link, and the things that you need to take care of when creating a D-Link. Here, we will:

- Show how to connect to data sources outside of IBM Cognos in order to bring data into the D-Cube

- Go through two special D-Links: the Look Up and Accumulation D-Links

- Demonstrate how to use D-List formatted items as virtual dimensions that can be paired with real dimensions in a D-Link.

- Show how to map data from sources to targets by using a local allocation table—an A-Table—and a D-Cube

- Explain the various options that gives the D-Link the additional functionality

- Describe how to move data from other IBM Cognos applications into your Analyst model

Overview of a D-Link

In a model that consists of several D-Cubes, data must be able to flow from one D-Cube to another. With a D-Link, you can move data from one D-Cube to another. You can also import data from a text file, a spreadsheet, or a database by using a File Map or an ODBC connection. When you create a D-Link, you pair the dimensions in the source to dimensions in the target. Then you allocate items in the source dimensions to their corresponding target items. Because data is stored in the intersection of multiple dimensions, how you map source and target dimensions determines how the data flows.

Creating a D-Link

Before creating a D-Link you must know where you will be getting the data and where it will go. Creating a D-Link is pretty straightforward. However, it is the process of figuring out your source and target dimensions, and then allocating the dimension items that requires some thought, especially if the source and target are not structurally consistent. Analyst provides a wide array of options which give you many ways to move the data.

Creating a D-Link between two D-Cubes

Most of the time, a D-Link will be between two D-Cubes. This is because cubes perform specific functions. When a cube completes its task, it passes its output to another cube which performs *its* task and then passes the output along to the next cube. This input-output process requires a number of D-Links.

To create a D-Link between D-Cubes:

1. Click on **File | New | D-Link**.
2. In the D-Link dialog box, click on **Source**. Next, click on **D-Cube**.
3. Select the source D-Cube from the menu.
4. Click on the **Target** button. Then click on **D-Cube**.
5. Select the target D-Cube from the menu.
6. Map the dimension items by using the following methods.
   More of these methods are discussed later in this chapter.
      ◦ Matched Descriptions
      ◦ Allocation
      ◦ Selection from Unpaired Dimensions

The D-Link dialog box

The D-Link dialog box has two sections. The upper section displays the dimensions of the source and the target. The lower section displays the dimension items belonging to the source and target dimensions. When dimensions are paired, the source dimension items are matched to their corresponding target dimension items. The items can be matched by their descriptions or through an allocation table. Source and target dimensions whose items are matched by a local allocation are connected by green and red arrows. In the following illustration, the **Sales** dimension is matched to the **Profit and Loss** dimension through a local allocation. Those dimensions whose items are matched by their descriptions are connected by a yellow arrow in the upper section of the dialog box, as in this case for the **Periods** and **Departments** dimensions.

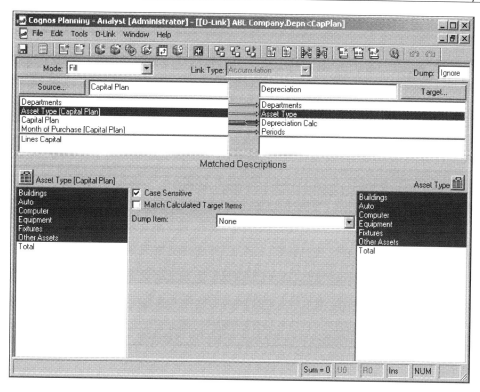

 If the source and target D-Cubes share the same D-Lists, the D-Link will automatically match the dimensions.

Connecting to external data sources

With Analyst, you can connect to a variety of data sources, such as a text file or a database. The simplest method of doing this is by using a File Map. With a File Map, you can connect to the delimited ASCII text files, and configure the file so that the data can be imported into a D-Cube. A more advanced method uses an ODBC connection. **ODBC** stands for **Open Database Connectivity**. This method allows you to connect to any data source for which you have configured a data source name. This includes text files, spreadsheets, and databases. To use this method, you must have the appropriate drivers installed on your computer, and you must be familiar with basic SQL. Once configured, the data source becomes available in a D-Link, and you can write SQL statements against the data source in order to bring data into the D-Cube.

File Map

The File Map allows you to connect to an ASCII file so that you can transfer the data into a D-Cube. You can configure the file as being delimited or using a fixed width file format. If the file has fixed width, you can parse the file and create separate fields for each data type. From the fields, you can define your dimension and data items. Then you can format the fields to the data type that corresponds to the items in the target D-Cube. Because the File Map is an Analyst object, it can be shared. Once the File Map is configured, it can be used by other objects, for instance, as a source for D-List items, data in another cube, or items in an A-Table. However, because the File Map is limited to text file, it requires that the text files be extracted from its original source and then delivered to you in the right format.

To create a File Map:

1. Click on **File | New | File Map**. Here, choose the file type, from:

   ○ **Fixed Width**

   ○ **Delimited**

2. In the **Start Import at Row** box, select the row number where you want the File Map to start importing.

3. Select the checkbox next to **Use row as column names** if the file contains field headers.

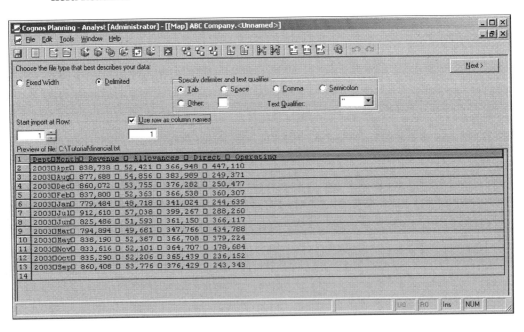

4. Click on **Next** to go to step 2.

5. The File Map wizard creates subcolumns in the file based on the delimiter that you selected.

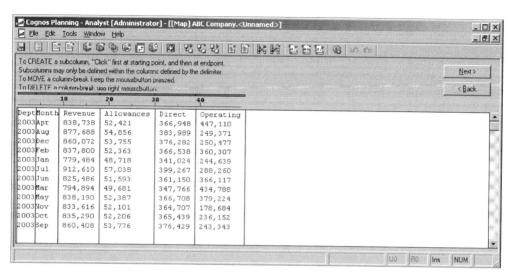

6. If you select **Fixed Width** in the previous box, you will be required to create the subcolumns by clicking on the space between the data, where you want the subcolumn to appear.

7. After you have defined the subcolumns, click on **Next** to get to step 3 of the File Map editor.

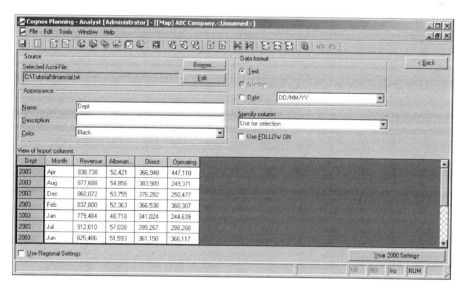

8. If you selected the **Use row as column names** option, then the column headers in the ASCII file will also be used as the column headers in the File Map. If the ASCII file has no headers, then you must provide column header names by highlighting each column and typing the **Name** under the **Appearance** section of the box. Continue doing this for each of the columns.

9. After you enter the column names, determine whether the columns in the ASCII file will be used as a dimension or as data. Click on the column and select **Use for selection** to configure the column as dimension. Otherwise, select **Use as data** to configure the field as a data item. If you select **Skip**, the File Map will ignore the field.

10. If you configure the field as a dimension, then the field becomes a dimension in a D-Link and the data becomes dimension items. If you configure the field as data, then the field becomes a data dimension item and the data becomes values. All of the fields that are configured as data comprise the DATA dimension in the D-Link.

11. Format the fields that are configured as data. The data can be numeric, text, or a date. Select the data format under the **Data format** section. If you select a date format, select the specific format from the drop-down list box next to the **Date** option.

12. By default, fields that are configured as dimensions assume a text format.

13. Save and name the File Map.

 In practice, File Maps are named by the source file. So if the file is called `products.txt`, it would be appropriate to name the File Map as **Products**.

Creating a D-Link using File Map as a source

Once you have configured the File Map, you can use it as a source in your D-Link. No additional configuration is required. You can pair the dimensions and allocate the dimension items just as you would with a D-Cube. The columns that you specified to be used for selection will become dimensions, and the columns that you specified to be used as data will become items in the DATA dimension.

To create a D-Link using a File Map as a source:

1. Click on **File | New | D-Link**.
2. Click on **Source** and select **Mapped ASCII File**.
3. Navigate to the ASCII file, select it, and then click on **Open**.
4. Allocate the dimensions and dimension items.
5. Save and close the D-Link.

Although you cannot use an unmapped ASCII file as your source in a D-Link, you can import D-List items or items in an A-Table directly from an unmapped ASCII file.

ODBC connection

Importing data using the ODBC connection gives you the ability to manipulate data by writing simple SQL queries. The ability to write SQL queries is most useful when the data source does not easily conform to the structural requirements of the target cube. Unlike a File Map, which needs to be configured only once, the ODBC connection option requires you to write a SQL statement each time the D-Link uses the ODBC connection for its source. That means you will have as many SQL statements as you will have D-Links using ODBC connections. However, the ODBC connection has many advantages. With this option, you can connect directly to production databases, giving your models direct access to real-time data. With SQL, you can modify the data without the need for a staging table. You can also insert calculations, parse or concatenate data, filter, join two or more tables, and much more.

Creating an ODBC data source name

Before creating the ODBC connection, you must know what your data source is and where it is stored. If the data source is a database, you must have permission to read the database as well as the necessary database information to configure the connection.

1. On your desktop, click on **Start | Control Panel**. Double-click on **Administrative Tools**, and then double-click on **Data Sources (ODBC)**.

2. Click on the **System DSN** tab. Although you can use the **User** or **File** DSN tabs, we recommend that you choose the **System DSN** so that all of the ODBC links will run, regardless of who logs on to the computer.

3. Click on the database driver that corresponds to the database type to which you are connecting, and then click on **Finish**.

4. Type the data source name, and a description (optional).

5. Enter the data source information pertaining to the data that you want to access, and follow the wizard to complete the connection. The required entries will vary depending on what database you are using. Refer to your database administrator for assistance in completing the entries required for your database. For more information on configuring the ODBC connection, refer to the Microsoft help and support web site.

Creating a D-Link using an ODBC connection as the source

Once the ODBC connection has been configured, you can connect to the data source within Analyst:

1. Click on **File | New | D-Link**.

2. Click on **Source** and select **ODBC (SQL) Database**.

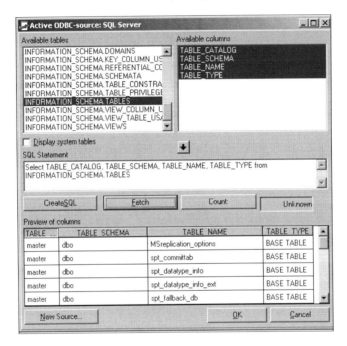

3. Select the table containing the data that you want to import.

4. In the **SQL Statement** box, write the SQL statement. You can create a simple `Select` statement by pressing the *Ctrl* key and clicking simultaneously on the fields that you want to select and finally clicking on the **CreateSQL** button.

5. Click on **Fetch** to view a sample of the data being extracted from the SQL statement.

6. Click on **OK** to bring the fields into the D-Link.

7. Click on **Mark as Data**.

8. On the list of sources, select the items that you want to use as data items and move them to the rightmost pane. Click on **OK**. The items that you selected become a part of the DATA dimension.

9. Select the target cube and allocate the items in the DATA dimension to their corresponding target dimension items.

10. Pair the other dimensions and allocate their dimension items as appropriate.

11. Close and save the D-Link.

Executing the D-Link

In Contributor, the D-Links are run automatically based on how they are set up in the D-Cube Update function, which we will discuss in the following sections. In Analyst, D-Links are run when you execute the command. When you run the D-Link, data from the source is copied to the target. By using D-Links, you can copy data from several sources to a single target D-Cube, and vice-versa. You can run a single D-Link or a group of D-Links at a time. When you have several D-Links targeting a single D-Cube, you must determine the sequence in which the D-Links will run.

Executing a D-Link

A D-Link will copy the data based on the allocation defined within the link. You can run a D-Link to view the data flow between D-Cubes. The ability to run a D-Link is most useful when you are developing the model and you want to test the data flow. If you have the target D-Cube open when you run the D-Link, you can view the results. You can then save the D-Cube after the data is copied, or close the D-Cube without saving the changes. If the target D-Cube is not open when you run the D-Link, the data copied will be saved automatically.

To execute a D-Link:

1. Open the D-Link.
2. Click on **D-Link | Execute**.

Running several D-Links into a single target D-Cube

When you have several D-Links targeting a single D-Cube, you can execute them with a single command through the D-Cube **Update** option. With this option, you can choose which D-Links to run along with the sequence in which they must run. Only D-Links targeting the D-Cube can be run using this option. Any D-Link that is not included in the D-Cube Update will not run. In Contributor, the D-Links are run automatically based on how you configure the D-Cube Update, whereas in Analyst, you have to run them by executing D-Cube Update.

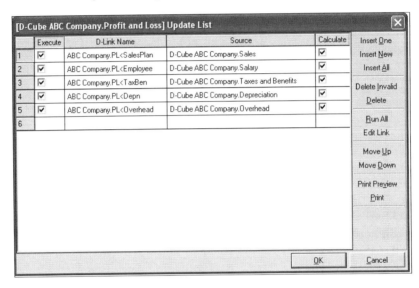

To execute D-Links using a D-Cube Update:

1. Open the target D-Cube.

2. Click on **D-Cube | D-Links | Update**.

3. Click on **Run All**.

You can disable a D-Link in the **Update List** by un-checking the **Execute** box next to it. This is useful when the link is necessary only in certain periods during the budget cycle and you don't want to recreate the link each time the D-Link is needed. You can also disable the **Calculate** option. When you do this, the D-Cube re-calculates at the next D-Link when the **Calculation** checkbox is selected or it re-calculates after all of the D-Links are run. This is helpful when you have a large cube that contains a lot of calculations and you want speed up re-calculation.

Executing a batch of D-Links

You can execute a number of D-Links in a single command. The D-Links do not have to target a single D-Cube or come from a single source. Any D-Link can be included in the batch including the ones residing in another library. The sequence in which the D-Links run will depend upon the order in which you have positioned the D-Links in the lower pane. The D-Link at the beginning of the list will run first, followed by the second, and so on.

To execute a batch of D-Links:

1. Click on **File | Library | D-Links**.
2. In the **D-Link Library Function** box, select the D-Links by pressing the *Ctrl* key and simultaneously clicking on the required D-Links to select them, and drop them onto the lower pane by using the down arrow button in the middle of the dialog box.
3. Click on the **Run** button to execute the D-Links that you selected.

It is not uncommon for a D-Cube to be targeted by several D-Links coming from a single source D-Cube. This happens when you want to allocate items from one source dimension to items that reside in several target dimensions. The same is true when you have items in several source dimensions that you want to allocate to a single target dimension.

Allocating dimension items

After you have selected the source and target of a D-Link, the next step is to establish the correspondence between the source and target items. There are two ways of doing this. The first way is to match the names of the items automatically. This method is the faster and more efficient way of mapping items, but it requires strict adherence to a naming convention. The second is to use an allocation table. With an allocation table, you can map items regardless of their name. This method is more time-consuming and not advisable if you have a long list of items that change frequently.

Allocating dimension items using Matched Description

When you link dimension items using the **Matched Description** option, you map the source and target dimension items by their display names. The connection will exist only if the name matches. If you change the name of either of the dimension items, the connection will be severed. Similarly, if you create new source or target dimension items that have matching names, D-Link will automatically create a connection between the two. You do not need to open or refresh the D-Link for the connection to be created.

To match dimension items by matching descriptions:

1. Click on the source dimension to open the dimension items in the source section.

2. Press the *Ctrl* key and simultaneously click on the target dimension to open the dimension items in the target section.

3. Click on **Matched Descriptions**.

Having a standard naming convention for D-List items can make it easier to map sources to targets. If the names are consistent throughout the model, use the matched description method to simplify your allocation.

In the following illustration, the **Periods** dimensions are matched by description. The D-Link maps the source and targets by matching their names. This approach is symbolized by the straight yellow arrow as shown:

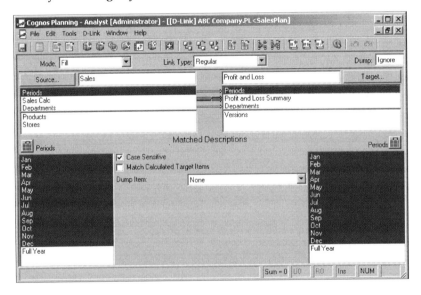

Using Cut Sub-Columns

You can still match the descriptions even if the descriptions are not entirely identical, as long as they contain a string of characters that are identical. Using the Cut Sub-Column option, you can parse the dimension items to expose only the characters that can be matched. For instance, if your source is "40000 Revenue" and your target if "40000", you can cut the source description so that the program only matches the first five characters. You can use this option either on the source or the target, or both.

To cut sub-columns:

1. Click on the **Cut Sub-Column** icon 🏛 immediately above source or target list box.

2. In the **Sub-Column** dialog box, parse the dimension items by clicking on the start and/or end of the string of characters containing the descriptions to be matched.

3. Click on **OK**.

4. Right-click on the parse line if you want to remove or change it.

Allocating dimension items using a local allocation

When you link two dimensions using a local allocation table, you need to specify the source and target dimension items. The relationship between the source and the target is based on an Internal ID (IID). If the description of either of the dimension items changes, the D-Link will update the description in the allocation table and preserve the relationship. However, if you delete either the source or the target dimension, you will need to remove the deleted item from the allocation table.

To allocate dimension items through a local allocation table:

1. Click on the source dimension to open the dimension items in the source section.

2. Press the *Ctrl* key and simultaneously click on the target dimension to open the dimension items in the target section.

3. Click on **Allocate Items**.

4. Click on the source dimension item. Then click on the target dimension item.

In the following illustration, the **Sales** and **Profit and Loss Summary** dimensions are linked by their dimension items: **Gross Sales**, **Allowance**, and **Cost of Sales**. Allocated items are symbolized by intertwined red and green arrows.

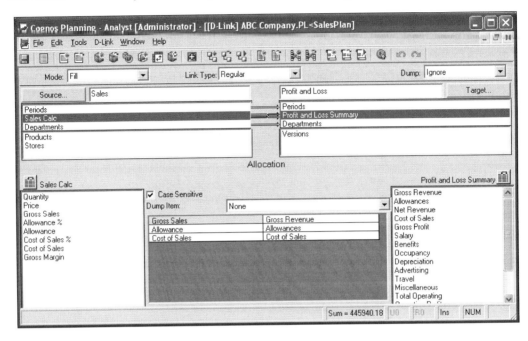

Matching descriptions within a local allocation table

You can match dimension item names in a local allocation table to facilitate your allocation. However, the relationship will be based on the internal ID. The D-Link will neither match the similar names outside the allocation table automatically, nor match them when new dimensions are added to the source and target.

To match descriptions in a local allocation table, click on **D-Link | Allocation Table | Match Descriptions**.

Selecting items from unpaired dimensions

When the number of dimensions in the source and target is uneven, one or more dimensions will be unpaired. In the unpaired dimension, you must specify the dimension item that you want to use as a source or target. By default, if an unpaired dimension is left unselected, all of its items will be selected. If the target dimension is left unselected, all dimension items will be targeted by the same data. If the source dimension is left unselected, all of its items will flow to the target.

To select a dimension item from an unpaired dimension:

1. Click on the source or target dimension to open the dimension items.
2. Highlight the dimension item and click on **Select**.

In the following illustration, the **Budget** item in the **Versions** dimension is selected as the target:

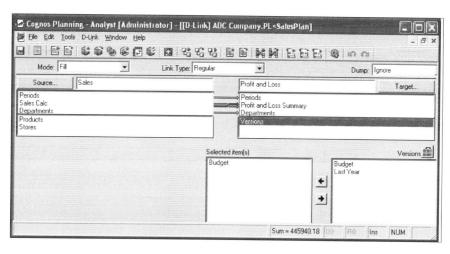

Many to one and one to many allocations

You can link multiple dimension items to one target and vice-versa. When you link multiple items, the data will be aggregated when it reaches the target. This is useful when you are aggregating data from several dimension items, in order to aggregate data into a summary item without having to write a subtotal in the source D-List. However, keep in mind that if you add another item to consolidate you will need to update the allocation table to include the new item. In a *one-to-many* allocation, the same data will populate each of the targets. This is useful when populating assumptions across several target dimension items.

Modes

In general, you use D-Link to copy data from a source to a target. However, there are several ways in which the data can reach the target:

- **Fill**: This is the default mode. The **Fill** mode will replace all of the targeted cells with new data. If the source is a file outside Analyst, a Look Up link, or an Accumulation link, the **Fill** mode will zero out the cube and then populate it with new data. Data in untargeted cells will be deleted.

- **Substitute:** The **Substitute** mode will replace only targeted cells with new data, leaving untargeted cells intact.

- **Add**: The **Add** mode adds the values in the source to the existing values in the target.

- **Subtract**: The **Subtract** mode reduces the values in the target by the value of the incoming data.

Dump option

When the source contains more data than the target can take, some data will be rejected. You can capture the rejected data by enabling one of the **Dump** options. There are four **Dump** options:

- **Ignore**: This is the default option. This option produces no record of rejected items.

- **Edit**: This option displays any dump item in a separate table. This table can be viewed but not saved. However, you can copy the contents into clipboard and paste them into Excel.

- **Print**: This option creates a print file that you can send to your printer.

- **File**: This option allows you to save the rejected items to a text file. When selecting this option, you will be prompted to select the location of the file.

Special D-Links

In Chapter 5, *Defining Data Structure: D-List* we explained that a D-List item can be formatted on another D-List: the format D-List. A D-List formatted item can become a virtual dimension when used in a D-Link. A virtual dimension is both data and dimension. It is data in a D-Cube, but can be paired with a real dimension in a D-Link. To convert the D-List formatted item into a virtual dimension, you need to select **Look Up** or **Accumulation** in the D-Link **Type** option. Once activated, the virtual dimension becomes available in the dimension section of the D-Link. If you click on the virtual dimension, it displays all of the items in the format D-List. Even though the format D-List is not a dimension of either the source or the target cube, the D-Link recognizes it as though it is. That is why, it's called virtual: it assumes the properties of a real dimension without truly being one. Virtual dimensions are especially useful because they perform special functions in addition to moving the data. They can look up or accumulate data before passing the data to the target cube.

You can distinguish a virtual dimension from a real dimension by its description. A virtual dimension is named after the D-List formatted item and the Format D-List enclosed in brackets. An example is "Grade [Employee Grades]" where Grade is the D-List Formatted item and Employee Grades is the Format D-List.

Limitations of special D-Links

There are limitations to what you can do with special links. You cannot pair a virtual dimension with another virtual dimension. Moreover, you cannot use any of the D-Link options such as scaling, rounding, and sign-changing.

Look Up D-Links

A Look Up D-Link performs a similar function to the look up function in Excel. The Look Up D-Link takes a value entered in a target D-Cube, looks for that value in the source D-Cube, and then returns another value that corresponds to the value entered. For Look Up to work, the source D-Cube must contain the association between the data entered and the data being looked up. In many cases, the source D-Cube would be an assumption cube, but it could also be an input cube. For example, suppose the employees are paid a bonus based on their employee grade. The amount of bonus is based on the employee's grade as illustrated in the following **Salary Assumptions** cube:

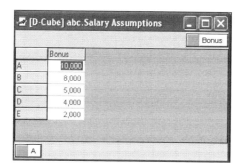

Using the Look Up D-Link, you can link the bonus amount from the **Salary Assumptions** cube above to each of the employees in the following **Salary** cube, based on the employee's grade:

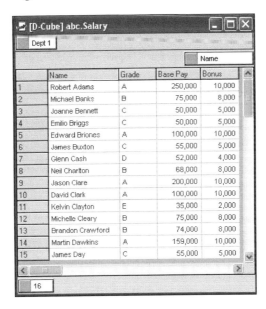

Creating a Look Up D-Link

Creating a Look Up D-Link is similar to creating a regular link. After you have selected the source and target D-Cubes, select Look Up in the **Link Type** box. By doing this, you display the virtual dimensions in the target cube. Once the virtual dimensions are available, you can pair the dimension items just as you would with real dimensions.

To create a Look Up D-Link:

1. Click on **File | New | D-Link**.
2. Select the source and target D-Cubes.
3. In the **Link Type** box, select **Look Up**.
4. Pair the dimensions as appropriate.
5. Save the D-Link.

Accumulation D-Links

An Accumulation D-Link groups data according to their attributes and sends their aggregated values to the target cube. This type of D-Link is often used to pass data from detailed calculation cubes to summarized reporting cubes. Continuing with the preceding example, the following **Bonus by Grade** D-Cube shows a summary of bonuses by grade. By using the Accumulation D-Link, you can add up the amount of bonus given to the employees and display the result by grade in another cube. Because the Salary D-Cube does not organize the employees by their grade, it would be impractical to create a calculation that would produce the same result without the use of the Accumulation D-Link.

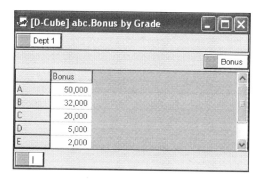

Creating an Accumulation D-Link

When you select **Accumulation** in the **Link Type** box, the virtual dimensions will appear on the source D-Cube. Then you can pair the virtual dimension and allocate the dimension items just as you would for a real dimension.

To create an Accumulation D-Link:

1. Click on **File | New | D-Link**.
2. Select the source and target D-Cubes.
3. In the **Link Type** box, select **Accumulation**.
4. Pair the dimensions as appropriate.
5. Save the D-Link.

Allocation tables (A-Table)

The A-Table is an Analyst object that lets you map source to target items in the same manner as a local allocation does. However, the A-Table has additional features that allow you to filter, sort, or re-arrange source and target items. Because it is an object, not a function within a D-Link, the A-Table can be used by more than one D Link. Thus any change to the A-Table will update the D-Links that use it. This is a powerful feature that can simplify the maintenance of your models. With an A-Table, you can have a central place where you control how data flows within several D-Links. Without an A-Table, updating D-Links that share the same allocation can be tedious. For instance, suppose you have a staging cube that loads actual data each month into five calculation cubes. Each time you update the calculation cubes, you have to open a local allocation table in each D-Link and map the current month from the source to its corresponding month in the target. This step will have to be performed five times to update all of the calculation cubes. With an A-Table, this task is done once.

In the following illustration, we have an A-Table that maps certain benefits and taxes to the Profit and Loss.

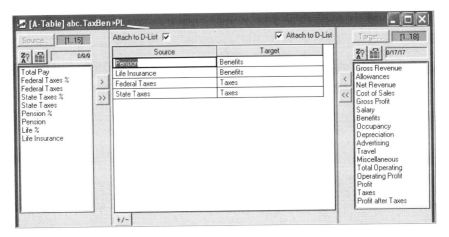

Creating the A-Table

Before you create an A-Table, you must consider the D-Links that will be using it. In general, you use an A-Table if you plan to share it. However, in some cases, you may use it for a single D-Link because of its sorting and filtering capabilities. If the allocation table is a part of routine maintenance, then it is appropriate to use an A-Table, instead of a local allocation table, even if it is used by only one D-Link.

To create an A-Table:

1. Click on **File | New | A-Table**.
2. Click on **Source** and select the source.
3. Click on **Target** and select the target.
4. Allocate the source and target items.
5. Save the A-Table.

Allocation items

In a local allocation table, you are limited to items that are available in the source and target D-Cubes. That is not the case with the A-Table. With the A-Table, you can define any source or target items. The A-Table allows you define any logical correspondence of source and target items using any list of items, even if an item on the list does not exist in the source or target. The list of source or target items can come from a D-List, an ASCII file, or a database. You can still use the A-Table even if the allocation that you need is only a subset of the A-Table, that is, if there are more source-to-target associations than you need. The D-Link will ignore any invalid association and will pass data only where a valid source and target correspondence exists.

Creating the source or target items from a D-List

You can use a D-List to provide the list of items that you want to allocate. You can only use one D-List as your source or target, so the D-List must contain all of the items that you want to allocate. You can use the same D-List as both the source and the target.

To use a D-List as source or target:

1. Click on **File | New | A-Table**.
2. Click on **Source** or **Target**, and then select the D-List.
3. Select the D-List from the menu. Then click on **OK**. The D-List items will appear on the source or target section of the A-Table.

To use a D-List from a D-Cube as source or target:

1. Click on **File | New | A-Table**.
2. Click on **Source** or **Target** and select the D-List from the D-Cube.
3. Select the D-Cube from the menu.
4. In the **Specify A-Table** box, select the D-List that you want to use, from the drop-down box.

Creating the source or target items from a delimited ASCII file

You can use a delimited ASCII file as your data source or target. When using a delimited ASCII file, you need to select two fields: one field as the source and the other as the target.

To use a File Map as your source or target:

1. Click on **File | New | A-Table**.
2. Click on **Source** or **Target**, and select **Delimited ASCII File**.
3. Locate the file, and then click on **Open**.
4. In the **Specify A-Table** box, select the delimiter type, and then select the number representing the field to be used.
5. Click on **OK**.

Creating the source or target items from a mapped ASCII file

Selecting from a File Map is similar to selecting from an ASCII file. In the File Map you will be able to read the headers defined in the File Map, instead of the position number.

To use a File Map as your source or target:

1. Click on **File | New | A-Table**.
2. Click on **Source**, and then select **Mapped ASCII File**.
3. Locate the File Map in the menu.
4. In the **Specify A-Table** box, select the delimiter type and then select the field to be used.
5. Click on **OK**.

Creating the source or target items from an ODBC data source

You can load your source or target list from a database by using an ODBC connection. You must have an ODBC connection configured before you can view the data source. With an ODBC connection, you can manipulate data using SQL queries before loading them into the A-Table.

1. Click on **File | New | A-Table**.
2. Click on **Source**, and then select **ODBC SQL (Database)**.
3. Select your data source.
4. In the **SQL Statement** box, type your SQL statement.
5. Click on **OK**.

Using a D-Cube as an allocation table

You can use a selection of a D-Cube as an allocation table. To be used as an allocation table, the D-Cube must be reduced to a two-dimensional slice. If the D-Cube contains more than two dimensions, you must select one item in each of the pages. The selection can have multiple rows. However, only one data item can be used as your column so that the table consists of two sides, similar to an A-Table. The row dimension is one side of the table and the column containing the data is the other. You can choose whether to use the row dimension or the data as your source. If you choose the data, the row dimension will default as the target, or vice versa.

To use a D-Cube as an allocation table:

1. Open a D-Link.
2. *Ctrl+* click on the source and target dimensions.
3. Click on **Allocate**.
4. Click on **D-Link | Allocation Table | Use D-Cube Data**.

 Instead of using a D-Cube, you can create a selection from the D-Cube and use the selection as your allocation table. In this case, you need to select **Use Saved Selection**, instead of **Use D-Cube Data**.

5. Select the D-Cube from the menu.
6. Select the dimensions that contain the data that you want to use as your allocation, and move the dimensions from the **Items Available pane** to the **Items Included** pane.

7. Click on **Slice**. Select the items that will become the row and column dimensions in the slice. Click on **OK** to accept the slice.

8. Click on **OK** to complete your D-Cube selection.

9. In the **Specify Allocation** box, select either **D-List as Source** or **D-Cube Data as Source**.

10. Click on **OK**.

Analyst <> Contributor links

You can import data from a Contributor application into an Analyst D-Cube and vice versa by using a D-Link. You can also move data from one Contributor application to another. With this method, you can make use of the D-Link options. You can link data items using a local allocation table, or you can match their description. You can load an A-Table or a D-Cube allocation, execute the D-Link modes, or use the dump options. The Analyst <> Contributor D-Link works well with small amounts of data and is handy for ad hoc data transfers. However, there are drawbacks. If you use this method to import large sets of data, you may encounter performance issues. Also, because Analyst is not scalable, you cannot distribute jobs to multiple servers, and thus it takes longer to load data this way.

To create an Analyst to Contributor D-Link:

1. Click on **File | New | D-Link**.
2. In the D-Link dialog box, click on **Source**. Then click on **D-Cube**.
3. Select the source D-Cube from the menu.
4. Click on **Target**. Then click on **Contributor Data**.
5. Select the Contributor application.
6. Select the target D-Cube, and then click on **OK**.
7. Pair the source and target dimensions, and allocate the dimension items accordingly.
8. Save and close the D-Link.

To create a Contributor to Analyst D-Link:

1. Click on **File | New | D-Link**.
2. In the D-Link dialog box, click on **Source**. Then click on **Contributor Data**.
3. Select the Contributor application.
4. Select the source D-Cube, and then click on **OK**.
5. Click on **Target**. Then click on **D-Cube**.

6. Select the target D-Cube, and then click on **OK**.

7. Pair the source and target dimensions, and allocate the dimension items accordingly.

8. Save and close the D-Link.

To create a Contributor to Contributor D-Link:

1. Click on **File | New | D-Link**.

2. In the D-Link dialog box, click on **Source**. Then click on **Contributor Data**.

3. Select the Contributor application.

4. Select the source D-Cube, and then click on **OK**.

5. Click on **Target**. Then click on **Contributor Data**.

6. Select the Contributor application.

7. Select the target D-Cube, and then click on **OK**.

8. Pair the source and target dimensions, and allocate the dimension items accordingly.

9. Save and close the D-Link.

Importing from IBM Cognos Package

You can import data from IBM Cognos Package by using a D-Link. Before creating the D-Link, you must have already created the Framework Manager model, and published the package in order to use it as your source.

To use an IBM Cognos Package as the source:

1. Click on **File | New | D-Link**.

2. Click on **Target**, and then select the D-Cube that you want to import data into.

3. Click on **Source**. Then click on **Cognos Package**.

4. Select the package from the drop-down list.

5. Select the **Query Subject**.

6. Select the **Query Items** within the **Query Subject**, and move them to the **Selected Query Items** pane.

7. Select the **Display preview of selected query item** check box to view the **Query Items**.

8. Click on **OK** to display the **Query Items** in the D-Link.

9. Click on **Mark Data**.

10. Move the items that you want to include as your data items in the DATA dimension.

11. Click on **D-Link | Options**. In the **Cognos Package – Alternative** temporary data storage path, enter the location where the data will temporarily be stored. The default will be the path to the `Filesys.ini` file. Make sure that the location is accessible and writeable from all Analyst clients and Planning servers.

12. Pair the source and target dimensions, and allocate the dimension items accordingly.

13. Save and close the D-Link.

Analyst <> Cognos Finance D-Links

You can import data from IBM Cognos Finance to an Analyst D-Cube or vice versa by using a D-Link. With this method, you can make use of the D-Link options. You can link data items using a local allocation table or can match their descriptions. You can load an A-Table or a D-Cube allocation, use the D-Link modes or use the dump options. IBM Cognos Finance must be installed and configured on your computer before you can use this option.

To create the IBM Cognos Finance <> Analyst D-Link:

1. Click on **File | New | D-Link**.

2. In the D-Link dialog box, click on **Source**. Then click on **Cognos Finance Data**.

3. Select the IBM Cognos Finance application.

4. Click on **Target**. Then click on the Analyst **D-Cube**.

5. Pair the source and target dimensions, and allocate the dimension items accordingly.

6. Save and close the D-Link.

To create the Analyst <> Cognos Finance D-Link:

1. Click on **File | New | D-Link**.

2. In the D-Link dialog box, click the **Target button**. Then click on **Cognos Finance Data**.

3. Select the IBM Cognos Finance application.

4. Click on **Source**. Then click on the Analyst **D-Cube**.

5. Pair the source and target dimensions, and allocate the dimension items accordingly.

6. Save and close the D-Link.

Summary

In this chapter, we discussed the various ways in which you can copy data by using a D-Link. We demonstrated how you can copy data from a D-Cube and from an ASCII file or a database. You can connect to an ASCII file by using a File Map. If your data source is a database, you can connect to it using an ODBC connection. An ODBC connection gives you the ability to write SQL statements against the database and to manipulate the data before extracting it. Once you have defined the data and dimensions from the source, you need to pair or allocate the dimension items. You can automatically match descriptions, or can manually allocate the dimension items by using an allocation table. The allocation table could be created locally within the D-Link, or as separate object that can used by other D-Links. You can also use data in a D-Cube as your allocation table. There are two special D-Links that allow you to look up or accumulate data before sending the data to the target cube. These D-Links make use of virtual dimensions that can be paired with real dimensions in a D-Link. Finally, you can link to other IBM Cognos applications such as Contributor or IBM Cognos Finance, and import data into a D-Cube from an IBM Cognos Package.

8

Understanding the Contributor Environment

Fundamentally, the IBM Cognos Planning System contains two core products: Analyst and Contributor. Analyst is used to build models, whereas Contributor is used to distribute models to a wider user base. We will cover the Contributor product and its features and functionalities (from Chapter 8-16), beginning with an overview in this chapter. After reading this chapter, you will be able to:

- Explain how various components are used in IBM Cognos Planning to configure and deploy planning models

- Describe the three-tier architecture of the IBM Cognos Planning System, and how these tiers interact with each other

- Identify and explain the purpose of the Toolbar, Menu items, and the Tree found in the Contributor Administration Console

Understanding IBM Cognos Planning components

It is essential to learn about the components used by IBM Cognos Planning in order to understand how all pieces of the Planning System work together. The following table lists seven components of the Planning System, the users of these components, and the environments in which these components are used.

Components	Who Uses it?	Web or Windows Environment?
IBM Cognos Connection	Users, Administrators	Web-based
IBM Cognos Planning – Contributor Web Client	Users	Web-based
IBM Cognos Planning - Contributor Administration	Administrators, Modelers	Client tool
IBM Cognos Planning - Contributor for Microsoft Excel	Users	Client tool
IBM Cognos Planning - Manager	Users, Administrators	Client tool
IBM Cognos Planning - Analyst	Administrators, Modelers	Client tool
IBM Cognos Planning - Analyst for Microsoft Excel	Users, Modelers	Client tool

IBM Cognos Planning uses some other components; however, you, as a planning modeler, or a planning administrator, do not regularly work directly with them. These components include server components, modeling components, and IBM Business Intelligence Studios.

IBM Cognos Connection

IBM Cognos Connection is a web portal. Users can access planning applications and Business Intelligence (BI) reports by using the IBM Cognos Connection. The administrators use it to perform administrative functions, such as user rights management and server monitoring.

IBM Cognos Planning - Contributor Web Client

Contributor Web Client, commonly known as 'Contributor', provides the Web-based interface, thereby allowing the users to submit their plans simultaneously. Contributor streamlines planning data collection and *budget submit-review-revision* workflow management.

IBM Cognos Planning - Contributor Administration Console

You, as a planning administrator, use the Console program to create the Contributor applications, configure application access, setup the screen layout, and distribute applications to users over the Web. In the upcoming chapters, we will discuss Contributor and Contributor Administration Console programs in greater detail.

IBM Cognos Planning - Contributor for Microsoft Excel

This is an Excel add-in program for the Contributor Web Client, and it provides a familiar Excel interface for working with Contributor tabs. Business users can import Contributor tabs into Excel, manipulate data, and then save it back to the application database. Although this add-in is a moderate substitute for the Contributor Web Client, organizations usually prefer not to deploy this tool to end users. For example, if an organization purchases IBM Cognos Planning to replace their Excel-based planning model, they may be reluctant to provide users with a Contributor model with an Excel interface. Note that if users are not careful when using a Contributor model that has been deployed using an Excel add-in program, then the model's underlying links can break, possibly resulting in users not being able to submit and save their plans to the application database.

IBM Cognos Planning - Analyst

Financial modelers use the Analyst tool to define their business model. A model includes the drivers and contents required for planning, budgeting, and forecasting. In most cases, the model is distributed to planners by using the web-based architecture of Contributor.

IBM Cognos Planning - Manager

Business users can use this tool to create reports, enter data into D-Cubes, and create a flowchart for the financial model. However, in practice, this tool is not used for these tasks very often.

IBM Cognos Planning - Analyst for Microsoft Excel

This is an Excel add-in program for Analyst, and provides a familiar Excel interface for working with the Analyst's D-Cubes. Business users can import the Analyst D-Cubes into Excel, manipulate data, and then save it back to the Analyst D-Cubes.

Understanding the IBM Cognos Planning technical architecture

As an administrator or a modeler, you need to understand how the IBM Cognos Planning architecture works, and how the various components of the Planning System communicate with each other. To illustrate these concepts, we will describe an analogy, and then relate it to the IBM Cognos Planning architecture. Later, we will describe the role of each component of the Planning System architecture.

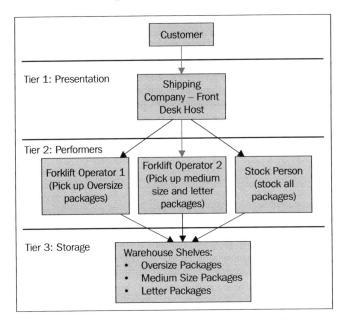

Let's assume that a shipping company (named Budget Shipping Company) has a branch office, where it stores packages to be dropped off and picked up. This branch has a **Front Desk Host**, and his role is to interact with customers and handle their shipping requests. There are two forklift operators who handle customers' pick-up requests. **Operator 1** handles requests for oversized packages, while **Operator 2** handles requests for medium-and letter-sized packages. In addition, a **Stock Person** is responsible for storing packages. The purpose of this analogy is to provide a conceptual framework for understanding IBM Cognos Planning architecture.

As illustrated below, IBM Cognos Planning uses a three-tiered architecture to create, configure, and distribute planning models. The three tiers are: Web Server, Application, and Data. The Web tier takes the browser's requests and services them, while working with the Application tier. In our analogy, the Front Desk Host functions as the Web Server tier. The application then takes the requests from the Web tier, performs security checks, and works with the Data tier in servicing the requests back to the Web tier. The Performers (Forklift Operators 1 and 2 and the Stock Person) function as the Application tier in our analogy. The role of the Data tier—the warehouse shelves in our analogy—is to store data in two separate datastores: Content Store and Planning Store.

In the following illustration, we assume that three computers are used to install these three tiers. You can install each tier on a single computer, or you can install the tiers on more than three computers.

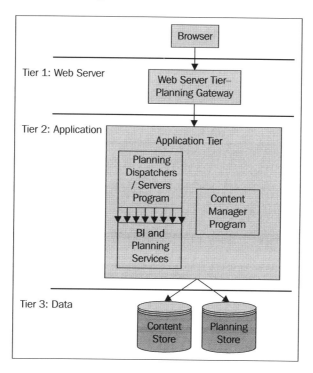

Tier 1: Web Server or Planning Gateway

The Web tier takes the browser's requests and passes them to the Application tier. When you install IBM Cognos Planning, you have to identify the computer on which the Web or HTTP server is running. You then install the Planning Gateway server components on that computer, so that this computer can function like the Front Desk Host of the Budget Shipping Company. IBM Cognos supports various types of web gateway technologies that generate dynamic web contents, such as CGI, Apache_mod, ISAPI, and so on.

Tier 2: Application

The Application tier is the central tier in which the coordination for servicing the browser's requests takes place. The following two components in this tier make things happen.

Content Manager

Similar to the Stock Person in our analogy, this component manages the storage of customer application data, such as security, configuration data, report specifications, scheduling information, and the IBM Cognos namespace. Content Manager stores information in a content store. We will refer to the *Data Tier* section discussed later.

Planning Dispatchers or Servers

Dispatchers handle requests from tier 1 web servers. They run various IBM Business Intelligence and Planning services in order to fulfill the requests, similar to our analogy where Forklift Operator 1 (a service) handles only oversized packages, versus Forklift Operator 2 (a service), who handles only medium-sized and letter packages. These are the main planning services run by dispatchers to support the Planning system.

- *Planning Job Service* manages the job servers' handling of administrative tasks, such as publishing users' submitted data to a database
- *Planning Data Service* provides real-time reporting and analysis, while working with IBM Business Intelligence tools
- *Planning Administration Service* manages communications with Contributor Administration, and performs other administrative tasks
- *Planning Web Service* manages communications for the Contributor Web Client and Contributor for Excel client

Tier 3: Data

In addition to a Content Store, which is a common datastore for the entire IBM Cognos environment, IBM Cognos Planning uses two types of datastores to store planning *system* data and planning *application* data.

Content Store

This database stores data necessary for operating the entire Planning System, such as packages, and the IBM Cognos namespace.

Planning Store

This database stores planning metadata for all planning applications and the planning environment, such as administration links and macros. Note that you can choose not to create and use a Planning store, as the information contained in this store can also be stored in a Content Store.

Application Store

This database stores the model's metadata and data. Each model creates a separate application datastore. For example, if your organization has three Profit and Loss models, you will find three application stores. Each application may also have a publish database or container. In simplest terms, the publish database stores users' submitted plan data for IBM Cognos reporting applications such as Report Studio. We will discuss the publishing process and publish containers in Chapter 13.

Using the Contributor Administration Console program

In this section, we will discuss the user interface of the Contributor Administration Console program. This console is used to create, configure, and distribute planning models.

We will cover three areas of the Contributor Administration Console interface: the Toolbar, Menus, and the Console Tree. We will explain the functionality of these items in the order in which they are used in the planning system:

1. System-wide settings, after installation of IBM Cognos Planning
2. Developing planning applications
3. Deploying, monitoring, and troubleshooting planning applications

The following sections briefly cover the interface and its functionality. More detailed information is provided in subsequent chapters.

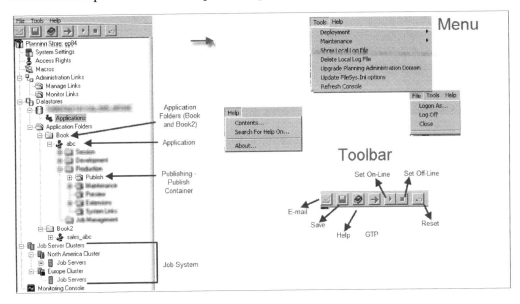

IBM Cognos Planning System settings

You need to perform these three steps in order to get IBM Cognos Planning up and running:

1. Install the IBM Cognos Planning components.
2. Configure the IBM Cognos Planning components via the IBM Cognos Configuration Program.
3. Apply IBM Cognos Planning System-wide settings by using the Contributor Administration Console program.

We will cover the last item in the following sections. The topic of installation and configuration of IBM Cognos Planning is beyond the scope of this book. There are several settings that you must attend immediately when you first open the Contributor Administration Console program, whereas other settings may be completed later, as needed.

Planning Store

Location: Console Tree

After installing IBM Cognos Planning products, Contributor prompts you to initially populate the Planning Store specified in IBM Cognos Configuration, when you launch the Contributor Administration Console for the first time. Note that the topic of IBM Cognos Planning installation is beyond the scope of this book, and it is, therefore, assumed that your software installation has been successfully completed.

The Planning Store holds information about:

- Datastore servers
- Contributor application datastores
- Job servers and job server clusters
- Security
- Macros
- Administration links
- Jobs

System settings

Location: Console Tree

You can perform the following types of system wide settings:

- **Scheduler credentials**: Occasionally, when unattended macros fail, you may need to validate the scheduler credentials on this tab. A scheduler credential is an authenticated session used to run scheduled, unattended macros, for example, running a GTP at 2 a.m. , in order to update model changes when an administrator is not physically present to open the Contributor Administration Console and run the macro.

- **Web Client settings**: The default Planning Rights Administrator can configure web client settings on this screen. Two key settings can be made here:

  ° You can allow automatic download and installations of Contributor Web Client. Otherwise, you have to install the client program in some other way, such as by using a command line script.

  ° You can limit the size of an attached document. A user of Contributor Web Client can attach various types of documents to their Web models. You need to limit its size to prevent users from (for example) attaching exceedingly-large Excel or Word files.

- **System settings**: You can change two types of settings here: how many e.List items you can see in a hierarchy format on the e.List screen, and the timeout value settings. This latter value may require changes if you experience timeout errors on long-running *Planning* server calls.

Access Rights

Location: Console Tree

Access to administrative functions in the Contributor Administration Console, such as synchronizing an application or publishing data, is granted by assigning Access Rights to groups or roles to perform these functions. For example, members of the Planning Rights Administration group may assign rights to import data or run GTP for specific contributor applications to other administrators. In a small installation with one or two administrators, the Access Rights setting does not require changing, and can be left to its default setting. In larger implementations with 15-20 administrators/developers, however, you should think about setting up Access Rights once the IBM Cognos Planning installation is complete. Note that you can modify these settings later, when you have started using the Contributor Administration Console. We will cover Access Rights settings in detail in Chapter 15.

DataStores

Location: Console Tree

To store an application's data, you need relational databases (such as SQL, Oracle, and DB2). When you open the Contributor Administration Console for the first time, you need to configure a database server computer on which to store the application's data. You can use more than one database server computer to store data.

Jobs, Job Servers, and Job Server Clusters

Location: Console Tree

Software development projects often require many varieties of jobs, for instance, programming, networking, database administration, testing, and so on. Similarly, the Contributor program uses various types of jobs to assist in the development and deployment of planning models. In the above example, programmers are hired to do programming jobs. Likewise, job servers (server computers) are configured to work on Contributor jobs. You can group job servers into clusters, just as you can group programmers by specialty, for example, Java programmers, or Visual Basic programmers. The entire architecture of job clusters and job servers is called the "job system".

Administrative activities or tasks such as a prepare import, reconcile, and publish are called jobs and run on single or multiple job servers. To increase the performance of jobs, additional job servers can be added that will pick up different job items. This will speed up processing time for the job being executed. The following factors need to be considered when determining how many jobs servers you will need:

- Model size—an estimate of the number of cells per slice that exist
- Model complexity—the number of links, number of calculations, and the complexity of calculations
- Number of applications—the number of Contributor applications that will be active and supported
- Processing needs—how many times a job is required to run on a specific schedule
- Processing window for administrative tasks—this is the amount of time available to perform normal administrative tasks, such as GTP or publish

A job cluster is a group of many job servers. You can designate job servers in various ways; for example, you can assign one job cluster with six job servers to your European applications and another job cluster with six job servers to your North American applications. Other possibilities include assigning a job cluster to a specific job type; for example, one job cluster may process all publishing jobs, and another cluster can run GTP or admin link jobs. The advantage of the job cluster is that you do not need to individually assign an application or object to a job server. When you assign an application or object to a job cluster, the jobs are executed on all job servers that are a part of this job cluster.

Please refer to Chapter 15 for a more in-depth explanation of how to maintain job servers and job clusters.

Upgrade the Planning Administration Domain (PAD)

Location: Menu

You can use this menu option to activate the Wizard for upgrading the PAD. In previous versions of IBM Cognos Planning (8.2 and earlier), the Planning Store was referred to as the PAD (Planning Administration Domain). This upgrade is a one-time exercise when upgrading from former versions.

Developing applications

Modelers and administrators typically use these options when developing and administrating applications. A few options are not used as frequently, for example the Reset Development to Production button; whereas other options, for example GTP, must be used regularly for developing and administering applications.

Logon As... and Log Off

Location: Menu

You can use these options to log on and log off from the Contributor Administration Console.

Email

Location: Toolbar

When you need to broadcast a message to users related to model operations and maintenance, for example, when taking the model down temporarily for routine maintenance, you can send emails to users defined in an application by using the default email program. The Contributor Administration Console pulls the email addresses from the mail servers.

Save

Location: Toolbar

Click on this button to save your work.

Go To Production (GTP)

Location: Toolbar

You initially run the GTP to make the application available over the web. You will need to run the GTP later to reflect any application change. The following are the very basic steps involved in creating and distributing planning models. We will cover these steps in greater detail in the next chapter.

- Create the planning model in Analyst
- Create the application from the Analyst model in the Contributor Administration Console

- Load an e.List (a distribution list)
- Run the GTP to make the application available over the web. You use the GTP button to run the GTP.

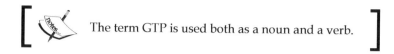 The term GTP is used both as a noun and a verb.

Set online and offline

Location: Toolbar

IBM Cognos Planning applications are typically available over the web 24x7 during the planning season. However, you may encounter situations in which you want to temporarily make applications unavailable to users. For example, when you have to make major structural changes that you don't want to show to the users until you're ready to re-open the application. You use these buttons to set the application online and offline.

Reset Development to Production

Location: Toolbar

An application always has two versions or copies, which we will discuss in detail in the next chapter. These are development and production. The development version is a staging area, and it is used to prepare an application for production. The production version is what the users see on the Web. You make changes to the development version of the application, and GTP the application to reflect those changes in the production version of the application. If you find that your saved changes to the development application are incorrect before you run the GTP, then you can use the **Reset** button to copy the production version of the application back to the development version. See **State 1** in the following illustration. Essentially, this is a big **Undo** button to correct any *saved* development changes since the last GTP.

As illustrated below in **State 2**, if you discover that the production version is not prepared correctly, then you have to restore the database to bring the production version of the application to the correct state. There is *no* undo button to rectify undesired production version changes. It is important to note that you may lose any data entries completed by users on the Web between the time that you GTP the application and restore the incorrect database.

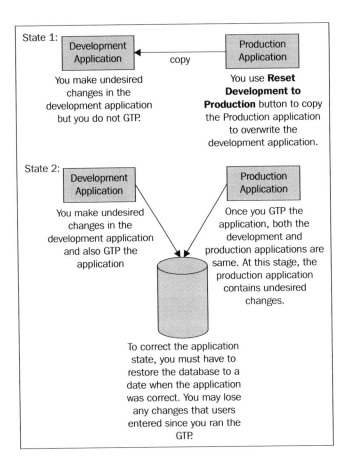

Refresh console

Location: Menu

This option refreshes the Contributor Administration Console, and it is similar to the **Refresh** button in the Web browser.

Application and Publish DataStores/Containers

Location: Tree

When you create an application from an Analyst model, the Contributor program creates a database (MS SQL) or schema (Oracle or DB2) in which to store the application's user-submitted data. Contributor stores users' submitted data in the IBM Cognos proprietary format. To convert the proprietary format to a format that can be easily used for reporting, Contributor uses the publishing process. It stores the published data in a database commonly referred to as a "publish container". It is important to note that the application store and publish datastore are two separate databases or schemas. You cannot use a single datastore to store both application data and published data.

Application folders

Location: Tree

Like Windows folders, in which you store related documents, Application folders are used to hold similar applications. For example, if your organization has two main business units, and each of these has four or five applications, then you can create two Application folders and move the applications to the correct folders. Organizing an application in Application folders is only a logical grouping and does not affect the way in which the applications are stored in the database.

Macros

Location: Tree

Like macro functionality in Microsoft Excel, you can create and execute Contributor macros in order to automate common administrative tasks performed by the administrator, such as publishing jobs, and GTP.

Administration links

Location: Tree

Administration links transfer data within an application or between two applications. You can create, manage, and monitor administration links by using two branches: Manage Link and Monitor Links.

Deploying, monitoring, and troubleshooting applications

Once an application has been developed, you have to deploy it to a production machine/server, monitor its ongoing administrative activities, and troubleshoot any program's technical issues. The following features help you to deploy, monitor, and troubleshoot an application.

Deployment

Location: Menu

In a typical IT environment, you will find three separate physical environments: development, QA, and production. The Deployment wizard helps to export and then import applications and data between these separate environments.

Monitor console

Location: Tree

From the Monitor console, you can monitor the progress of the following processes:

- Applications
- Job Server Clusters
- Administration links
- Macros
- Deployments

Local log files

Location: Menu

Log files record errors initiated by the Contributor Administration Console. You can open the log file to see details of program-generated errors.

Help

Location: Menu and Toolbar

IBM Cognos Planning provides extensive help resources that explain features, options, and the troubleshooting program's errors and issues.

Summary

In this chapter, you have learned the purpose and capabilities of the Web- and Windows-based components of the IBM Cognos Planning System. We have also discussed the three-tier architecture of IBM Cognos Planning, which are the Web server, the Application, and the Data tier. You have also discovered how these tiers interact with each other, through a description of the Shipping Company's analogy. Lastly, we listed and described the functions of the Contributor Administration Console, toolbars, menu items, and the tree.

9

Building, Configuring, and Updating the Contributor Application

In the previous chapters, we have covered the building blocks of Analyst models, such as D-Cubes, D-Links, and D-Lists. We have also visited the interface of the Analyst program and the Contributor Administration Console program and presented the information on the Contributor program's technical architecture.

In this chapter, you will learn the process of creating, configuring, and deploying a Contributor application. We will then cover the synchronization feature. The synchronization feature keeps both the Analyst model and the Contributor application in sync. Lastly, we will discuss the Contributor Extensions, which are mini programs that extend the functionality of the Contributor client web site.

 When we use the term "Contributor" in this chapter, we generically refer to the Contributor program, not the specific components of Contributor program—Contributor Administrator Console and Contributor Web Client.

Creating the Contributor application

Your Analyst model is ready and you want to distribute the model to users so that they can submit the plan. To distribute the model, you will use the Contributor Administration Console program to create, configure, and then deploy the Contributor application. Once deployed, the Contributor application will be available on the Contributor client web site for users to interact with and submit their plan.

An Analyst model becomes an application in the Contributor program. In practice, the terms **model** and **application** are used interchangeably.

First, we will discuss the pre-requisites for creating the Contributor application. Then, we will walk through the Contributor application creation process. Finally, we will cover the steps that you need to take once you have created the Contributor application.

Determining the Contributor application prerequisites

To create the Contributor application successfully, you must produce and get to know these three prerequisites: the Analyst model, the e.List, and an understanding of your organization's technical environment configured for IBM Cognos Planning.

Analyst model

In the previous chapters, we have covered in great detail the elements of designing an Analyst model for building a Contributor application. A partial list of model designing elements is repeated here:

- Check that the Analyst library is self-contained, having objects in a maximum of two different libraries. With the exception of the D-List that has been designated as an e.List, other D-Lists used in the model can be stored in the second Analyst library. The Contributor program requires all D-Cubes, D-Links, and the D-List designated as an e.List used in the model to be stored in the **main** Analyst library. The Contributor program will not permit the creation of an application if these rules are not adhered to.

- Check the naming convention of the Analyst library and objects for two reasons: D-Cube names are user friendly, and Analyst objects names can be easily identified in database tables. The Contributor program trims Analyst objects names when creating applications, for example, Contributor will name an import table as `im_geographic_regi` (15 characters) for an Analyst D-Cube named Geographic Regions.

- Check the order of your D-Lists within the D-Cubes, keeping in mind the different behavior of intersecting formats.

- Check that all D-Cubes, except for assumption D-Cubes, have the e.List.

- Fix an invalid D-Link; for example, deleted D-List items in an allocation table.

- Check that the Built-in Functions (BiF), used in the model, are supported in Contributor.

- Check that the Analyst objects meet the Contributor sizing specifications.

- Check that all relevant D-Links are listed in the D-Cube update list.

- Check to avoid any circular linkage.

Technical environment

You're ready to create the Contributor application once your Analyst model and e.List are ready. At this stage, you must know the configurations of your technical environments.

In a large, multi-server installation of IBM Cognos Planning, you need to know the name of the database server in which the Contributor application is stored, and then names of the job servers and clusters that will process administrative jobs.

You need database creation rights, specifically Data Definition Language (DDL) rights, in order to create the Contributor application. Contributor creates a database and various database objects, in order to store the Contributor application structure and data during the application creation process. It is not uncommon for the database administrator (a.k.a. the DBA) in your organization to not allow you to create the Contributor application database and database objects. In such a situation, the Contributor Administration Console offers an option to generate the database script for a database administrator, which allows the creation of the database and database objects after reviewing the script.

e.List

The e.List is an essential dimension in the Contributor application. You use the e.List to distribute the model template to users. Essentially, the e.List is a distribution list of budget holders. In the following illustration, the structure of the e.List shows a regional hierarchy. This e.List has many child nodes (countries) and parent nodes (continental regions).

Item Display Name	Item Id	Publish	View Depth	Review Depth
Global	1000	Yes	All	All
North America	1001	Yes	2	2
US	1002	Yes	1	1
Canada	1003	Yes	1	1
International	1004	Yes	3	3
Europe	1005	Yes	2	2
UK	1006	Yes	1	1
France	1007	Yes	1	1
Germany	1008	Yes	1	1
Spain	1009	Yes	1	1
Asia Pacific	1010	Yes	2	2
Australia	1011	Yes	1	1
Japan	1012	Yes	1	1

Do not substitute the D-List designated as an e.List with another D-List once a Contributor application has been completed. The Contributor application cannot be synchronized, as discussed later in this chapter, If you substitute a D-List designated as an e.List with another D-List, The application will require a total rebuild.

Setting up an incorrect e.List produces inaccurate budget roll-up and violates data security. For example, if you incorrectly setup Canada as a child of the Europe roll-up node, your North America roll-up will be inaccurate and European planners will be able to see the Canada budget.

The following are common methods of creating and maintaining an e.List, in practice:

- Add, edit, and delete e.List items on the Contributor Administration Console's e.List screen.
- Add, edit, and delete e.List items in a spreadsheet or Notepad program (we will provide more details about these methods in the next chapter).
- Add, edit, and delete e.List items by using a customized program or script to extract, clean, and prepare an e.List load file.
- Add, edit, and delete e.List items by using a master metadata management (MDM) tool, such as IBM Cognos 8 Business Viewpoint. Such tools ensure dimensional integration between Contributor and any underlying transactional system.

Chapter 10 covers the building and maintenance of an e.List.

Creating the Contributor application—the process

We will walk through the process of creating the Contributor application using the ABC Company's Analyst model.

1. Open the **Contributor Administration Console** from the Windows **Start** menu.
2. Click on the + sign to expand the **Datastores** branch.
3. Click on the + sign of the selected datastore (if more than one datastore) to expand it.

4. You will notice the **Applications** branch. Right-click on the **Applications** branch and click **Create New Application**...

Here is the summary of the **Link to existing Applications**... and **Upgrade Application**... options:

- **Link to existing Applications**: This option allows you to link to an already-created application on the data server, for example, an application that was created using the **Generate datastore scripts and data files** option.

- **Upgrade Application**: You can use this option to upgrade Contributor applications if your organization has recently upgraded the IBM Cognos Planning installation from a previous version.

5. Select the Analyst library on this screen. You will find the list of available libraries on the left, and the list of D-Cubes available in a specific library on the right:

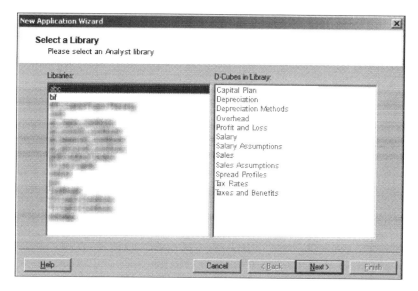

6. Select the placeholder e.List on this screen.

    On the left-hand side of the screen, you will see the list of available D-Lists in this library. It is very common that you save the placeholder D-List in the Analyst model with the name **e.List**. This helps you to identify the placeholder D-List/e.List from the available D-Lists. We have saved the placeholder D-List with the name e.List for the **ABC** company model.

    On the right-hand side of the screen, you can see the list of D-Cubes in this library. The highlighted data collection D-Cubes use the e.List, while un-highlighted D-Cubes are assumption D-Cubes. Refer to Chapter 5 to see the difference between an assumption D-cube and a data collection D-Cube. Occasionally, modelers choose to name D-Lists using numbering conventions, for example, 1=Calculation D-list, 2=Aggregation D-list, and so on. This naming convention provides visual assistance when looking at long lists of D-Lists; however, this is **not** a widespread practice. Giving names to D-lists using the above convention is optional, and is not required by Analyst or the Contributor Administration Console program.

    If the model contains erroneous codes, for example, a missing D-Link or a broken allocation table, the Contributor Administration Console displays an error or warning dialog box, once you click the **Next** button on the screen, as shown:

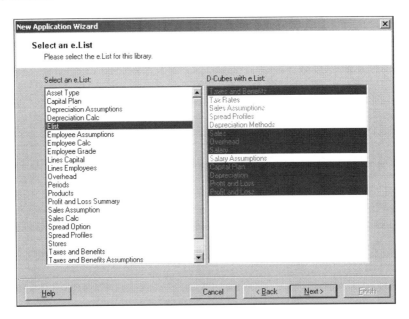

7. This screen displays the statistics of the Analyst model. You must follow the IBM Cognos guidelines provided below to build the model objects.

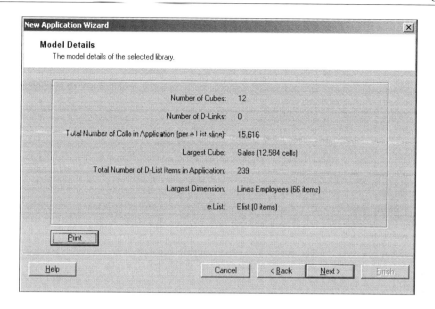

The following numerical limits provide model-building guidelines for an application. An application built using the following guidelines performs optimally. Although features, such as cut down and no data settings, are available to optimize performance when an application exceeds the following limits, IBM Cognos suggests that modelers follow these limits when designing models. We will discuss the cut down and no data settings features later in this book.

- ° Total number of D-Cubes: 10
- ° Total number of D-Links: 25
- ° Total cells per application (per e.List slice): 500,000
- ° Largest D-Cube cell size: 200,000
- ° Total D-List items per application: 2500 items
- ° Largest D-List size: 1000 items

8. Fill out the fields with the necessary information in the **Application Details** screen.

- ° **Application Display Name:** Enter the editable application name, up to a maximum length of 250 characters.
- ° **Datastore Name**: Enter the editable datastore name, for the SQL server using lowercase letters "a - z" and numeric characters, up to a maximum length of 30 characters.

○ **Application ID**: Enter the editable application name displayed
on the Web browser, using lowercase letters "a - z" and
numeric characters.
In practice, the aforementioned editable fields are occasionally
changed once an application is in production. Many organizations
have established a naming convention for their models, applications,
and datastore.

Keep a consistent naming convention for the above fields.

○ **Location of datastore** and **datastore backup files**: Enter the
file path of the location in which to store the database files.

○ Select the **Create and populate datastore now** option if you
have full rights to create the database and database objects.
Otherwise, select the **Generate datastore scripts and data
files** option to generate a script (named `script.sql`) that
you can pass to the database administrator. The database
administrator can run the script and create the application's
datastore after changing some syntax in the script. Make sure
that the **Generate Script** option is set to **Yes** in the Admin
Options branch when using **Generate datastore scripts and
data files** option.

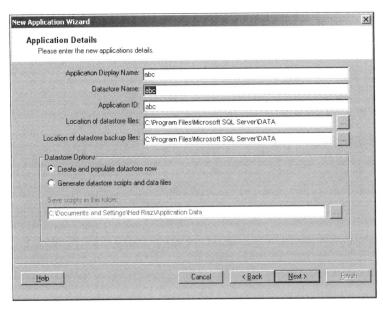

9. Select the job clusters or job servers on the following screen. Consult your technical team to select the appropriate checkbox on this screen. Generally the most common way of assigning applications to a job cluster is to put it to the uppermost level.

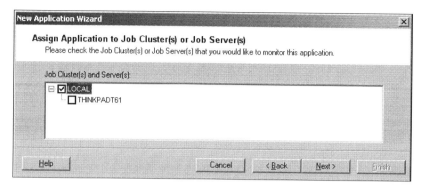

10. Click **Finish** on the following screen to let the Contributor Administration Console create the application. This screen shows the steps that the Contributor Administration Console takes in order to create the application.

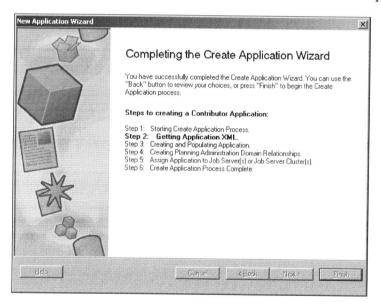

11. The following screenshot shows that the Contributor Administration Console has created the ABC Company application:

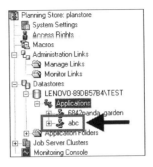

Understanding the post application creation steps

Before we configure the newly-created application, you need to understand the development and production areas of the Contributor Administration Console.

The application's development and production areas

The Contributor Administration Console offers two working areas for an application:

1. **Development** (also called development application)
2. **Production** (also called production application)

The development area is used to configure and update the model structure and data. The production area is what users see on the Contributor client web site. A process called GTP (Go to Production) moves the model and data changes from the development area to the production area.

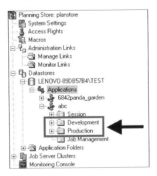

The screenshot above shows the Contributor Administration Console's **Development** and **Production** areas and their branches.

In a typical IT environment, the development and production environments refer to the physical separation of servers. This is not true when we refer the development and production areas in the Contributor Administration Console. These development and production areas must reside on one physical server or laptop. The development and production areas in the Contributor Administration Console provide a virtual environment for separating the administration functions used to prepare the application and then deploy the application for live usage.

We are now ready to configure the application, as we have created the application, and learned the concepts of development and production areas.

Configuring the Contributor application for the user web interface

In this section, we will first discuss the most commonly-used configurations in greater detail, and then briefly cover some less-commonly-used configurations.

Configuring commonly used options

You will most likely configure these seven options for a Contributor application in addition to configuring e.List, rights, and access tables. The topics of configuring e.List, rights, and access tables are discussed in Chapter 10.

- Navigation
- Orientation
- Breakback
- Multi-view
- Slice and dice
- Multiple Owner
- Planner Only Cubes

The following screenshot of the Contributor Administration Console shows the location of these options in the development branch of the Contributor application. A pane appears on the right-hand side when you click on each folder. Each pane provides several configuration options.

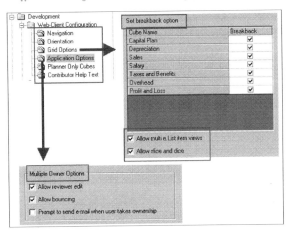

 The topics of e.List, rights, access tables, saved selections, and data validation are covered comprehensively in Chapter 10. These options significantly impact the user web interface.

Navigation

The **Navigation** option reorders cubes on the Contributor client web site. The following screenshot displays the order of cubes on the **Navigation** screen of the Contributor Administration Console, and demonstrates the same order of tabs on the Contributor client web site.

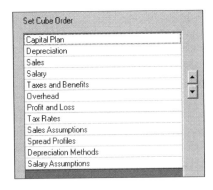

The following screenshot shows how the **Set Cube Order** appears on the Contributor client's screen:

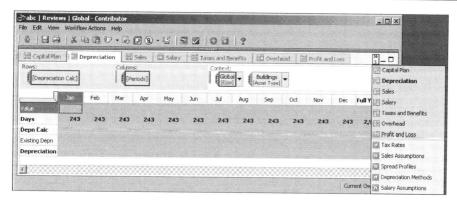

 An Analyst D-Cube is called a Tab in Contributor.
The terms **cubes** and **tabs** are used interchangeably.

It is a good practice to group related tabs together in an application. For instance, you may group input tabs together and output tabs together, so that users can easily follow the model flow. Unlike previous versions (8.3 or before), version 8.4 allows users to change the order of the tabs.

Orientation

A multi-dimensional cube can have one or more column dimensions, one or more row dimensions, and one or more pages. The **Orientation** option allows the cube's dimension to become a column, a row, or a page. Using the slice and dice feature, a user can re-orient default rows, columns, and pages, once they are inside the application on the Web. Additionally, the orientation feature allows the combining or nesting of two dimensions as a row or a column. Unlike previous versions (8.3 or before), version 8.4 allows users to nest and un-nest dimensions. For the ABC Company's application, we have oriented the dimensions as follows: **Depreciation Calc** as rowrows; **Periods** as columncolumns; **e.List** (country) as a page/context; **Asset Type** as a page/context. The first screenshot shows the orientation configured in the Contributor Administration Console. The second screenshot shows the row, column, and contexts/pages on the Contributor Web Client.

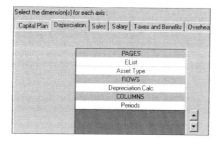

The following screenshot shows the default orientation appearing on the Contributor client's screen:

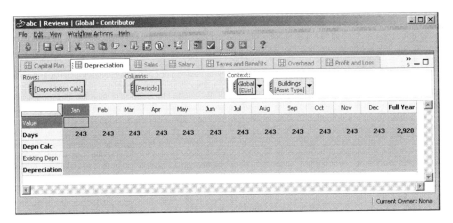

Financial users favor the timescale dimension, for example, calendar months, as a column. Using the Orientation feature, and selecting the period D-List as a column for all cubes in an application, provides a consistent look-and-feel to financial users.

The major difference between both configuration options is that the navigation option applies to all cubes in an application, whereas the orientation option applies to a specific cube.

Breakback (Grid options)

When you enter an amount to breakback a subtotal, for example, a year subtotal made up of twelve months; the yearly amount (say, $1200) changes the values of monthly numbers equally (say, $100), or changes the values of monthly numbers in the ratio of previously stored values.

You can activate or disable this feature for individual cubes. All formulas and subtotal cells are grayed out when you turn off the breakback feature for a cube. Moreover, users cannot enter values into these cells.

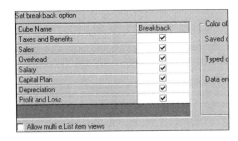

Although breakback is a powerful feature, it may mess up the budget templates if users don't fully recognize its power. For example, if a user inadvertently enters a value on a net profit subtotal for a group of cost centres, the breakback feature would change the sales, cost of sales, and expense values, because the net profit subtotal is normally dependent on those P&L accounts.

Multi-view

As demonstrated here, when the multi-view option is on, a user can see all of the **Europe** nodes in one window. On the other hand, when this option is off, a user can only see one **UK** node (e.List item). This shortcoming intensifies in a scenario when a user is responsible for planning many nodes, and they have to open and close individual nodes to finish their planning submissions or when they want to breakback a target number over the e.List items.

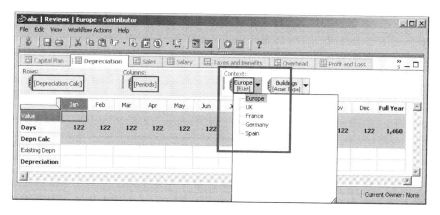

Compared to the above illustration, where planners can see all nodes, the following screenshot shows that planners can view only one **UK** node:

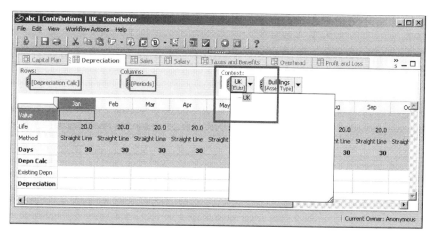

Turning the multi-view feature on and off involves a trade-off between usability and performance. When users open the Contributor client web site, the Contributor program loads the budget model into the computer's memory. Opening one slice of the model takes less memory, whereas opening multiple slices takes more memory, hence slowing the client's computer's processing power. Therefore, when this feature is on, users can open all nodes under a roll-up node in one view simultaneously, but it can affect program performance. The opposite is true when the feature is off. With multi-view turned on, the web client may not be able to open an application having many child nodes under a roll-up node.

Slice and dice

Slice and dice is a great analysis feature in OLAP applications, such as IBM Cognos Planning. Compare the illustration given here, where we have sliced the version/budget dimension as a row in the "After" view, and analyze the gross revenue amounts between the current year's budget and the last year's actual. In the following illustration, the store dimension is a context/page.

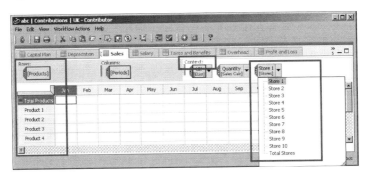

In the second illustration below, a user replaces the **Products** dimension (now a context/page) with the **Stores** dimension (now a row). Slicing and dicing provides analytical insight to plan data.

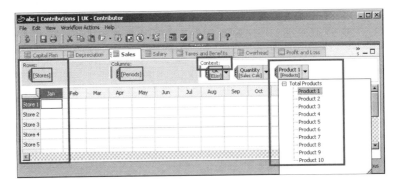

A likely challenge occurs when a new user, unfamiliar with the OLAP tool, slices and transposes the dimensions in a cube, and then gets lost in the cube orientation. Hence, consider your user's experience when you turn this feature off.

Multiple owner

When this option is turned on, users can take the ownership of nodes or e.List items from each other. Imagine a situation in which a planner, responsible for submitting the Canada node, is sick on budget submission day. If this feature is turned-on, another business user, if allowed, can take ownership of the Canada node and submit the budget on behalf of their sick colleague.

Planner Only cubes

The Contributor client web site has two key roles: Planner and Reviewer. Planners enter and submit budget holders, and Reviewers can review the budget submission. When you assign a cube as the **Planner Only** cube, it does not become visible in the Reviewer's view or node.

The following screenshot shows that, when certain cubes are configured as **Planner Only** they don't appear in the Reviewer's view. A reviewer of the Europe node only sees the **Profit and Loss** tab.

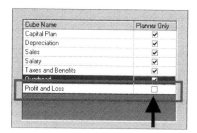

In the following illustration, reviewers can view *only* the **Profit and Loss** tab.

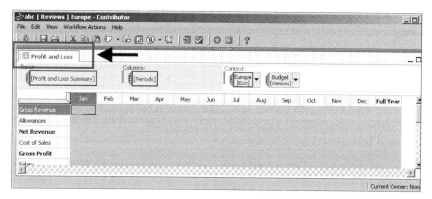

There are two key benefits of this feature. First, when a reviewer opens the aggregation node, the **Planner Only** cubes do not initiate the aggregation algorithm that takes place behind the scenes. Non-initiation of the algorithm speeds up the aggregation process and the appearance of the aggregated view. Secondly, reviewers see a less cluttered view, as they don't see the **Planner Only** cubes.

Understanding uncommonly used options

In practice, you will most likely not change the following options, and leave them set to their defaults:

- Data color
- Recalculate after every cell change
- Audit annotation
- Users instructions
- Translation

Deploying a Contributor application to the Web: The GTP and Reconciliation process

The GTP and Reconciliation process moves the application from development to production, and prepares the application for Web use. We will discuss the topics of GTP and Reconciliation in the following sections.

Understanding GTP

As discussed previously in this chapter, you complete application changes in the Development Area, and then move those changes to the Production Area.

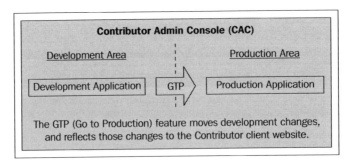

You will need to run the GTP in the following situations:

- After creating the application
- After changing the application's configurations
- After updating the e.List
- After adding, deleting, or editing access tables and saved selections
- After importing data
- After changing or synchronizing the Analyst model
- After setting up data validation rules

 The GTP operation moves the development model to production. It is a demarcation line between the development and production models with no point of return, once the GTP is executed. Make sure that you are satisfied with your development model changes before you execute the GTP operation.

Executing the GTP—the process

We will GTP the ABC Company application to walk you through the GTP steps:

1. Select the application and click on the green arrow button on the Contributor Administration Console menu.

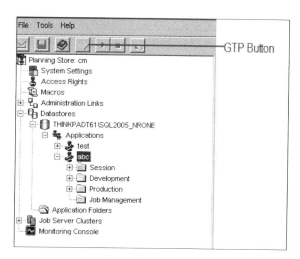

2. Click on **Next**, on the welcome screen.

3. Click on **Next** on the **Go To Production Options** screen, after changing any necessary options, as shown:

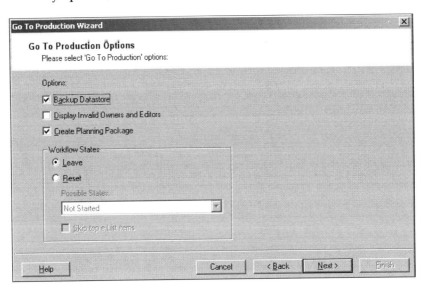

- ○ **Backup Datastore**: This option backs up the development and production application and stores them in the location specified by the database administrator during the application creation process. In practice, your database administrators will advise against using this feature as most organizations have already implemented a comprehensive database backup/restore plan.

- ○ **Create Planning Package**: To access Contributor applications, you, having the directory capability, must select the option to create the package when you run Go to Production. A Planning package, appearing as a folder in IBM Cognos Connection, contains only information regarding the connection to the cubes in a Planning application. The option of **Create Planning Package** also gives users access to IBM Cognos 8 studios from the Contributor application if they have BI studios installed, and enables users to report against live Contributor data by using the Planning Data Service (See Chapter 13).

 Cognos Connection, a portal to IBM Cognos 8, provides a single access point to all IBM Cognos 8 reporting, planning, score carding, and notification products.

- ○ **Display Invalid Owners and Editors**: Select this option to show invalid owners and editors. Example: Joe was responsible for submitting the monthly forecast of the Canada node last month, Sarah replaces Joe this month when Joe is promoted; you update the ownership of the Canada node to reflect the node ownership change. When you run the GTP next time, the **Show Changes** screen will show that the Canada node has an invalid editor/owner.

- ○ **Workflow States**: This option resets the state of the e.List items in the Contributor client web site (See Chapter 12).

4. Select **Next** on the **Show Changes** screen. The message that appears next will vary depending whether this is a first-time GTP or a subsequent GTP. The **Show Changes** screen shows the following tabs: Analyst model changes, data import details, invalid owners and editors, e.List items to be reconciled.

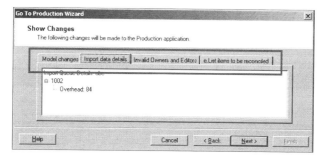

5. Click on **Finish** on the last screen to kick off the GTP. The Contributor Administration Console will show a message to confirm (**OK**)or **Cancel** the GTP.

Understanding the Reconciliation job

You may have two separate versions of the application, namely a development model or application and a production model or application. A discrepancy between the two can occur when you have made changes, for example, adding a few new e.List items or importing actual from the general ledger system to the model, in the development model and have not run the GTP to reflect those changes in the production model. Kicking off the GTP process moves the development changes to production behind the scenes. It fires up an admin job called "Reconciliation". This job reconciles the development model with the production model and ensures that the copy of the application that the users will see on the web is up-to-date. Reconciliation is an admin job and uses Contributor job architecture for job processing. Analogously, the process of reconciliation is no different than the process that you use to reconcile the difference between your bank statement and your check book.

Many factors determine the speed and performance of the Reconciliation job. A small model, a smaller e.List, and the availability of many job servers will speed the Reconciliation job.

As discussed in Chapter 15, a **Monitoring Console** feature is available in Contributor Administration Console to monitor the progress of Reconciliation and other jobs.

Users see a Reconciliation State icon when the Contributor program reconciles the application. Read Chapter 12 to learn more about this icon.

Making Analyst model changes (synchronize)

Your Contributor application is ready and being tested by quality assurance staff members. A quality assurance analyst discovers that a calculation does not work correctly in the application. You, as a modeler, review the calculation in the Analyst model, and find that the calculation needs fixing. You fix the calculation in the Analyst program and are now wondering how to reflect this fix in the Contributor application. This is where the Contributor synchronization feature comes into play.

Understanding synchronization

Suitably named, the synchronization feature synchronizes the Analyst model with the Contributor application. Note that the synchronization feature is a part of the development area in the Contributor Administration Console. To reflect the synchronized model changes in the Contributor production application, you have to run the GTP.

The following are typical situations in which you need to synchronize the Analyst model with the Contributor application:

- **Changes of business assumptions**: In a typical budget application, you use many business assumptions, for example, tax rates to calculate corporate tax or payroll tax amounts. Stored in the Analyst model, these assumptions are updated periodically, and require synchronization with the Contributor application.

- **Enhanced/revised business logic and features**: Users are pleased with the way model is working; however, business changes require certain logic changes in the model. Synchronization will be necessary in order to update the Contributor application once the model revision is complete in Analyst.

- **D-List changes**: D-Lists in the Analyst model store lists of dynamic items, for example products, employees, cost centre lists, and so on. These dynamic D-Lists require periodic updates as the business changes, for example, when new employees are hired. The Contributor application needs to be synchronized with the Analyst model when these changes occur.

Synchronizing the Contributor application—steps

To illustrate the steps, we will change the ABC Company Analyst model, and then synchronize the application to reflect that change. The following two screenshots show the change in the Analyst model (one account label has been changed), and no change in the Contributor application, as no Analyst to Contributor synchronization has taken place yet.

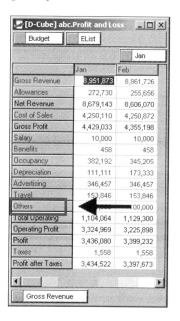

You will execute the following steps in order to complete the synchronization of an application:

1. Select the **Synchronize with Analyst** branch of the application.
2. Click on the **Synchronize** button on the right, under the **Library** name.

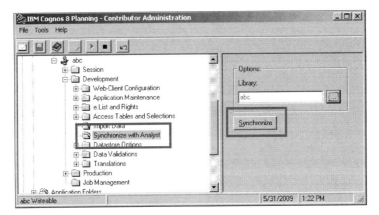

3. The Contributor Administration Console will show a number of warnings or error messages.
4. The next screen previews the model changes. It is a good idea that you check all changes, as an incorrect change may result in data loss. See the next section on this topic.

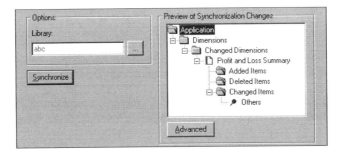

5. Save the changes by clicking on the **Save** button on the Contributor Administration Console menu. You have to run the GTP to reflect the Analyst model changes in the production application.

    The following is the list of changes in the Analyst model that require synchronization:

    ○ Changing D-List items, including additions, deletions, editing, format changes, calculation changes
    ○ Add, delete, or edit D-Links and D-Links pairing

  ○ Add, or delete a D-Cube in the model

  ○ Add, delete, substitute, or reorder dimensions in a cube

  ○ Add, delete, or edit assumption cube data

  ○ Change a data cube to an assumption cube or vice versa

Determining the synchronization impact

As illustrated here, certain model changes cause data loss, prompting Contributor to display a message stating **Destructive Synchronize detected**. Therefore, you must carefully examine all messages that the Contributor Administration Console displays during the synchronization process, in order to determine the impact of synchronization on the model structure and data. A few examples of synchronization impacts on the model structure and data are provided as shown:

- **Business assumptions**: As many revenue and expense calculations are built using business assumptions, changing business assumptions in the Analyst model, and synchronizing the application, would change the planned numbers and calculations depending on those numbers. For example, a change in the tax rate assumption would change the after-tax net income amount.

- **Removal of a D-List item**: Suppose that a planner has entered sales numbers for product Z in the contributor application. Their input will be irreversibly lost if you accidently delete product Z in the Analyst model and synchronize the application.

- **Adding, deleting, or reordering a D-Cube**: If you add, delete, or reorder D-Lists in a D-Cube in the Analyst model, you will lose planning data once you synchronize and GTP the application.

You should back up the production application regularly. It is possible that you may need to import data back into the application when you have to synchronize the application, in order to fix a scenario, as described previously.

 IBM Cognos Planning stores both model structure and data together as binary large object (BLOB) fields in the relational database.

Enabling Contributor extensions

Just as many universities offer extension courses to extend the offering of their education programs, IBM Cognos Contributor offers extension programs to extend the functionality of the Contributor product. Extensions are not third-party programs; they are IBM Cognos Planning mini programs. The following screenshot displays an example of the **Print to Excel** extension—an extension that expands the printing functionality of the Contributor client web site by providing users with Excel printing features.

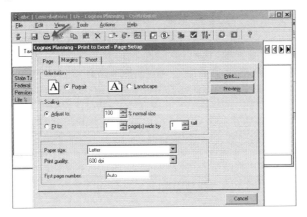

The Contributor program offers two types of extensions: Admin and Client. You, as an administrator, configure both types of extensions. We will discuss the client extensions in greater detail later, after briefly covering the admin extensions.

Configuring admin extensions

Admin extensions generate IBM Cognos BI models from the Planning application and data structure. You, as a BI modeler, can fine-tune these BI models and deploy them to deliver BI canned and query-driven reports and analysis. Users do not directly interact with the admin extensions; instead, they use BI reports and analysis. This screenshot displays the administrator extension configuration screen:

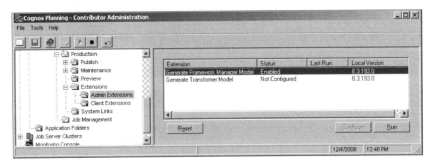

This table describes the purposes of the two admin extensions.

Admin Extensions	Purpose
Generate Framework Manager Model	The Generate Framework Manager Model extension creates two Framework Manager models: a base model and a user model. You, as a BI modeler, use the IBM Cognos Framework Manager program to fine-tune the models and deploy them to deliver the BI canned and query driven reports and analysis.
Generate Transformer Model	The Generate Transformer Model extension generates a Transformer Model and creates IBM Cognos Power Cubes. You, as a BI modeler, use the IBM Cognos Transformer program to fine-tune the models and deploy them in order to deliver the BI OLAP analysis.

Configuring client extensions

Client extensions, extending the functionality of the Contributor client web site, are available to the users on the Contributor client web site. You, as an administrator, configure client extensions. Users directly interact with the client extensions. We will discuss three commonly-used client extensions in the following sections, and illustrate the configuration steps for the **Print to Excel** extension.

Print to Excel

When this extension is enabled, users can print cube or tab contents using the printing features offered by MS Excel. The three required configuration steps are:

1. Select the **Client Extensions** branch of the application, and then click on the **Configure** button in the **Configure Extensions** tab, as shown:

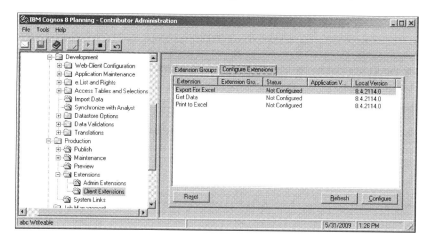

2. Click on **Next**, on the **Extension Properties** screen, as shown:

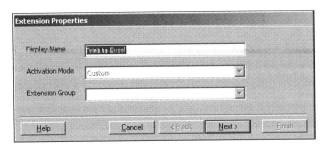

3. You can limit the availability of the client extensions by selecting a specific group or users. Select either **All Users** or **Selected Users**.

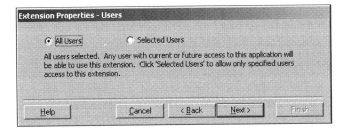

4. Select whether you want to enable the extension or leave the extension disabled. You can enable or disable an extension at any time. There is no need for a GTP to make the extensions available to the users in the web client.

Export to Excel

With this extension, users can perform a static export of the data from the Contributor client web site to an Excel file. They can analyze the exported data and link the exported data to an Excel report. Once the data has been exported, the data becomes part of the Excel program. Further data changes in the web client will not be reflected in the Excel file until a user re-exports data.

Get data

Users can import data into the Contributor client web site by using this extension. Users can import data from the following sources:

- Import data from an external flat file or an Excel file
- Import data between an application's tabs
- Import data from other application

Summary

In this chapter, we have discussed the process of creating and configuring a Contributor application before deploying it to the web for budgeting and forecasting. We also described the need for application synchronization after changing the Analyst model. Finally, we covered Contributor extensions, which can be used to extend the Contributor administrative and client functionality.

10
Securing and Controlling Contributor Web Client Template/Application

In this chapter, we will cover various features of IBM Cognos Planning that facilitate securing and controlling the Contributor Web Client template to be rolled out to users.

Securing application access

After creating the application, you need to enter or import an e.List and its rights to roll out the application to business users. We will cover the topics of e.List and rights in this section.

Understanding e.List dimensions

An e.List typically reflects the organization chart, for example, regions, departments, branches, and so on. It is the list to distribute the planning model template to business users, called planners, and reviewers in IBM Cognos Planning. You can occasionally find a product or project list as the e.List in planning models. However, the e.List typically represents an organizational hierarchy with a valid parent-child relationship.

As illustrated in the following screenshot, the ABC Company is organizationally structured around geographic regions, and that structure is reflected in its e.List. A valid parent-child relationship exists in the e.List. The parents are called reviewer or roll-up nodes, and lowest level children (leaves) are called Contributor or Planner nodes in IBM Cognos Planning. For example, France is a child or planner node, and Europe is a roll-up or parent node.

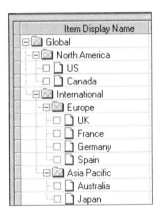

The planning workflow in IBM Cognos Planning works as follows. Planners submit their plan to reviewers. Reviewers can accept or reject the plan. If rejected, the plan goes back to the original planners who can then revise the plans and resubmit them. This workflow continues until all of the planning numbers are correctly submitted from the bottom level to the top level of the organizational hierarchy.

When working with the e.List dimension, the Analyst and Contributor programs operate differently. You create a **placeholder dimension** as the e.List in the Analyst model, and then replace that placeholder dimension by importing an e.List in the Contributor Administration Console (CAC). The e.List may be prepared in an external program, such as MS Excel or directly maintained within the Contributor Administration Console. In the following Analyst cube, a placeholder e.List/ D-List dimension exists with three *dummy* e.List items. The program requires one D-List item in this placeholder e.List/D-List. However, to test the Analyst model's aggregation logic, such as weighted averages, you want to use two detailed dummy e.List items and one subtotal item. After you create the application in the CAC, import the full e.List hierarchy in the CAC program from an external file to replace the placeholder dimension.

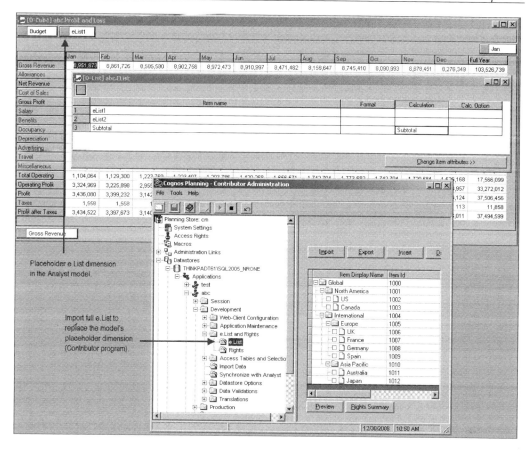

Determining the e.List ownership

An e.List can have a single owner or multiple owners. When you assign one user to a node, he/she becomes the single owner of the node. However, in certain shared or delegated budgeting responsibility situations, you may assign two users to a node to make them the shared or multiple node owners. Note that both owners cannot edit the node simultaneously.

When you import the e.List and then GTP the application for the first time, nobody owns the e.List nodes. This is called an un-owned node. Once a user opens the Contributor Web Client, and takes ownership of the node, he/she becomes the current owner of the node. Multiple owners can switch the node's ownership back and forth among themselves when the **Allow Bouncing** option for the application is checked by the administrator in the CAC.

[No more than 20 child items should be assigned to a parent. This will help performance and aggregation speed.]

Creating and maintaining an e.List

You can create an e.List in two ways:

1. Manually add and delete an e.List entry on the CAC screen.
2. Import the e.List from an external file.

We will cover the import process in greater detail, as it is the most common method of creating the e.List.

Preparing an e.List file

The Contributor Administration Console supports the following types of files to import e.List information: an Excel workbook, and a flat file with a delimiter. Most planning administrators maintain e.List information in an Excel file after sourcing the hierarchy from one or more general ledger or ERP systems. You find the file layout below with the comments on key fields. The following screenshot also shows the mapping of fields in the external e.List file to the Contributor Administration Console's e.List screen. We use the ABC Company's e.List in this example.

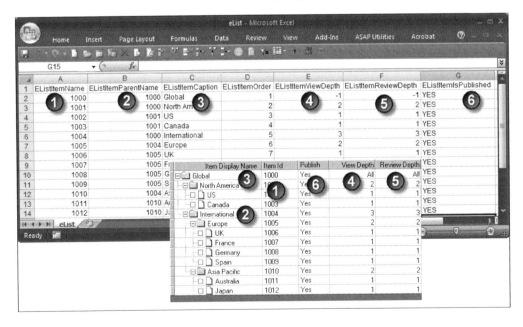

- **EListItemName**: A case sensitive, unique ID of an e.List item name (parent or child). The IDs are typically the cost center number, product number, and department number. These IDs are generally retrieved from the general ledger or ERP system.

- **EListItemParentName**: A case sensitive parent node ID. For example, in row 3 column A, the e.List item **1001 (North America)** rolls-up to the e.List item **1000 (Global)** in row 3 column B.

- **EListItemCaption**: This caption appears on the Contributor Web Client for users.

 The last four fields/columns, illustrated in the preceding Excel file, are optional.

- **EListItemOrder**: An optional field to setup the order of the e.List appearing on the Contributor Administration Console's e.List screen.

- **EListItemViewDepth** and **E.ListItemReviewDepth**: The Level of Depth determines how far down in the hierarchy a user can edit/view a node. As demonstrated in the following screenshot, when you set the Level of Depth 1, the Global user can edit/view only one level down. If you set the Level of Depth 2, now the Global user can edit/view two levels down, as shown next:

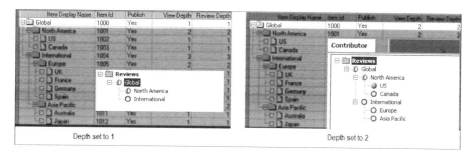

- **EListItemIsPublished**: Select **Yes** to publish this node (see Chapter 13).

Importing an e.List file

Once the external e.List file is ready, you can import the file into the Contributor Administration Console's e.List screen. The following is a description of the fields on the e.List screen;

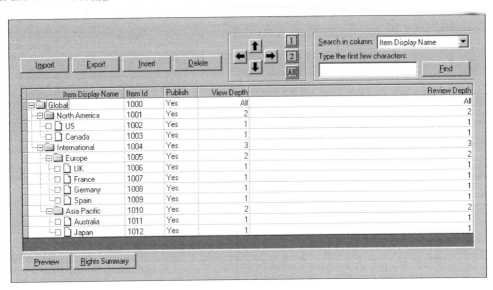

- **Import** and **Export**: Import and export the e.List using these buttons and save the e.List as a file.

- **Insert** and **Delete**: Use these buttons to manually add and delete an e.List entry on this screen. Be careful when inserting and deleting e.List items manually, as this feature may produce unintended results.

- **Arrows**: Reorder the e.List items manually using these arrows.

- **Search**: Find an item on the e.List screen.

- **Preview**: Preview the Contributor Web Client template for the selected e.List item. This option opens a pop-up window showing a light version of the Contributor Web Client grid. Data entry and printing a tab is possible from this pop-up window, but no saving or submitting can be done. This preview option is also available under the **Production** branch of an application.

- **Rights Summary**: Show the rights assigned to an e.List item.

The process of e.List import, demonstrated with the ABC Company's e.List, is described as follows:

1. Prepare the e.List file.
2. Click on **Import** button and locate the **Source file**.
3. Click on **OK** to start the import process.

    The following is a description of the key import options:

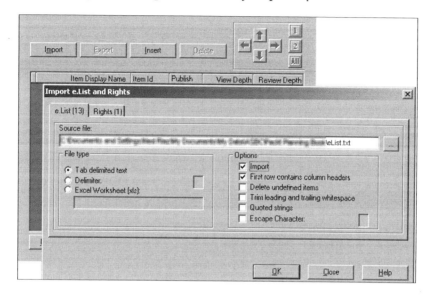

-   °   **Delete undefined items**: Delete the existing e.List items that are not included in the external file. Beware that this will result in an unrecoverable data loss of those e.List nodes that are no more included.

-   °   **Trim leading and trailing whitespace**: Remove extra spaces at the beginning and ending of text strings on import.

-   °   **Quoted strings**: Remove quotation marks.

-   °   **Escape Character**: Type a character to escape it from processing.

-   °   **File Type**: Select an Excel file and sheet name, or a flat file with a proper delimiter.

4. You will receive an error warning with error descriptions, if the file format is incorrect, or if there is any issue with the hierarchy. Troubleshoot the issue and re-import the file.
5. Configure the **Rights** (see next section) before running the GTP.

Impact on reconciliation job

The first e.List import requires a full reconciliation of all of the e.List items. Future changes in the e.List may require a reconciliation of all or just affected e.List items.

Changing e.List manually

Although the import of the e.List is the preferred method, you can add, delete, reorder, and rename an e.List on the **e.List** screen. However, you must fill out all of the fields on the e.List's screen.

[It is good practice to modify e.List information in the source file and re-import it using the e.List import feature.]

Securing an application with Rights

Rights assignments determine what actions a user can perform on a specific planner or reviewer node. In the following example, Joe and Sara are assigned to the Canada node, but only Joe can submit the plan. Sara can only view the Canada node and view Joe's submitted plan throughout the plan development.

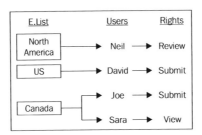

The Contributor program offers the following types of Rights for the planner and reviewer nodes:

- **Rights for Planner or Contributor nodes**: Submit, edit, and view
- **Rights for Reviewer or roll-up nodes**: Submit, review, and view

You explicitly declare the rights of the Contributor node by each e.List item. However, the reviewer's node rights are produced from the configuration of the following items:

- Explicitly declared review rights to the review node
- The view and review depth setting of the review node
- Checking the **Allow Reviewer Edit** option in the **Application Options** screen

Assigning the Rights to e.List items

You can assign rights in two ways:

1. Manually add and delete rights entries on the CAC screen
2. Import rights from an external file

We will cover the import process in greater detail, as it is the most common method of assigning rights.

Preparing the Rights file

The Contributor Administration Console supports the following types of files to import rights information: an Excel workbook, and a flat file with a delimiter. Most planning administrators maintain rights information in Microsoft Excel file, but export it as a text file. You will find the file layout below with comments on key fields. The following screenshot also shows the mapping of fields in the external rights file to the Contributor Administration Console's rights screen. We use the ABC Company's rights assignment in this example.

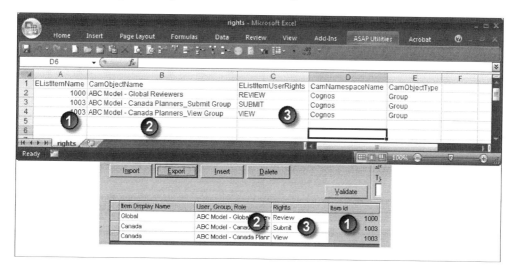

- **E.ListItemName**: The e.List item (ID) for which the rights need to be defined.
- **CamObjectName**: Entries of users, groups, and roles as displayed in the namespace (see the following section, which provides a brief overview of users, groups, and roles). A namespace is a way of naming things, for example, the home addressing convention used by the postal service is sort of a namespace.

- **E.ListItemUserRights**: The type of rights for the planner and reviewer nodes.
- **CamNamespaceName**: The namespace where the users, groups, and roles are stored.
- **CamObjectType**. Can be either a user, group, or role

Users, groups, and roles

Just as shown above, a human user (Joe) is responsible to submit or view the Canada node in real life. However, from the system's perspective, it is more efficient to maintain a user group, or user role, and then assign users to a group or role. Imagine you are the Cash Register Security Administrator of a Walmart store, which has about 20 cashiers. You can create a group called *Cashier*, and provide this group with similar cash register access. By doing this, you would avoid the maintenance of granting or revoking register access when a cashier leaves or joins your store. IBM Cognos Planning deals with groups or roles, which are stored in an external security database, for example, Microsoft Active Directory. Note, IBM Cognos Planning does not provide that security database to store users and security information. We will discuss how to maintain users, groups, and roles in Chapter 16. To focus on our discussion on Rights, we assume that the security administrator in your organization has already created proper groups or rights for your planning applications.

 Groups and roles can behave exactly the same way. The difference is that a role can contain users, groups, and other roles, while a group can only contain users and other groups, but no roles.

Importing the Rights file

Once the external rights file is ready, you can import the file into the Contributor Administration Console's rights screen. The following is a description of the fields on the rights screen:

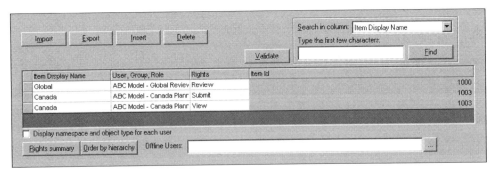

- **Import** and **Export**: Import and export rights using these buttons and save the rights as a flat file.

- **Insert** and **Delete**: Use these buttons to manually add and delete a rights entry on this screen.

- **Validate**: Clean up and update any old or removed entry of users, groups, and roles defined in the namespace.

- **Search**: Find an item on the rights screen.

- **Rights summary**: Show the rights assigned to an e.List item.

- **Order by hierarchy**: Reorder the **Item Display Name** column as laid out for the e.List hierarchy.

The process of rights import, demonstrated with the ABC Company's rights, is described as follows:

1. Prepare the Rights file.

2. Click on the **Import** button and locate the source file. Click on **OK** to start the import process. The options on the **Rights** screen are same as the options available for the e.List import screen. See the e.List section discussed previously.

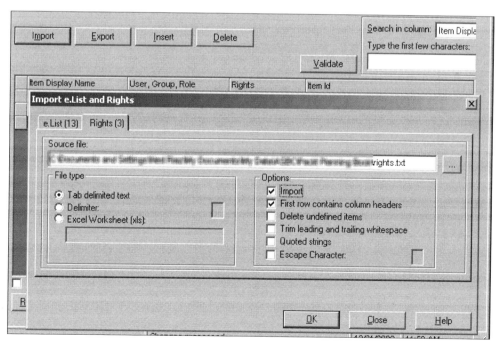

3. Troubleshoot the issue and re-import the file if you receive an error warning.

4. Run the GTP after you have finished importing the e.List and rights files (or continue setting up further configurations before GTP).

Changing Rights manually

Although the import of rights is the preferred method, you can add, delete, and change a rights entry on the **Rights** screen. However, you must fill out all of the fields.

 It is a good practice to modify rights information in the source file and re-import it using the rights import feature.

Securing the application data

You have created the application, imported the e.List and rights, and now the application is ready for users. However, you determine that you do not want to show a specific cube, or you want to make a range of cells *Read Only* in your application due to a data security issue. You will use Access Tables to secure data access in IBM Cognos Planning.

Understanding access tables

You, as an administrator, create Access Tables to determine the level of access users should have to the application's cubes and dimension items in a cube.

IBM Cognos Planning provides four types of access levels to secure the data access: Write, Read, Hidden, and No Data access. You can secure the data access for all of the planning nodes, or a group of planning nodes. You cannot explicitly create an access table on a review e.List item.

In the following illustration for the ABC Company, we hide an assumption cube (**Tax Rates**) from users due to a data security concern, even though this cube is available in the Analyst model. We use an access table to hide that assumption cube.

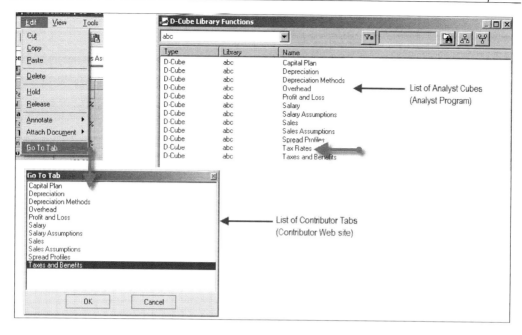

Differentiating access levels

IBM Cognos Planning provides four types of access levels to secure data access.

Read

Users cannot change these visible cubes or cells. Cells targeted by an Analyst D-Link are always *Read Only* in the Contributor application. System Links targeting read-only cells can change these cells. Assumption cubes are always read-only; and therefore cannot be changed to a different access level.

Write

Users with appropriate rights can write to cubes or cells for an unlocked e.List node. The write access level is the default for all of the cubes except assumption cubes.

Hidden

Hidden cubes or cells are not visible to users.

 The breakback feature behaves restrictively when above access levels are defined on cubes or cells.

No Data

Like Hidden cubes, No Data cubes or cells are not visible to users. However, the No Data access level provides greater benefit on the Contributor Web Client side. When the access table uses No Data access, the system removes selected dimensional items from the planning model definition, and therefore this access level improves application performance at the client side.

Defining Access Table

You can define Access Tables in two ways:

- Define rule based Access Tables manually
- Import Access Tables from an external file

We will cover the manual process in greater detail, as it is the most common method of creating Access Tables.

Creating Access Table manually

We will discuss the access table screen and create an access table for the ABC Company's application in the following paragraphs.

Access Table interface

The Access Table interface has three panels: **Assumption Cube** panel, **Cubes without Access Tables** panel, and **Cubes with Access Tables** panel.

You can find the **Assumption Cube** panel on the bottom-right of the **Access Table** screen. *Assumptions* cubes, for example, tax rate cubes, are global cubes and apply to all of the e.List items. They do not contain an e.List dimension. You can define only two types of access levels for the assumption cubes: **READ** and **HIDDEN**.

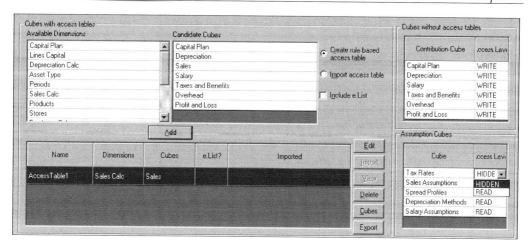

You use **Cubes with Access Tables** and **Cubes without Access Tables** panels to define the access level on contribution cubes (cubes with an e.List or non-assumption cubes). The differences between both panels are:

- **Cubes without Access Tables**: Use this panel to define the access level for the entire cube. For example, make the entire **Profit and Loss** cube readable from the default setting of **WRITE** (as shown in above screenshot).

- **Cubes with Access Tables**: Use this panel to define the access level on a specific D-List or D-List items. We will demonstrate this feature soon, using the ABC Company's application.

Creating a rule based Access Table

We define an Access Table for the ABC Company's application by making all of the items *Read Only*, and making one item writable in the **Sales** cube.

1. Open A**pplication | Development | Access Table** and **Selection | Access Tables** branch. Select the D-List to define the access level. We select the D-List **Sale Calc** that contains dimensional items we want to work with.

 You can open the Analyst cube to find the D-List used in a cube requiring data security.

2. Select the **Create rule based access table** option, and click on the **Add** button.

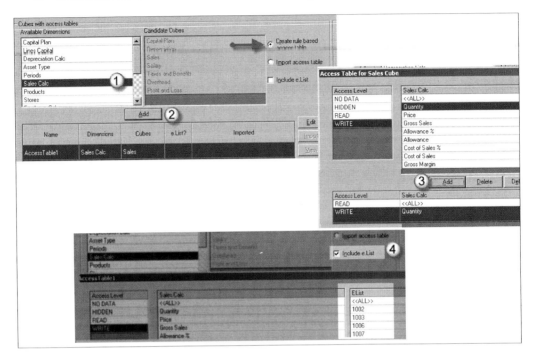

3. Clicking on the **Edit** button opens up another window where you can define the access rules. In the ABC Company's application example, we first make all of the D-List items *Read Only*, and then we make the **Quantity** item writable. Note that the lowest item in the bottom pane gets the highest priority. Thus, we are commanding the Contributor program to 'Show all of the D-List items in the **Sales** cube as read only, but let the users input to the **Quantity** field'. Click on **OK** and save your work.

4. You can select the **Include e.List** checkbox to customize the Access Table by e.List items. In the illustration above, we provide different access levels to different e.List items by selecting an **Access Level** (write, read, hidden, no data) from the left panel, and selecting **Sales Calc** and **e.List** items from the right panels.

Importing Access Table

You can import Access Tables from a flat file or an Excel workbook. However, you must define the Access Tables in the external program before importing them. Defining the Access Table in the external program uses the same principles we have just discussed. In practice, you create the Access Tables manually, export them, and then maintain them in the external program for future imports.

 To get a good understanding of how the Access Table's import file needs to be structured, you can export a test Access Table. Then you can fill out this exported file with correct entries and import back.

Applying Access Table cautiously

Avoid defining a **large multi-dimensional** Access Tables, unless you come across a situation which requires the use of a multi-dimensional Access Tables. For instance, we would create a large multi-dimensional Access Tables if we used the Sales Calc, Products, and e.List dimensions to define the Access Tables in the ABC Company's example above. Several small single-dimensional Access Tabless are easy to maintain, and improve the performance of the Contributor Administration Console.

When you change the Access Tabless, the system determines the impact of no data cells. If there is an impact, then all of the e.List items must be **reconciled**, otherwise, no reconciliation job is triggered. Adding and deleting an entire access table requires the reconciliation of all of the e.List items.

Data import queue, discussed in the next chapter, is impacted by the change of Access Tables and the pattern of No Data cells.

 Always try to keep Access Tables as small and simple as possible.

Understanding saved selections

Imagine that you have 3000 employees in your organization (employees D-List), and you want to restrict planners to viewing only their own department's employees in the application (don't show employees of department X to department Y). It would be a painstaking task to define the Access Table (employees and e.List dimension with no data and write access levels) for the entire organization right on Contributor Administration Console screen. Using the **Saved Selection** feature eases this task.

The saved selections feature groups dimensional items, for example, employees of department X, and simplifies the Access Tables build. It also significantly reduces the maintenance of a large dimensional list.

Creating saved selections for Access Table

For demonstration, we will use the ABC Company's product D-List to create the saved selections. We will then use saved selections in the access table to hide certain inactive products for a few e.List nodes.

1. Open **Application | Development | Access Table and Selection | Saved Selections** branch.

2. Select the D-List to define the saved selections and name the saved selection. We use the **Product** D-List.

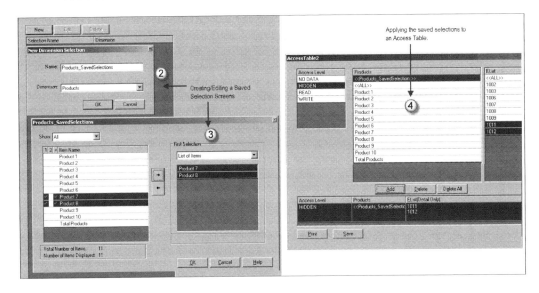

3. Select the dimension items you want to use to create the saved selection and move them to the right on the **SavedSelections** editor screen. We choose two inactive products (product 7 and 8). Click on **OK** and save your work.

4. Open **Application | Development | Access Table and Selection | Access Table** branch. Create a new, or edit an existing, access table, and then use the saved selection in the access table. Notice that we hide product 7 and 8 (bundled and shown as a saved selection) from two e.List nodes in the previous screenshot.

Use the No Data access level if you want to remove data from any calculations and roll-ups for these inactive products; otherwise, use hide or read only options to include data for these inactive products in cubes calculations and aggregations.

Validating users' data input

What is the value of planning numbers if they are incomplete and don't comply with business rules? As a custodian of the planning system, you want to make sure that you collect complete and accurate planning information from users over the Contributor Web Client.

Understanding the Data Validations feature

The **Data Validations** feature in IBM Cognos Planning ensures that incoming data, entered by users on Contributor Web Client templates, is in the right format, complete, and conforming to business rules. For example, if the organization's capital policy dictates that the organization must capitalize spending over $5K, the data validation feature evaluates that business rule, and warns users if they do not follow that business rule. You use the following area of the Contributor Administration Console to implement the Data Validations feature.

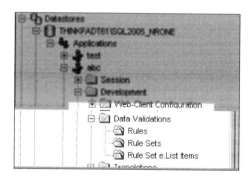

Terminology

You need to be familiar with the following terms to understand how the IBM Cognos Planning data validation feature works.

- **Data Validation Rule:** A validation rule is a data entry requirement imposed on a range of cells in a cube. For example, "Do not pay more than 5% raise to an employee in the employee grade X".

- **Validation Rule Scope:** The scope tells the Contributor program to what extent a validation rule affects dimensional items. For example, the bonus field (payroll dimension) should not be zero in the month of April and May (period dimension), when a company rewards bonuses to its employees. The validation rule scope extends for April and May, but not from Jan to Mar and Jun to Dec.

- **Rule Sets:** A rule set contains one or more data validation rules. For example, you can add the following two validation rules in one rule set: do not pay more than 5% raise to an employee in the employee grade X, the Overtime field must contain a value. You can program the rule set to either inform users of their errors, or force the Contributor program not to allow users to submit or save their plans until they conform to the business rules.

- **e.List Assignment:** Telling the Contributor program how you want to apply the rule set to e.List items. You can apply a rule set to: all of the e.List items, all of the planner nodes (detail), and all of the reviewer nodes (aggregate).

Configuring the Data Validations feature

The following flowchart shows the steps you take to generate the data validation rules. We discuss each step in subsequent paragraphs.

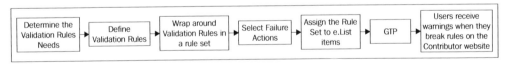

Deciding to validate or not to validate

You need to consider the following alternatives before using the data validation feature.

- What do you want to validate? Do you want to check the business rules? Do you want to make sure that users do not skip the required field?

- Is the Analyst model ready? Does the Analyst model have all of the necessary conditional logic built in? Should you build the business rules logic in the Analyst model, or should you use the data validation feature?

For the ABC Company's application, we enforce two validation rules (see the application's screenshot below):

- Users must input quantity in the Sales cube (Input presence check).
- Users' capital requests must be between $5K and $100K (Business rule check).

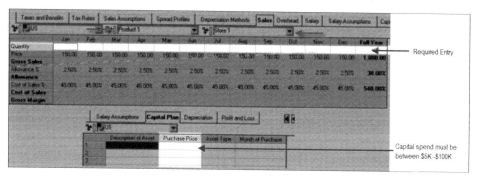

Defining the validation rules

The steps to define the validations are as follows:

1. Click on the **New** button under the **Rules** branch of the **Data Validations**. Enter the descriptive **Rule Name** and the **Rule Message** to appear on the Contributor Web Client. Click on **Next**.

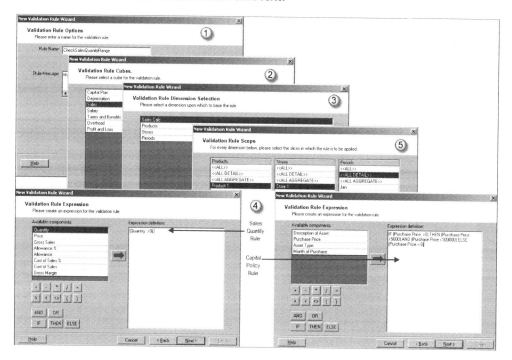

1. Select the cube in which you will create the rule. We select the **Sales** cube for the ABC Company's application. Click on **Next.**

2. Select the D-List in which you will create the rule. We select the **Sales Calc** D-List. Click on **Next.**

3. Select the D-List item(s) to create the formula. See the example of **Sales Quantity** rule and **Capital Policy** rule formulae above for the ABC Company. Click on **Next.**

4. Select an item from the list of all of the D-Lists in this cube to apply the rule (the scope of the rule). We select the **Product 1, Store 1**, all of the months to check the sales quantity formula, and select **<<ALL DETAIL>>** to check the Capital Policy formula. Click on **Next.**

5. Save your work after clicking on the **Finish** button on the last screen.

Defining the Rule Sets

You define the rule sets after you have defined the data validation rules. Click on the **New** button under the **Rules Sets** branch of the **Data Validations**. In the following **New Validation Rule Set** screen, you complete these steps:

1. Enter the descriptive name of the Rule Set.

2. Select the **Restrict Submit** radio button in the **Fail Action** section. The Contributor Web Client evaluates the data validation rules, and if a rule fails, then it triggers a fail action which you select here.

3. Click on the **Add** button to add the rule(s) you want to include in this rule set. We include both rules in this rule set for the ABC Company's application. We restrict users' submissions if users do not comply with the rules. Click on **OK**.

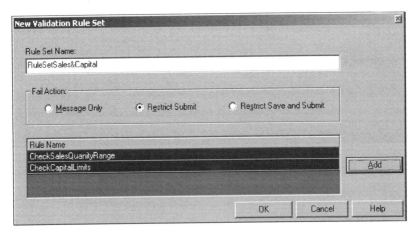

Assigning the Rule Set to e.List items

The last step in this process is to assign e.List items to the rule set as follows:

1. Click on the **Rule Set e.List Items** branch of the **Data Validations**.

2. On this screen, you select the rule set on the left side, and the select either **ALL** e.List items, or **All Detail** e.List items, or **All Aggregate** nodes, or a specific node on the right side. You click on the **Add** button to apply the rule set to e.List items. For ABC Company's application, we add the rule set to **All Detail** e.List items (Contributor or planner nodes).

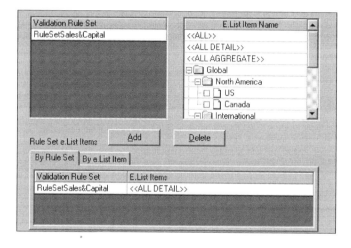

3. You need to run the GTP. The GTP does not kick off the reconciliation job.

Applying the validation rule on the Contributor Web Client

When users enter plan numbers on the Contributor Web Client, IBM Cognos Planning either provides a warning message for non-compliance with the rules, or allows them to save and submit their plans when they are in compliance with the rules. As demonstrated below, an ABC Company's user:

- Does not enter sales quantity in all of the months, and enters only $4K for the capital request.

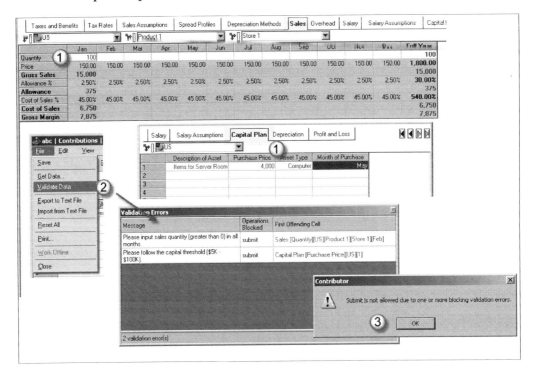

- Once the user clicks on the **Validation Data** menu (*manually triggered*), they receive a warning regarding the data validation rules and the cells where the error occurs.
- If the user ignores the error warning and tries to submit, the data validation feature blocks their submission (*system triggered*). The user must comply with the validation rules to submit their plan.

Improving the application performance: The cut-down feature

You have just deployed a large application (for example, an application containing an employee D-List with 5000 items), and you find out that users are not satisfied with the application's performance. So what do you do in this situation? IBM Cognos Planning offers the 'cut-down' feature to improve application performance. Although this feature is tricky to use, it can improve the performance of a large application, if you use this feature correctly.

This feature may not be as attractive to use now as when it was introduced in 2002 (Contributor 2.2) when the client machine specs and network bandwidth was not as powerful as it is now.

Understanding cut-down feature

Like the mail merge function in a word processing program, in which you create a master letter and then use a list of recipients to customize the master letter for individual recipients, the cut-down feature creates customized copies of the master planning model for planner and reviewer nodes. This feature compresses the master planning model to include only relevant dimensional elements in the model for each planner or reviewer.

The following diagram and example are provided to explain the cut-down feature:

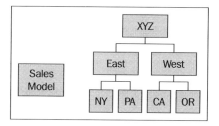

Suppose you roll out the sales planning model to the branches of your company (XYZ) in the Eastern and Western US States. Assume the XYZ Company is a publishing company and it sells products (books) to its customers on the State Income Tax Laws in the above States. Further assume that the product D-List in the sales planning model contains about 3200 products (800 products per State), and your planners complain that the planning application performance is poor. If you do not use the cut-down feature, all of the planners in these States generally receive one model definition, even though you hide the irrelevant products (other States' products) from their view using the Access Table (No Data). As each planner in each State just sells and plans for his/her own State Income Tax Laws products, this is a good opportunity to use the cut-down feature with the No Data Setting by e.List. This feature reduces the planning model size and distributes a condensed and precalculated model definition, with the optimized model performance, to each planner.

Selecting cut-down options

Before configuring the cut-down model, you need to select the appropriate cut-down option.

Cut-down configuration options

You have three options for configuring cut-down models.

1. **No cut-down models**: The Contributor program does not cut-down the planning model.

2. **For each aggregate e.List item**: The program cuts down the aggregated or roll-up nodes. For example, if you cut-down only the roll-up nodes for the XYZ Company, then the PA and NY branches in the East region receive only the model definitions (PA and NY products list) of the Eastern States branches. The Contributor program removes the model definitions (CA and OR products list) in their planning model.

3. **For every e.List item**: The program cuts down the model to the lowest level (planner level). For example, if you cut-down the model to every e.List item, then NY receives only the NYs model definition (NY products list).

Cutting-down an application

The configuration of the cut-down feature requires the following steps:

1. Open the **Application Options** under the **Web-Client Configuration** branch.

2. Select the appropriate cut-down option from the drop-down menu. The cut down feature works in conjunction with the No Data setting.

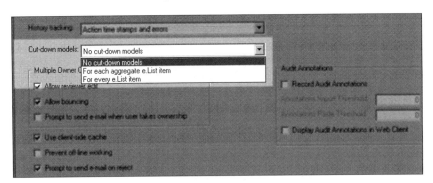

3. Save the application.

4. Execute the GTP. The Contributor Administration Console fires up the cut-down job as shown:

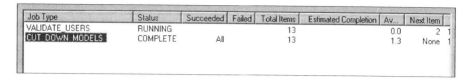

Job Type	Status	Succeeded	Failed	Total Items	Estimated Completion	Av...	Next Item
VALIDATE_USERS	RUNNING			13		0.0	2 1
CUT_DOWN_MODELS	COMPLETE	All		13		1.3	None 1

Applying the cut-down feature carefully

You have learned the idea behind the cut-down feature and how to configure it; however, the following background information will assist you before turning the cut-down option on.

IBM Cognos provides a utility called epModelSizeReader (see bin directory of C8 installation location). This utility reveals model information and helps determine model size. The following illustration provides an overview of the technical side of the planning model and demonstrates "what happens when you turn on the cut-down option".

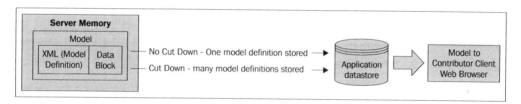

The Contributor client receives two pieces of information when users download and open the application: XML definition and data block. The smaller these pieces are, the faster the download and the planning model performance. The cut-down feature precalculates and stores a reduced planning model definition by removing irrelevant elements, thereby improving model performance on the client-side when opening the node. This is a noticable advantage of the cut-down feature.

However, the cut-down feature comes with a cost on the server-side. When you have a long e.List with a large model size, and you have selected the **For every e.List item** option, the system loads the model in the server's memory and makes calls to the datastore to save a customized model definition of each e.List node. The system uses significant server resources when performing these operations. The cut-down job may fail if there are not enough server resources available, or the cut-down job may take a considerably long time to finish up. It is important to note that the cut-down job is not a one time operation. It kicks off every time you save various Contributor Administration Console configurations while maintaining the application.

Summary

We have covered various features of IBM Cognos Planning pertaining to securing and controlling the Contributor Web Client templates. First, we have discussed the role of the e.List and rights configuration in securing a planning application. We have shown how to create and import the e.List and rights information. Then, we covered data and content security. We talked about the importance of Access Tables in securing Contributor Web Client template contents. We also demonstrated the purpose of the saved selections in defining Access Tables. Next, we discussed the feature of data validation, and how to setup the validation feature for the ABC Company's application. Lastly, we briefly covered how the cut-down functional can improve the performance of Contributor Web Client templates.

11
Importing Data into a Contributor Application

The purpose of the data import is to load and populate data in the Contributor application from the external systems. In this chapter, we will cover various methods of data import to Contributor applications. Refer to Chapter 7 to learn how to import data into the Analyst program.

Two types of data are populated in the Contributor Web Client: assumptions data, non-assumptions data, which we will just call 'data' in this chapter. Some examples of 'data' are general ledger actuals or existing depreciation details from the Fixed Assets System. The following table lists the import methods discussed in this chapter. It also shows the individuals responsible for administering or importing data, and the type of data to be imported.

Import Methods	Importer	Type of Data Import
Updating assumptions cubes in Analyst	System Administrator or Planning Modeler	Business Assumptions
Analyst to Contributor D-Links	System Administrator or Planning Modeler	Data
Importing Data from other Planning applications (Administration Links)	System Administrator, Planning Modeler or users if allowed	Data
Importing Data from External Files/ Database	System Administrator or Planning Modeler	Data
Importing Data Using IBM Cognos Packages (Administration Links)	System Administrator or Planning Modeler	Data
System Links	Business Users	Data
Local Links	Business Users	Data

Updating assumption cubes in Analyst

Assumption cubes do not contain an e.List dimension. The assumptions data, which are stored in assumption cubes, apply globally to all e.List items in an application. Good examples of assumptions data include a standard product price list and payroll tax rates.

You follow these steps to update the assumptions data in a Contributor application:

- Open the assumptions D-Cubes in the Analyst program for the selected model and update assumptions values before saving the D-Cubes.

- Open the Contributor Administration Console program and then synchronize the selected application.

- Run GTP. The reconciliation job will kick off.

- The assumption cubes in the selected Contributor application should now show the revised assumption values.

Importing data from external files/databases

The Contributor import feature is the primary method of loading data into the Contributor database from external sources. The Contributor database is created when you create an application. This database contains many tables which support the application, including an import table for each cube.

Understanding the import process—concepts

In this section, we will explain how Contributor imports data from external sources. You can find step-by-step instructions of data import in the next section.

Contributor transfers data from external sources to the Contributor database, or the Contributor Web Client, using a four-step process:

- **Copy**: In this step, Contributor copies the data file from a local PC to the Contributor Administration Server.

- **Load**: Contributor loads the data file from the Contributor Administration Server to the application's import tables (**im_table**) using the database bulk load utility program.

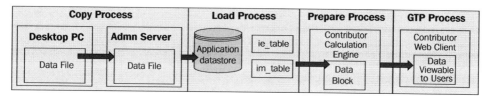

- **Prepare**: The Contributor Calculation Engine, which is a part of the Contributor program, validates data contents and prepares proprietary import data blocks. The proprietary data blocks contain the data required for an individual e.List item. Any rejected items are stored in **ie_tables**.

- **GTP**: Contributor makes the data available on the Contributor Web Client.

Importing data

We will use the ABC Company's example to illustrate the data import steps. We will load sales data into the Sales cube.

1. Open the **Import Data** branch of the application.

2. Select the cube in which you want to load data. We select the **Sales** cube. Also select or **browse** the file that contains data. You must have the correct data format in the file. For example, the correct spelling of dimensional items, and the order of columns. An incorrect data format will result in complete or partial file rejection.

3. Click on **Copy**. The **File copied successfully** message appears.

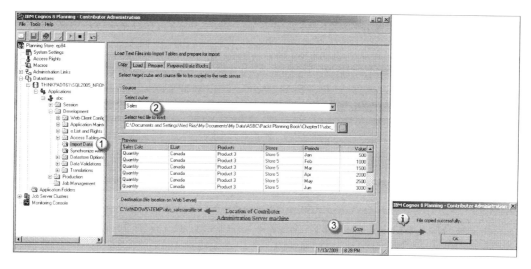

4. Click the **Load** tab to view the data available by cubes to be loaded into the database. Check the checkboxes from those D-Cubes that you want data to be loaded. If you want to remove previously loaded data from the database tables, then check the **Delete Existing Rows** box. Click **Load** once you have finished auditing this tab.

5. This screenshot shows the database tables in which Contributor has loaded data. Database tables cannot be viewed through the Contributor Administration Console. To view these tables, you have to logon to the database server. The `im_cubename` tables store the loaded data, while the `ie_cubename` tables store rejected records. You can view rejected records in the `ie_cubename` table once you have completed step 7 as discussed later.

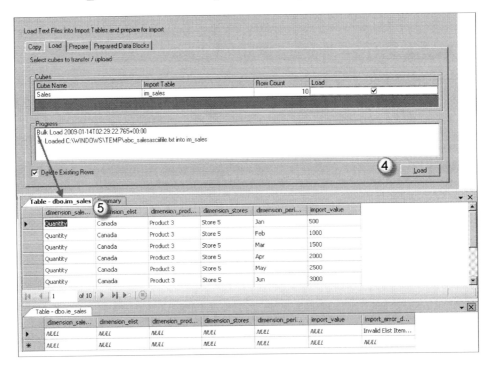

6. Click the **Prepare** tab when the load process is complete. Click the **Prepare** checkbox to identify the cube in which you want to load data. Click the optional **Test** button to verify the data format and data integrity.

7. Click the **Prepare** button to prompt Contributor to start preparing the import data blocks. Unlike the copy and load processes, the prepare process is a multi-threaded process that uses the Contributor's job system.

8. Once the import job is complete, you can click on the **Prepared Data Blocks** tab to view the completed data blocks. This screen shows the number of rows processed by Contributor for each e.List item. However, if you find that the import data blocks are not correct, for example, when you have revised the actuals extracted from the general ledger system, you can click on the **Delete Import Queue** button to remove the data blocks. You need to re-import the revised data.

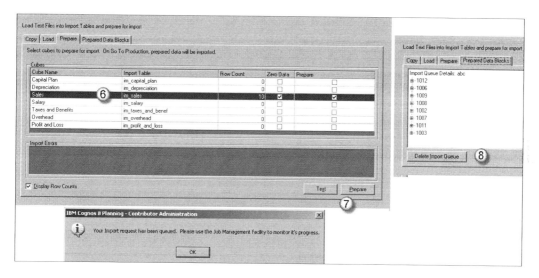

Bypassing importing data steps

In some situations, you can bypass the *Copy* and *Load* steps, and directly import data into database tables using an external data loader program, such as Informatica or Microsoft Integration Services. This can be done when, for example, you have to move a large volume of data, or when you have sufficient internal IT/database expertise to program data loader utilities. Although you can skip the Copy and Load process, you must run the *Prepare* and *GTP* process to transfer data to the Contributor Web Client.

Administration Links

Administration links facilitate transferring data between Contributor applications or from IBM Cognos packages. Let's assume that you administer detailed sales, workforce, and expense applications to collect data from numerous departments throughout the world. A consolidate application showing P&L requires the consolidation of a plan data from these sales, workforce, and expense applications. You can use other import methods described in this chapter; however, each import method carries pros and cons. IBM Cognos Planning offers administration links which are optimal and scalable solutions for importing large amounts of data between applications and from multiple datastores.

An administration link can store multiple data transfer components, which are called **elements**. Analogously, one element is equal to one D-Link. Each element can transfer data between a source and a target D-Cube from different applications as well as within one application. Since you are required to transfer plan data from three detailed sales, workforce, and expense applications to the Consolidated P&L application in above example, you must create three individual data transfer elements (one element per application).

The steps to create administration links are as follows:

Creating Administration Links

1. Open the **Manage Links** branch of the **Administration Links** tree. Since administration links move data between the applications, the functionality for their creation and editing cannot be found in the tree of a specific application. Instead, the functionality for creation and editing an administration link is available at the Planning Store level. As a repository, the Planning Store stores the definitions and relationships of *all* Contributor applications. The following is a description of the options available on the administration link screen:

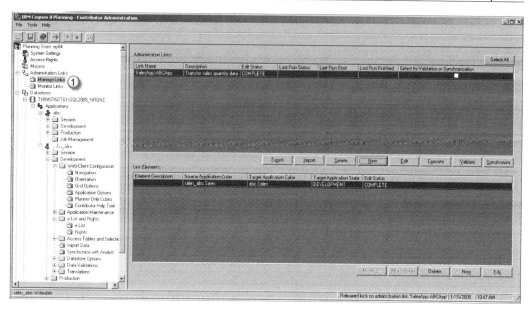

Top Panel: This panel shows the list of available administration links in this PAD.

- ○ **New**: Click this button to create a new administration link.
- ○ **Edit**: Click this button to edit the setting of an existing administration link.
- ○ **Execute**: Click this button to run an administration link.
- ○ **Validate** and **Synchronize**: Click these buttons to validate and synchronize the allocation table—stored in Analyst—used in this link.
- ○ **Import/Export**: Click these buttons to export the links definition and import it back. You can use this feature when you have to move an application from a development to production environment, for example.
- ○ **Delete**: Click this button to delete a link.

Bottom Panel: This panel shows the list of elements for a specific link.

- ○ **New**: Click this button to create a new element.
- ○ **Edit**: Click this button to edit the settings of an existing element.
- ○ **Move Up/Move Down**: Click these buttons to order elements in which you want them to get executed.
- ○ **Delete**: Click this button to delete an element.

2. Click on the **New** button in the top panel. This button opens the following screen where you define the properties of a link. Enter the **Name** and **Description** of the link and select the **Data Source Types** (Contributor Application or IBM Cognos Package). We will discuss the IBM Cognos Package later. When link performance is poor, you can tune up a link using the features available under the **Advanced** button. Click **OK** to go to the **Map Source to Target** screen.

3. On the **Map Source to Target** screen, you:
    - select the source and target applications
    - choose the development or production area of the application to target data transfer
    - select a source and a target cube

    If you target the development application, then you have to run the GTP so that users are able to see the data on the Web. Mistakes in creating or running an administration link can be fixed before running the GTP. On the other hand, when you target the production application, there is no recovery possible, with the exception of the database backup, if an administration link is incorrectly built.

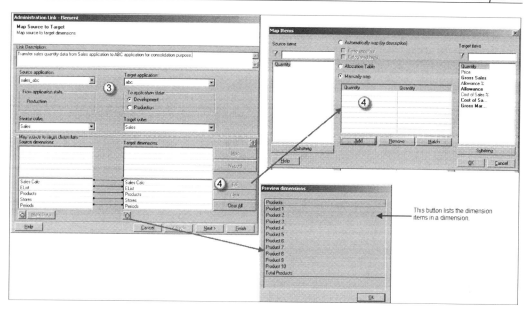

4. You must map each source and target dimension on the **Map Source to Target** screen. You can select *individual* source and target dimensions and click on **Map** or you can select *all* source and target dimensions and click on **Map All**. The **Edit** button opens the **Map Editor** screen where you can map each dimension item individually. See the description below for three mapping options available on the **Map Editor** screen. Click **OK** on the **Map Editor** screen, and then click **Finish** on the **Map Source to Target** screen to get to the final configuration screen.

   ○ **Automatically Map**: You can let the program match each item when both source and target items have exact descriptions. You can use the substring function on both source and target sides. For example, if you have D-List items named Quarter 1, Quarter 2, Quarter 3, and Quarter 4, and you applied the substring QUARTER, all four items would be rolled into one dimension item to be loaded into the target dimension.

   ○ **Manually Map**: You need to select the dimensional items from source and target sides, and then map them according to business rules.

- ○ **Allocation Table**: Rather than mapping each source and target item on this screen, which could be a laborious task when mapping hundreds of items, you can create the mapping in the Analyst program and import it onto this screen. You would want to use the Analyst program because it provides a more robust mapping and allocation table option. When you click on the **Allocation Table** button, the program opens a **Select A-Table** screen which allows you to select the library where the **A-Table** is stored. Click **OK** to import the mapping.

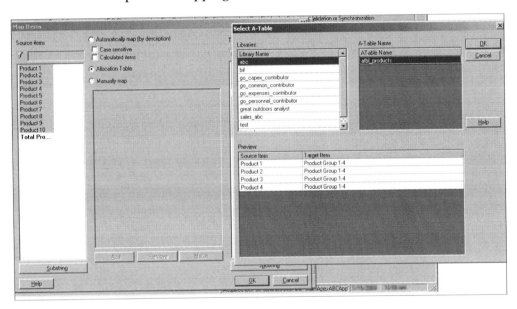

5. Check the **Additional Options** boxes to indicate whether you want to bring the **Annotations** and **Attached Documents** from the source application. Once you click on the **Finish** button on the **Additional Options** screen, the program provides an option to add another element to the administration link. Clicking on **Yes** brings up the **Map Source to Target** screen again.

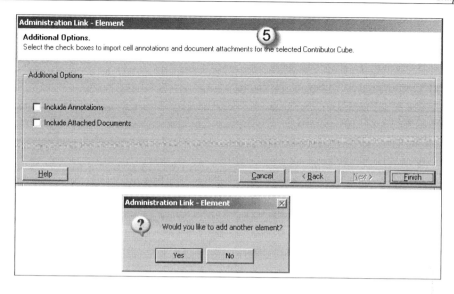

The steps to execute the administration links are discussed in the next section.

Running Administration Links

1. The administration link runs when you click on the **Execute** button on the **Manage Links** screen. You can monitor the progress of an administration link job on the **Manage Links** screen. Note that administration links use the Contributor's job system.

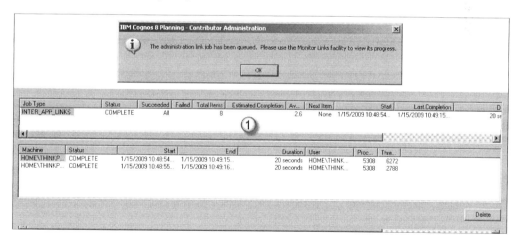

2. If the administration link runs to the development section of your target application you can view the **Prepared Data Blocks** (Import Data screen) in the target application once the administration link job is complete.

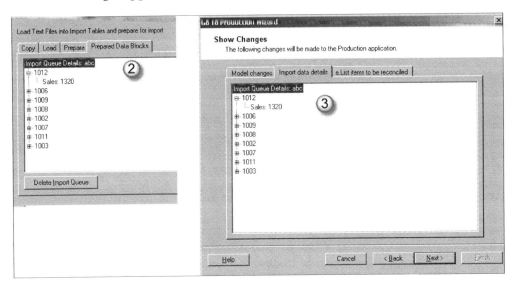

3. When you import data to the development area of the target application, you must run the GTP process to import data to the Contributor Web Client. The GTP screen, shown above, *also* presents the status of **Import Data Details**.

Importing data using IBM Cognos packages

IBM Cognos unveiled a variety of data import methods in recent IBM Cognos Planning versions. A new import method—Importing Data Using IBM Cognos Packages—was introduced in version 8.2. With IBM Cognos Packages, you can import data into Contributor and Analyst programs by leveraging IBM Cognos BI modeling toolsets. In the following illustration, we explain how to import data using IBM Cognos packages:

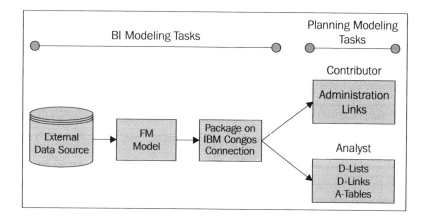

Using the Framework Manager (FM), you, as a BI modeler, create and program the FM model. The Framework Manager program is an IBM Cognos metadata modeling tool. You can define and program SQL query statements in the FM model to pull external data either into reporting tools, such as Query Studio, or into a planning application. Once the FM model is completely defined, you publish the model as an IBM Cognos Connection package. The package is a pointer or a link, and it contains an FM model and relevant security information.

Once the package is published, you, as a planning modeler, can pull data into Contributor or Analyst programs from an external data source. When using the Contributor program, you can use the IBM Cognos package to import data into a planning application using administration links. When using the Analyst program, you can use the IBM Cognos package to import data into a D-Cube using D-Links, and to import data structure into D-Lists and A-Tables.

Analyst to Contributor D-Links

It is not uncommon for planning modelers and system administrators to store planning data in the Analyst program for analysis, reporting, or loading to Contributor. You have two choices for loading data from the Analyst program to the Contributor program.

- Export data from Analyst and import into the Contributor database using the import feature of the Contributor program. We described this method in previous section.

- Use Analyst to Contributor D-Links. **Analyst to Contributor D-Links** are normal Analyst D-Links, except they target data to the Contributor application rather than an Analyst D-Cube.

Creating and running Analyst to Contributor D-Links

The following is a description of the process used for creating and running the Analyst to Contributor D-Links:

1. Open the Analyst program and create a new D-Link. Select the source Analyst D-Cube and select the **Contributor Data** as the target.

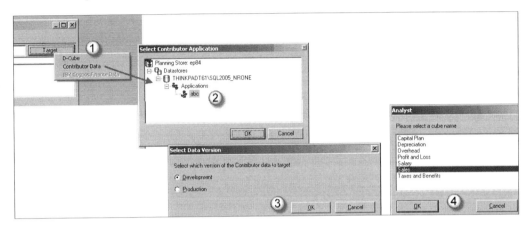

2. On the **Select Contributor Application** screen, select the target application where you want to load data. Click on **OK**.

> Generally, you must have Analyst and the Contributor Administration Console installed on the same machine, which is used to create and run a Contributor<>Analyst link. You must also belong to a user class which gives you rights to Analyst and the appropriate Contributor applications.

3. Select the **Development** or **Production** area of the application. You need to run the GTP when transferring Analyst data into the development area of the application. Data transfer to the production area does not require a GTP.

4. Select the cube in which you want to load data. Pair the dimensions in the D-Link before saving it.

5. Run the D-Link so the Contributor program creates the import queue.

6. If applicable, run the GTP to process the import queue so users can view data on the Contributor Web Client. Note we have a full ABC Company's e.List stored in the Analyst program; therefore, we are able to transfer data from Analyst to Contributor.

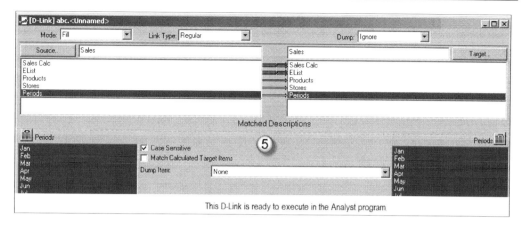

This D-Link is ready to execute in the Analyst program

Unlike admin links, the Analyst to Contributor D-Links do not use the Contributor's job system and, as a result, they are not scalable. Therefore, you only use them when you have to move a small set of data from Analyst to Contributor.

When you create an Analyst to Contributor D-Link, you can use **all** standard D-Link features, for example, local allocation table, and sub-cut string operations. However, certain exceptions exist. For example, you cannot target an assumption cube in Contributor, and you cannot target cells with an access level set as *No Data,* as defined in the access tables.

Although, we have discussed only Analyst to Contributor D-Links in this section, you can also create a *Contributor to Analyst* D-Link or a *Contributor to Contributor* D-Link. Conceptually and mechanically, the last two types of D-Links work the same way as the Analyst to Contributor D-Links.

System Links

So far you have learned how you, as a system administrator, import data in the Contributor application using various import methods. We will now discuss how users can control the import of data in the Contributor Web Client. Rather than waiting for a system administrator to move data using the methods described in previous sections, users can perform ad hoc data transfer between applications in an IBM Cognos Planning environment. A system link can be seen as a pull method, whereas an administration link can be seen as a push method.

It is important to understand that business users must run the system link, *configured by the system administrator,* to move data from a cube in a source application to a cube in a target application.

Creating System Links

Before you, as a system administrator, create the system link, you must ensure that:

- The proper Access Rights to configure the system link on an application have been granted to you.

- The **Act as system link** source is checked as **Yes** on the **Admin Option** screen of the source application.

- The Get Data Extension has been configured (applies when using the Classic Contributor Web Client) in the target application.

The following are the steps to create the system link:

1. Open the **System Links** branch under the production tree of the target application. Click the **New** or **Edit** button to add or edit a system link. Provide a user friendly name to the system link. Click on **OK**.

2. In the second screen, select the cube of the source application. Do the same steps for the target application and target cube. Note, both source and target applications must be the production applications (GTP ran previously). To demonstrate the system link functionality, we use the ABC Company's application as the target application and a sample Sales Application as the source application.

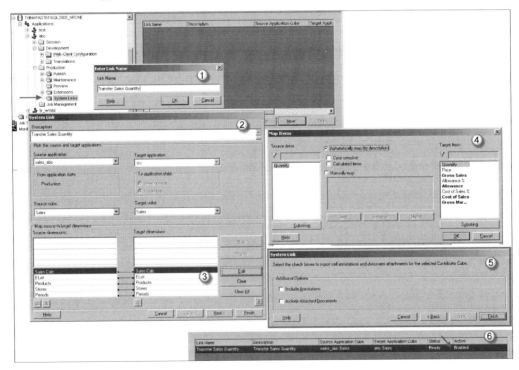

3. Pair the dimensional items from the source to target and click **Map**.

 Rule: A source e.List dimension must be paired with the target e.List dimension. You cannot map a source e.List item data to multiple target e.List items.

4. In the **Map Items** screen, you can either manually map each item or let the system automatically map each item. Click on **OK** when you finish mapping all items in all dimensions. Click **Next** on the **System Link** screen.

5. On the **Additional Options** screen, check whether you want to move the annotations and documents when users run the system link. Click on **Finish**.

6. The new system link is added to the main **System Links** screen. The status of the system link shows **Enabled**. You do not need to run the GTP to make the system link available to users.

Running System Links

Once you have configured the system link, users can run the link to transfer data from the source to the target application. Training your users to run the system links is recommended.

1. Users logon to the Contributor Web Client, open a node, select a target cube, and then click on the **Get Data** tab under the **File** menu. Users will need the *write* access (ownership) on the target application's node to run the system link. A system link can transfer data from the source application to a hidden, *Read Only*, and writable cell in the target application.

The following screenshot explains the data transfer procedure:

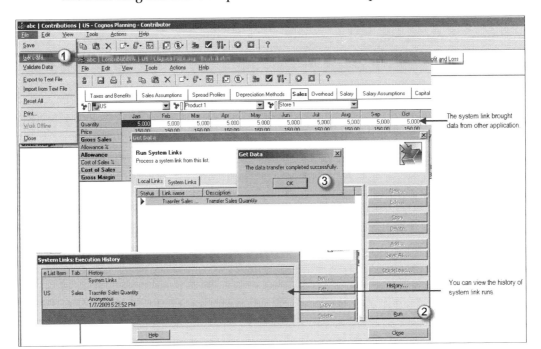

2. Users select the system link they want to run on the **Get Data** screen and click the **Run** button to execute the link.

3. Within few moments, users are notified that the data transfer is complete. In the ABC Company's example above, we have transferred the quantity information from the source application to this target application. The changed numbers are in blue. Users can view the history of the system links runs by clicking the **History** button.

Local Links

You, as a system administrator, receive a call from a user who tells you that she has an Excel file with planning data, and she wonders if she can load that data in the Contributor Web Client, rather than manually re-keying it. She asks whether you can help her to load the file. You explain that she can use the local link feature of IBM Cognos Planning.

Users, with edit or submit rights, can create and run local links to load data into the Contributor Web Client from various *external* sources. They can also transfer data *between Contributor tabs* using local links. The external source can be an Excel file or an ASCII file. Users — not system administrators — set up and execute the local links. The system administrator has only to configure the Get Data extension, so that users can create the local links.

As illustrated: a user, Sara, creates a local link named **Overhead**, she sources the data from an Excel file, she uses (A) the **Map Source to Target** screen to (B) map the Excel file to the cube dimensions (C), then she runs the local link to populate the values from the Excel file to the Contributor Web Client (D).

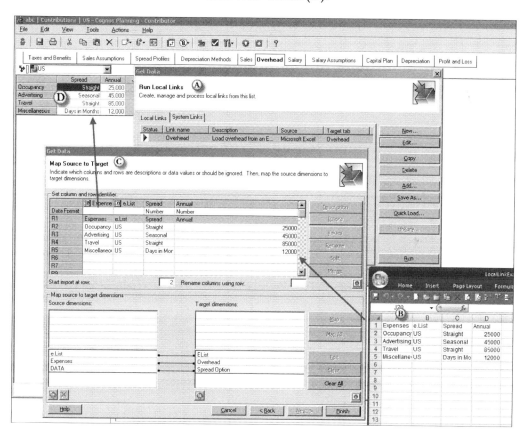

Summary

In this chapter, we have described various data import methods for pulling data into a Contributor application from internal and external sources. First, we discussed updating business assumptions in the Analyst program. Next, we discussed various methods administrators use to load into a Contributor application, namely, the Contributor import feature, Administration Links, and Analyst to Contributor D-links. Lastly, we presented information on importing data via system and Local Links by users.

12
Working with the Contributor Web Client

The previous chapters have focused on the application development tasks that are performed in order to design and build a forecasting and budgeting application. This chapter explains how the Contributor end user can use this application to forecast and budget for the entities that they are responsible for within a company during a typical planning cycle. After you have read this chapter, you will fully understand:

- The Contributor workflow process
- The roles of a planner and a reviewer within the planning process
- The rights of a planner and a reviewer
- How to monitor the current status of the forecast and budget process within a cycle, by using the workflow screen
- How to log on to and navigate in the Contributor Web Client
- How to enter planning data in various ways, including how to use effective shortcut commands
- How to validate the data that you are entering into the plan
- How to use the powerful breakback functionality
- How to add, browse, and copy annotations and documents
- How to export data from and import data into the Contributor Web Client, by using various techniques
- How to work offline
- How to use Contributor for Excel

The last section of this chapter will introduce you to the very well designed new Contributor Web Client, which was made available during the release of IBM Cognos 8 Planning 8.4.

The Contributor Web Client is used by planners to enter planning data for the organizational entities that they are responsible for. In this chapter, we will refer to these entities as e.List items. Typical examples of these e.List items may be geographical regions, countries, departments, or products. For our ABC Company, the e.List is the geographical hierarchy within the company, and the e.List items are the members of this hierarchy. The following is the e.List for ABC Company:

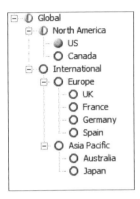

Any number of planners or reviewers can be involved in the process, simultaneously, by logging on to the Contributor web site through a web browser and accessing the application for the e.List item that they are responsible for. Planners can enter data manually or import data by using various methods.

Managing the Contributor workflow

The Contributor workflow engages two sets of users in the planning process: the planner and the reviewer. The planner enters the planning data for the e.List items that they are responsible for and submits the planning data for review. The reviewer examines the submitted planning data and can either accept it or reject it, and request that the planner make changes. This section explains the roles of the planner and the reviewer within this cycle. Additionally, we examine a typical workflow for a company and show how planners and reviewers can monitor the progress of the planning cycle by checking the workflow states of the e.List items they are planning for or reviewing.

The roles of the planner and reviewer

The two roles within a traditional workflow cycle are the planner and the reviewer.

The planner

The planner can typically be anyone who enters planning data into the planning process. They could be a sales manager responsible for a geographical region who is accountable to the regional sales director, or they could be an analyst accountable to the head of the planning department for the brand division of a retail company. If their role is to enter planning data for managerial review for their e.List items during the cycle, then they are a planner. The planner may be responsible for single or multiple e.List items, and can view, enter, save, and submit this planning data for review. A planner cannot review their own submission unless they occupy both roles within the planning process.

The reviewer

The reviewer is usually a manager who reviews the planning data that the planner has entered and submitted. They can accept this data, make any additional changes if appropriate, and submit it to the next reviewer in the hierarchy, which is usually their manager. Alternatively, if they are not happy with the submission by the planner, they can reject it and request that the data be changed and the plan resubmitted.

In some cases, a user may have both the roles. They may be both the planner and the reviewer. This may happen where a person is responsible for entering and reviewing plan data for their e.List item. A reviewer can review data and may edit, save, and submit data, if the administrator has given them the right to perform these actions.

Examine a typical workflow for an organization

Let us examine the workflow of the monthly sales planning cycle for the North America division of ABC Company. The following schematic demonstrates the workflow:

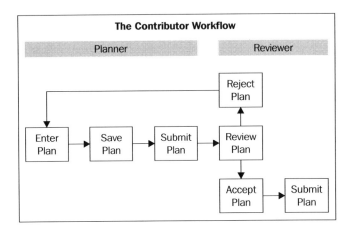

In this scenario, there are four people involved in the planning process for North America sales. There are the sales managers for the US and Canada territories who are responsible for planning unit sales and pricing for the US and Canada territories, respectively. It is their role to gather this data and enter it into the Contributor Web Client on a monthly basis. There is also the Sales Director for North America, whose role is to manage the sales for this region. His role is to review the sales submitted to him by the two sales managers. He subsequently submits this data to the Global Sales Director, whose role is to oversee global sales. He reviews the sales plan submitted to him by the Sales Director. Within this planning process, the two sales managers are planners, given that their role is to enter planning data. The Sales Director for North America and the Global Sales Director are reviewers, as they review the plan data submitted to them.

The two sales managers will set the process in motion by opening their e.List items in the Contributor Web Client , in order to enter unit sales and price data. At this point, if the managers are not finished with entering the plan data, they can save the data and continue at a later stage. Alternatively, if the managers are happy with their data, they can submit it to the Sales Director for North America for review. Once one or both of the managers have submitted the data, the Sales Director for North America can begin to review the information. If he is unhappy with the submission, he can reject it and request that the manager make changes and submit it again. Alternatively, he can accept it and either make changes to the submission himself or leave it as it is and submit up the hierarchy to his senior, the Global Sales Director, for review. The Global Sales Director, as a reviewer, can either accept the plan or reject it, and request changes if he is unhappy with the submission.

At the end of the cycle, the forecast is signed off by the Global Sales Director. The same process begins again in the next financial period.

Working with the Contributor Web Client

The Contributor Web Client can be accessed by clicking on a web link to the application supplied by an administrator or through IBM Cognos Connection. The ABC Company application has been published as a package to a sub-folder in the Public Folders in IBM Cognos Connection. The e.List item can now be accessed through IBM Cognos Connection, for entering planning data.

Exploring the Contributor Web Client

In this section, we explain how to log on to the Contributor web client, and examine the workflow screen. We also show you how to open an application for entering plan data, and explore the menu bar and its buttons.

To log on to the Contributor web client:

1. Open **IBM Cognos Connection**.
2. Click on **Launch**.
2. Click on **Contributor** .

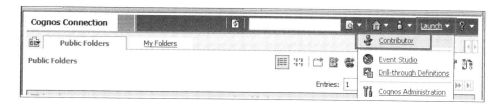

4. Click on the **ABC Company** application.

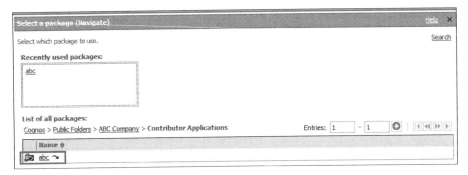

The **Contributor** workflow screen appears, as shown in the screenshot below:

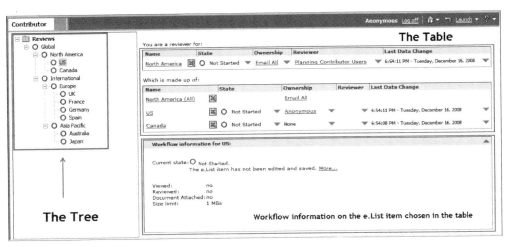

The tree and e.List

The tree on the leftmost side of the screen is the e.List for the ABC Company and represents the geographical hierarchy of the company's territories. The countries, US, Canada, UK, France, Germany, Spain, Australia, and Japan are at the lowest level of the e.List. It is at this level that the sales managers enter their forecast for the territory they are responsible for. The international territories are grouped under their parents, Europe and Asia Pacific.

Europe and Asia Pacific are children of the International parent, whereas the US and Canada territories are children of the North America parent. Both of the North America and International regions group into the top level node of the e.List, Global. The review of the forecast is done at each parent level. Each e.List item is preceded by a workflow state icon. All of the workflow states are explained in the following sections.

The Table

When you click on an e.List item, the information on the current status of this node will appear in the section on the right-hand side of the Contributor Workflow screen. This section is called the "The Table" and provides information on the e.List item such as the current **State, Owner, Reviewer**, and **Last Date Changed**. The state of the e.List item is represented by an icon and a short description. All of the workflow states are detailed in the next section of this chapter. The owner of the e.List item is the user who is currently editing it or who last edited this item.

Workflow states

During the planning cycle, planners and reviewers can check or monitor the status of each e.List item by looking at the workflow table. When they click on an e.List item, its state will be represented in the table by an icon and a short description. The table below displays all of the workflow states.

Icon	State	Description
O	**Not Started**	There have been no changes made to the forecast data for this e.List item. The e.List item may have been opened but not saved.
	Work in progress	Changes have been made to the forecast data for this e.List item, and saved but not submitted.
	Locked	The forecast data for this e.List item has been submitted for review. The e.List item is now locked and cannot be edited by the planner.
	Incomplete	This state only occurs for review level e.List items. It indicates that there is at least one child e.List item that is Not Started and at least one other child e.List item that is Work in Progress, Locked or Ready.
	Ready	This state only occurs for review level e.List items. It indicates that all of the child e.List items for this node have been submitted and locked. This e.List item and its children are ready for review.

Icon	State	Description
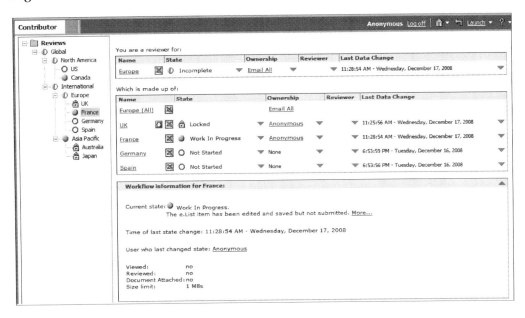	**Currently being edited or annotated**	This e.List item has been opened for editing or adding annotations.
	Out of date	This e.List item needs updating to reflect application changes and restructuring.
	Currently being edited or annotated and is out of date	This e.List item has been opened for editing or adding annotations and is out of date.

The Global Sales Director of the ABC Company wants to see the current status of the planning cycle. To do this, he can log on to the Contributor application through IBM Cognos Connection and review the workflow screen for the application.

By looking at the workflow screen above, he can see that the two sales managers for Australia and Japan in the Asia Pacific region have submitted their forecast for review. The consolidated forecast for Europe is incomplete, because only the **UK** forecast has been submitted; **France** is **Work in Progress** and **Germany** and **Spain** have not yet been started. North America is also incomplete as the US forecast has not yet been started, and **Canada** is **Work in Progress**. The CEO has decided to send an email to both the North America and International Sales directors to remind them that these forecasts are due by the end of the week.

Emails can be sent directly from the Contributor client by clicking on the name of the current owner of an e.List item in the ownership column of the table on the rightmost side of the workflow screen.

The workflow screen also contains a number of icons.

Icon	Action
☒	This icon means that the application for this e.List item can be opened in Excel. The Excel Add-in for Contributor must be installed.
⬇	A reviewer may click on this icon to reject a submission.
📎	The annotation icon indicates that an annotation is attached to this e.List item.

Opening the application grid for inputting data

To begin inputting planning data, open the application grid for an e.List item. On the workflow screen, click on an e.List item to open the grid as shown:

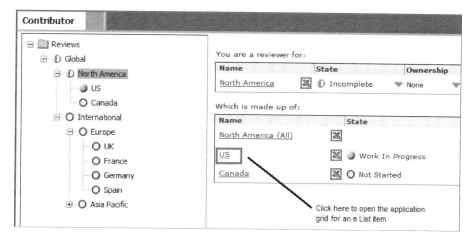

The menu bar and its buttons

The menu bar allows you to perform actions such as save, export, copy, paste, and other import tasks, by clicking on an icon. The following is a list of icons on the menu bar and their functionality.

Icon	Functionality
	Take ownership of the application and start editing it
	Save data
	Print
	Cut
	Copy
	Paste
	Delete
	Annotate — Add, edit, view or delete annotations to a cell, column or model
	Attach Document - Add, edit, view or delete documents for a cell, column, or model
	Browse commentary
	Transpose rows and columns
	Suppress rows, columns or pages
	Get Data – Import data using local or system links
	Validate Data – Ensure that data entered is compliant with defined formats and business rules as laid out by the Contributor Administrator
	Tools
	Submit
	Reject
	Help

Entering data

In this section, we will look at how you can edit, save, and submit data in the Contributor Web Client, focusing on various shortcuts. We will also look at validating data and also briefly discuss the functionality of breakback. Finally, we will explain how you can add, edit, and browse commentary and documents.

Editing and saving data

The Contributor Web Client has to be open in order for you to be able to start entering forecast data. Ensure that the application grid is open by clicking on an e.List item.

The application contains tabs that represent the underlying D-Cubes created in Analyst. Each tab consists of columns, rows, and page dimensions (if there are more than two dimensions in a tab). Forecast data is entered into any cells with a white background in the grid.

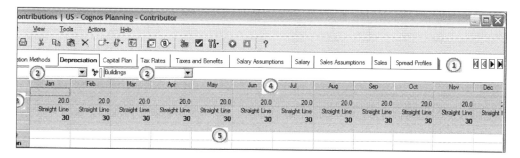

Note the following items identified on this screen:

1. These are the tabs that represent the D-Cubes created in Analyst.

2. These are the page dimensions. Clicking on the down arrow will display all of the items for that dimension. Any item in this list can be selected.

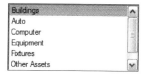

3. The row dimension.

4. The column dimension.

5. The grid. Only cells with a white background are editable; the cells with a gray background are read-only.

If you are not the current owner, then all of the cells will have a gray background and will not be editable. To commence entering forecast data, click on the **Take Ownership** icon (⚙). All of the editable cells will now have a white background.

Data entered into the grid is green. You can use the arrow keys to move to different cells to continue data entry without running calculations. When the *Enter* key is pressed, the entered data turns blue. You will immediately see the change in totals or any other calculations in all of the dimensions for this tab. All of the calculation changes will appear in bold and blue.

To save the data, click on the save 🖫 icon.

Editing data using shortcuts

In this section, we will explain how data can be edited in the Contributor Web Client by using copy commands and data entry commands.

Copy commands

Data can be copied, cut, pasted, and deleted by selecting a cell or cell range and right-clicking and then selecting one of the edit commands you want to perform from the context menu.

Additionally, the user can use copy commands to facilitate the editing process. Copy commands are processed when the *Enter* key is pressed.

The following is the list of copy commands available for the user to use when entering data:

Command	Action		Example
<	Copy across	<100	Copy the value 100 forward across cells
>	Copy back	>100	Copy the value 100 backwards across cells
|	Copy down	|100	Copy the value 100 down across cells
^	Copy up	^100	Copy the value 100 up across cells
:	Copy stopper		Use with another copy command to denote which cell to end the copy action on

Data entry commands

Data entry commands are used to facilitate the entry of data into cells.

The following is the list of data entry commands available to the user when entering data:

Command	Action	Example	
K or k	Enter value in thousands	100K	100,000
M or m	Enter value in millions	20M	20,000,000
Add or +	Add a number to an existing cell value	add1000	Add 1000 to existing cell value
Subtract or Sub	Subtract a number from an existing cell value	sub400	Subtract 400 from existing cell value
Multiply or Mul or *	Multiply an existing cell value by a number	mul2	Multiply existing cell value by 2
Divide or Div	Divide an existing cell value by a number	Div4	Divides existing cell value by 4
Increase or Inc	Increase an existing cell value by a percentage	Increase8	Increases existing cell value by 8%
Decrease	Decrease an existing cell value by a percentage	Decrease12	Increases existing cell value by 12%
GrowLinear or GroLin or GL*	Increase the existing value by a percentage for each period on a linear basis	G2L	Grow each value on a linear basis by 2%
GrowCompound or GroCom or GC*	Increase the existing value by a percentage for each period on a compound basis	G2C	Grow each value on a compound basis by 2%
Power or Pow	Raise the existing cell value to the specified power	power8	Raise the existing cell value to the power of 8
Zero or Zer	Make the existing cell value a zero	Zero8	Zero out a cell
Reset or Res	Reset cell values to what they were when last saved	Reset	
Round or Rou	Round existing cell values	Round100	Round existing cell values to nearest 100
Hold or Hol	Hold the cell value against breakback	Hold	
Release or Rel	Release cells that are held	Release	

 *Grow Command – Insert the value between Grow and Compound. For example: Grow2Compound, Gro2Com, or g2c.

Data entry commands can also be used in conjunction with copy commands. Some examples of this are shown below:

Command	Example
<100k	Copy the value 100,000 forward across cells
>10m	Copy the value 10 million backwards across cells
ADD1K>	Add 1,000 to a cell and spread across forward cells
INC10>	Increase a cell by 10% and spread across forward cells

Validating data

Data validation forces you to enter forecast data that complies with a set of business rules defined by the Contributor Administrator. You can validate all of the data entered into the application at any time by clicking on the Validate Data icon ☑. When the icon is clicked, the **Data Validation** dialog box appears, displaying any errors. You can double-click on an error message to locate the cells that contain the errors.

As an example, the Contributor Administrator has added a data validation rule in the Contributor model that provides a warning to the user if they have selected an End Month that is before the Start Month in the **Salary** tab. Additionally, the data validation rule has been configured so that the user is prohibited from saving his changes if this rule is broken. When the user saves the changes, the **Validation Errors** box pops up displaying an error message. When the box is closed, another box pops up with a message that saving is not allowed due to the validation error. To continue saving changes, the user will need to click on **OK** and edit the **End Month** entry to specify a month prior to the **Start Month**, in order to abide by the rule.

Swapping rows and columns

You can transpose rows and columns easily by clicking on the **Swap Rows and Columns** icon ▣. The following is an example of how rows and columns can be swapped, along with the current layout of the **Sales** tab:

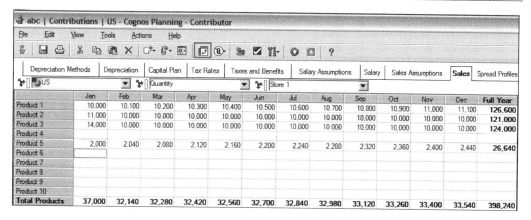

The following is the layout of the sales tab after transposing rows and columns:

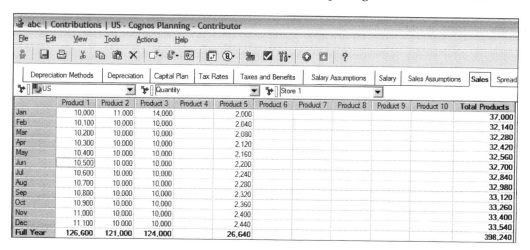

Breakback

Breakback allows you to enter data into a calculated cell and change the underlying cells that make up this total in a linear or given proportion. Holds can be applied to individual underlying cells to prevent them from being changed during the breakback process. To hold a cell or a range of cells, select the cell or range, right-click on the cell to bring up the context menu, and then select **Hold**. To release the hold so that the underlying cell will change, right-click on the cell and select **Release**.

Annotations

You can add commentary or user annotations when entering forecast data. You can add annotations to a cell, tab, or a model by clicking on the Annotate icon 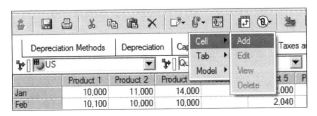. You will see additional options to edit, view, or delete annotations.

To add an annotation to a cell, click the **Annotate** icon , select **Cell**, and then select **Add**. An **Add Annotation** box is displayed, allowing you to enter the annotation. Enter the commentary, and then click on **OK**.

To view, edit, or delete an annotation, click on the Annotate icon, select **Cell**, and then select **Edit, View**, or **Delete**. Cells that contain annotations contain a red triangle in the upper-right corner. You can also enter links to web pages, email addresses, and files, by using the following example:

Web Pages: `http://www.webpage.com`

Email Addresses: `mailto:email address`

File links: `file:\\servername\fileshare path\filename.doc`

Adding documents

Depending on how the Contributor Administrator has configured the web settings in the Contributor Administration Console, you can add documents to cells, tabs, or models. Some of the standard file formats supported are Word docs (`.doc`), Excel spreadsheets (`.xls`), PowerPoint presentations (`.ppt`), ZIP files (`.zip`), PDF files (`.pdf`), and text files (`.txt`).

To add a document to a tab, click on the **Attach Document** icon 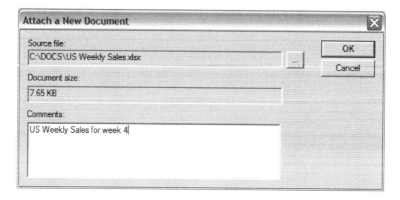. In the pop-up menu box, click on **Tab**, and then click on **Add**. The **Attach a New Document** box will allow you to select a document to add to the tab, and also make comments.

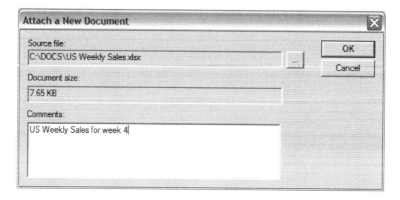

Submitting data

Once you have finished entering forecast data into the application and are ready to have it reviewed by a reviewer, you submit the data by clicking on the **Submit** icon ⊙. Once you have submitted the forecast for review, the application becomes locked. No additional editing can be made to a submission unless it has been rejected by a reviewer.

Importing and exporting data from Web Client

You can import data to the application and export Contributor data to various file formats by using a variety of techniques.

Exporting Contributor data

You can export Contributor data to a text file or to Excel.

To export Contributor data to a text file, select the tab that you want to export data from. Click on **File**, and then on **Export to Text File** and select a location to save the exported data to.

Contributor data can be exported to Excel if the Contributor Administrator has enabled this functionality. To export data to Excel, click on the **Tools** icon 🍴,
and then select the option **Export to Excel**.

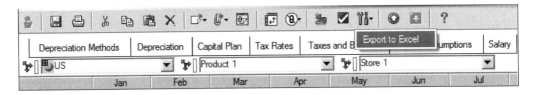

A pop-up box will be displayed, with three export options, as follows:

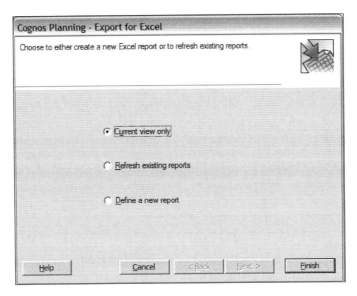

- **Current view only**: Selecting this option will export the current slice to Excel.
- **Refresh existing reports**: This option will refresh a report that was previously created with the latest Contributor data.
- **Define a new report**: This will create a new report. This report can be refreshed with the latest Contributor data at later date.

Importing data to Contributor

As a planner or reviewer, you can import data from flat files, Excel files, or a Contributor application. There are two methods of importing data from a flat file. You can click on **File** and then **Import from Text File**, and select a flat file to import to Contributor.

The second method uses the Get Data tool.

The Get Data tool makes use of local and system links, and is used to import data from various data sources into Contributor.

Local links

Local links are links that a planner or reviewer can create and configure in the Contributor Web Client. They can be used to import data from ASCII files, Excel, or a Contributor tab. Local links can be edited, copied, or deleted by the planner or reviewer. They can only import data in editable cells.

Follow the steps below to create a local link:

1. Click on the **Get Data** icon .
2. The **Get Data** dialog box is displayed. Select **Local Links**.
3. Select the **New** tab, and enter the following data:
   a. Enter **Sales Data Import** as the link name.
   b. Enter **Import of weekly sales data** as the description.
   c. Select a data source type of **ASCII**. The available sources are Contributor Tab, ASCII, and Excel.
   d. Choose the **Sales** tab as the target tab to import the data into.

e. Click on **Next**.

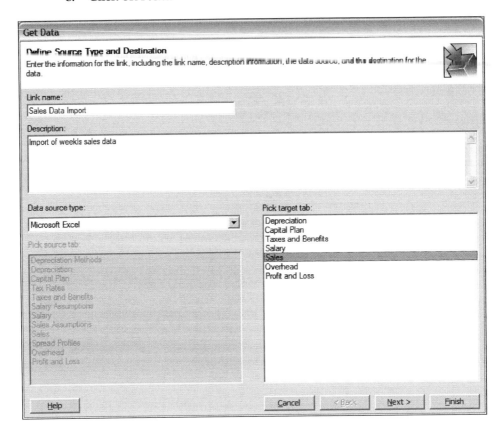

4. Select the source file and the worksheet. Click on **Next**.

5. Map the dimensions in the data to the target tab.

a. Identify the columns to map as a dimension to the target tab by highlighting them and clicking on **Description**.

b. Rename the column heading as required.

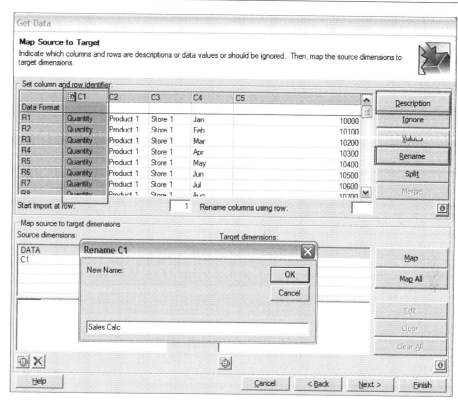

c.   Select the dimensions to map, and then click on **Map**.

d.   You can map items in each dimension either manually or automatically.

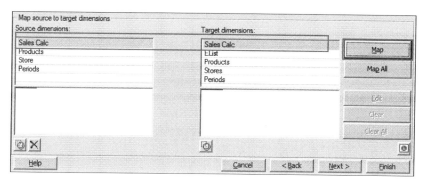

e.   Click on **Next**.

6.   Run the link to validate the results. Save the link.

System links

System links are created and configured by the Contributor Administrator in the Contributor Administration Console. Planners or reviewers cannot construct or configure system links. System links can be target writable, hidden, and read-only cells. System links are used to import data from the same, or a different, Contributor application. Link states define whether a system link is "Ready" or "Incomplete". A system link that exists in a Ready state has all of its dimensions correctly mapped between the source and the target, and is ready to be run by the planner or reviewer. System links that are in an incomplete state do not have their dimensions correctly mapped and cannot be run (this should not be the case if the System link is configured correctly). Follow the steps below to run a system link:

1. Click on the **Get Data** icon .
2. Select the **System Link** tab in the **Get Data** pop-up box.
3. Click on **Run**.

Working offline

Imagine that you are going to be traveling and that you will need to access the Contributor application in an airport, in order to update the sales information before an important meeting. You also anticipate that you will not be able to connect to the server during this period. While you are connected to the server, Contributor allows you to bring an e.List item offline. Forecasting changes for this e.List item can then be made in offline mode. You can then bring your forecasting changes back online at a later date, when you are ready.

To work offline, click on an e.List item to open the Contributor application. Click on **File**, and then click on **Work Offline**, a dialog box will be displayed to indicate that the e.List item is offline.

To bring your data back online, click on **File**, and then click on **Work Online**. Click on **Yes** when you are prompted to bring the data online.

Please note the following when working in offline mode:

- The Contributor Administrator configures offline rights in the Contributor Administration console.
- You can only bring an e.List item offline when you are connected to the server.
- Any changes made offline are saved to the offline store and not to the server.
- You need to be connected to the server to bring your forecasting changes for the e.List item back online. Your forecasting changes made offline are only updated to the server when you save or submit when online.

- Annotations cannot be edited, and automatically become read-only in offline mode.

- Attached documents cannot be opened in offline mode.

- Extreme care should be taken when working offline, in particular when structural changes have been made to an application while forecasting changes have been made offline.

Using Contributor with Excel

An e.List item can be opened in Excel to combine the use of Excel's familiar formatting features with much of the functionality of Contributor. The Contributor add-in for Excel must be installed to be able to do this.

On the workflow page for an application, click on the Excel icon . This will open the e.List item in excel. Each tab will be opened in a separate Excel worksheet. The Contributor add-in for Excel allows you to perform, in Excel, many of the functions that you can carry out via the Web interface. The following are all of the Contributor operations that can be performed in Excel:

1. View, edit, save, submit, and reject data
2. View the current workflow
3. Print
4. Run local links and system links
5. Add annotations
6. Add documents
7. Browse commentary
8. Swap rows and columns

The new Contributor Web Client

With the release of IBM Cognos 8 Planning 8.4 came the much-anticipated new Contributor Web Client. There are a number of new and exciting features that will be discussed briefly in this section. The Contributor web user will easily be able to pick up these new features and at the same time use much of the functionality that existed with the previous version of the web client that they are accustomed to using.

The new interface

Let's start by looking at the interface of the new Contributor Web Client.

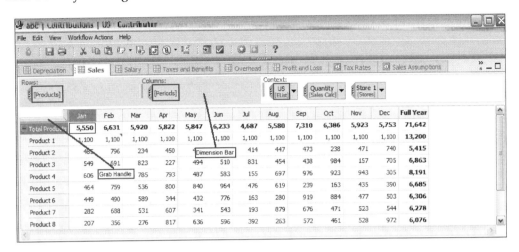

The dimension bar underneath the tab names shows the dimensions that are rows and columns. The layout here shows a basic view of one row (**Products**) and one column (**Periods**). Note that the names of the row and column dimensions are clearly labeled on the dimension bar. The Grab Handle allows you to easily move dimensions around on the screen in order to customize the Contributor web view, as explored in the next section.

New features

In this section, we will explore some of the new features of the new Contributor Web Client.

Customization of the Contributor web view

The following sections explain how the Contributor web view can be customized in the new Contributor Web Client.

Nesting dimensions

You can now freely nest dimensions by dragging and dropping dimensions as you wish, without depending on Contributor Administrators to configure the nesting functionality in the Contributor Administration Console. To illustrate this, we will nest the Sales Calc dimension within the Products dimension, so that both dimensions are rows.

Drag the **Sales Calc** dimension to the rows, and position it before the **Products** dimension. Ensure that the black line is placed before the **Products** dimension as shown:

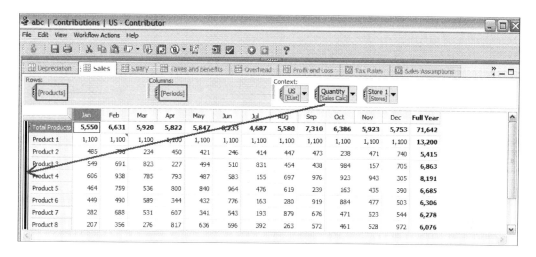

The result is shown in the following screenshot:

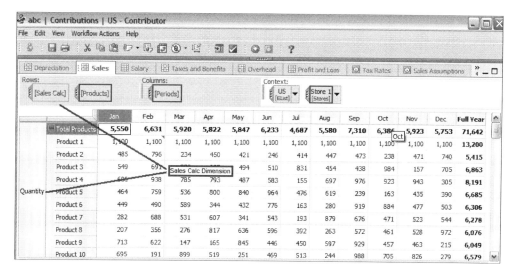

The effect of nesting is that you can see more information on the screen. You can scroll down to see the remaining items of the Sales Calc dimension, such as prices.

Freeze Panes

You can now freeze panes by clicking on **View | Freeze Panes** on the menu bar. The following example shows where we have frozen the **Total Products** row. You will be able to scroll down and continue to view the Total Products line as shown in the screenshot below:

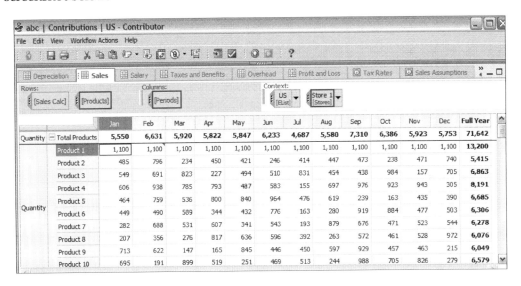

You can now change the order of tabs by grabbing a tab and dragging it to position it before or after another tab.

Viewing multiple tabs in one view

You can now view multiple tabs in a single view. To do this, grab hold of a tab and tear it off by dragging it down to the center of the view. In the following example, we want to see the **Sales** and **Sales Assumption** tabs in one view. Grab the **Sales Assumption** tab and tear it off. The cursor will switch to an image of multiple folders. Drag it down to the bottom of the view, until you see the highlighted drop area with a black arrow, and release the tab. You will now be able to see two tabs in a single view, as shown in the following screenshot:

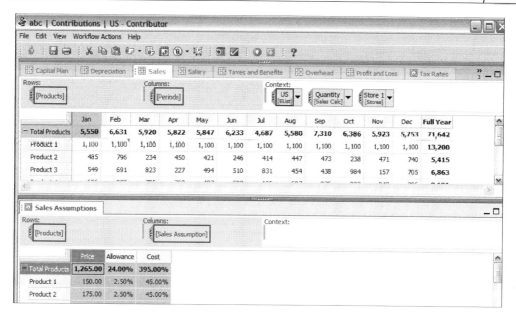

To return the view to a single tab, grab one of the tabs and drag it to the middle of the other tab area. Additionally, the tab view can be reset by clicking on **View|Reset Views|Reset Tabs only**.

Collapsing or expanding dimension hierarchies

Dimension hierarchies can be collapsed or expanded by clicking on the + (to expand) or - (to collapse) sign on a dimension, as shown in the following screenshot:

Click on the - sign to collapse the hierarchy.

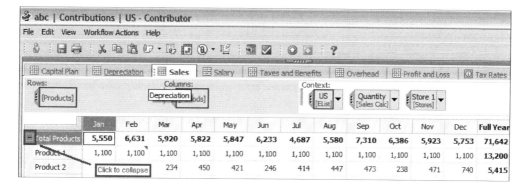

Click the + sign to expand the hierarchy.

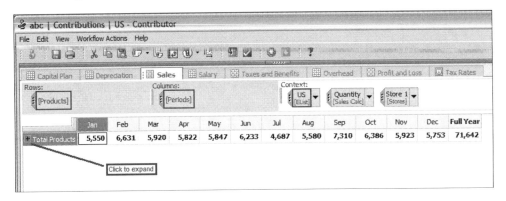

Hiding dimension items

Dimension items can be hidden by highlighting them, right-clicking on the highlighted selection, and selecting **Hide Selected**, as shown below. To unhide them, select the dimension name, right-click on the highlighted selection, and then select **Unhide Selected**.

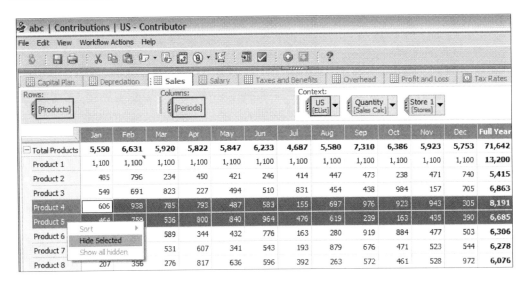

Sorting dimension items

Dimension items can be sorted in ascending or descending order as explained
in the following example. Let's sort the Full Year values of the Products dimension
in ascending order. Right-click on the Full Year column name, and then select
Sort | Ascending, as shown in the following screenshot:

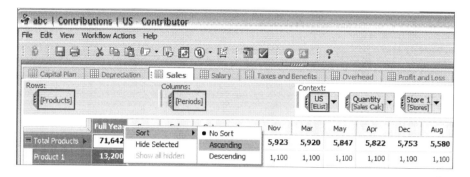

The results will appear as follows, clearly showing that **Product 2** has the lowest
amount of unit sales for the Full Year.

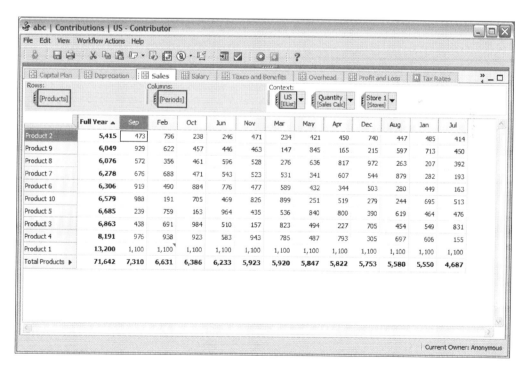

	Full Year ▲	Sep	Feb	Oct	Jun	Nov	Mar	May	Apr	Dec	Aug	Jan	Jul
Product 2	5,415	473	796	238	246	471	234	421	450	740	447	485	414
Product 9	6,049	929	622	457	446	463	147	845	165	215	597	713	450
Product 8	6,076	572	356	461	596	528	276	636	817	972	263	207	392
Product 7	6,278	676	688	471	543	523	531	341	607	544	879	282	193
Product 6	6,306	919	490	884	776	477	589	432	344	503	280	449	163
Product 10	6,579	988	191	705	469	826	899	251	519	279	244	695	513
Product 5	6,685	239	759	163	964	435	536	840	800	390	619	464	476
Product 3	6,863	438	691	984	510	157	823	494	227	705	454	549	831
Product 4	8,191	976	938	923	583	943	785	487	793	305	697	606	155
Product 1	13,200	1,100	1,100	1,100	1,100	1,100	1,100	1,100	1,100	1,100	1,100	1,100	1,100
Total Products ▶	71,642	7,310	6,631	6,386	6,233	5,923	5,920	5,847	5,822	5,753	5,580	5,550	4,687

Resetting tabs and grids to their original state

All tabs and grids can be reset to their original state by clicking on **Views | Reset Views**, and then selecting either **Reset Tabs only**, **Reset Grid only**, or **Reset both Tabs and Grid**.

Summary

In this chapter, we explained the Contributor workflow process, explored the roles of the reviewer and the planner, and also explained how the current status of the forecast cycle can be monitored by using the Contributor workflow screen. We then showed you how to log on to and navigate in the Contributor Web Client. We also explored how the entry of planning data can be facilitated by the use of copy and data commands. Additionally, we looked at breakback, working with annotations and documents, exporting data from and importing data to the client, data validation, Contributor for Excel, and working offline. Finally, we explored the new Contributor Web Client that was released with IBM Cognos 8 Planning 8.4.

13
Reporting Planning Data— Publish and BI Integration

In this chapter, we will explain how planning data that has been entered and saved in the Contributor Web Client can be made available for reporting purposes by using the publish process. We then explain the different options that can be used for accessing this data for reporting in real time and through the publish process. After reading this chapter, you should be able to:

- Make the user-submitted plan data available, by using the Contributor Web Client, for reporting, analytics, and export this data to other databases.

- Understand how to access this data for IBM Cognos BI reporting in real time or through the publish process

Accessing planning data

There are two elementary methods in which planning data can be accessed for reporting. The first method allows you to access real-time data either by creating a planning package during a GTP or through the Planning Data Service (PDS). The data is revealed by opening up a slice of the application. This process is slow and is better suited to ad hoc reporting rather than for full-scale reporting purposes. The second method involves moving the planning data to a separate star schema datastore by using the publish process and reporting off of this database. This option is far more suited to reporting and ETL purposes.

Publish

When your users save and submit plans on the Contributor Web Client, Contributor saves and stores this data in XML format in a relational database. The stored data needs to be translated into a format that is easily readable and accessible to other IBM Cognos tools and databases. The publishing feature in Contributor works like a translator and converts the XML format data into a readable format. Publishing is an administrative task, and it is executed by the Contributor job system. You, as an administrator, can either manually publish data or automate the publishing task by using a Contributor macro. The frequency of data publishing is dictated by the needs of the consumers' tools, such as IBM Cognos Report Studio, or as an enterprise data warehouse.

Although Contributor-published data can be used for various purposes, the following are the most common business uses of published data:

- Reporting plan data using IBM Cognos reporting tools, such as Report Studio, Analysis Studio, and Query Studio
- Performing additional analysis on submitted plan data by using IBM Cognos Planning Analyst
- Loading plan data back into a general ledger or ERP system

Storing published data

Contributor stores published data in a separate datastore, which IBM Cognos documentation refers to as the 'publish container'. Unlike the Contributor application datastore, which is a transactional database, the publish container has a different life cycle and contains a significantly different storage and performance profile. There are two different types of publish containers available, and we will examine both types of containers in the next section. The two types of containers are:

- The Table-only Layout Publish Container
- The View Layout Publish Container

The following are the steps required to create a publish container. Note that the steps to create a publish container apply to both types of publish layouts.

1. Select the application and click on the **Production** branch.
2. Select either the **Table-only** Layout or the **View Layout** from the **Publish** branch.

3. Click on the **Configure** button on the **Option** tab. You may or may not have the required rights to create the publish container. See the following section.

4. Click on the **Create New** button on the **Select Publish Datastore Container** screen.

5. Click on the **Star** icon on the **Configure Datastore Server Connection** screen. This opens the **Create a New Publish Container** screen.

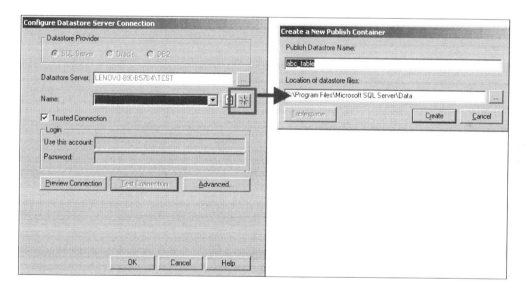

6. Type the name of the publish container and the location of the database files on the **Create a New Publish Container** screen. Click on the **Create** button.

7. Click on the **Test Connection** button on the **Configure Datastore Server Connection** screen to test the configuration. Click on **OK** twice on the next two messages.

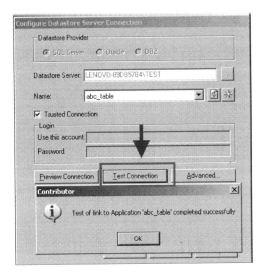

8. Add this new publish container to the Job system by opening the **Job Server Cluster** branch and selecting a cluster or job server. You are ready to publish data.

Who can publish?

You need the following rights to successfully complete the administrative duties related to creating the publish container and publishing data.

*   **Access Rights**: This gives you rights to perform publishing tasks. You can configure these rights on the following **Access Rights** screen. Note that the default Access Rights should work in most cases.

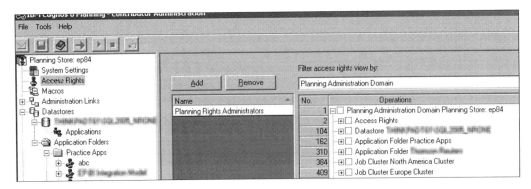

- **Database Rights**: Published data is stored in a database (called Container). The account that creates the publish container needs database creation rights (DDL) to create and modify a publish container. If this account does not have DDL rights, you can ask the database administrator to create and modify a publish container. In the Contributor Administration Console, you can generate a script for the database administrators, so that they can create and modify a publish container.

Publishing using the Table-only layout

The recommended Table-only layout is an optimized publish layout for IBM Cognos BI reporting tools. As discussed later in this chapter, the Framework Manager (FM) model, which uses the Framework Manager Extension, requires this layout. You can also transmit data from the Table-only layout published tables to external databases, such as data mart or data warehouse.

Several tables are created when you run the Table-only publish layout. Three important types of tables are D-List items tables, hierarchy tables, and D-Cube export tables. The following is a description of these tables. You can create reporting models from these key tables to report on planning data.

- **D-List items tables** (`it_table`): One table is created for each D-List in the planning model. Each item table describes the contents of a D-List. For example, you may find a month item table storing month details, such as Jan, Feb, Mar, and so on.

- **Hierarchy tables** (`sy_` and `cy_table`): The two most commonly used hierarchy tables are `cy_` (Calculated hierarchy) and `sy_` (Simple hierarchy). In most of the cases, the contents of these two tables will be very similar. Derived hierarchy lists found in `sy_table` allow reporting tools to automatically generate summaries for each level of the hierarchy. The complete hierarchy lists found in `cy_table` are intended to be used when a D-List contains complex calculations between D-List items. You can use complete hierarchy lists, which are already in the Planning application, to avoid having to recreate calculations in your IBM Cognos 8 report.

- **Export tables** (`et_table`): One table is created for each D-Cube in the planning model. For example, you may find the Sales cube export table when we publish the Sales cube of the ABC Company's model.

The following are the steps to publish the Table-only Layout:

1. Select **Production | Publish | Table-only Layout**.

2. Select the cube that is to be published, and then select a dimension to be published. The dimension for publish reduces the data volume to be published. It provides the measure dimension for the reporting environment. The measure dimension is typically referred to as a calculation D-List in the planning model, for example, the PL D-List in the ABC Company model. The following illustration identifies the differences in the table structures when you choose or do not choose a dimension for publish:

With No Dimension for Publish Selected

Cost Centers	Months	PL Calc	Amount
1001	May	Sales	1000
1001	May	Cost of Sales	350
1001	May	Gross Profit	650
1001	May	Operating Exper	300
1001	May	Net Profit	350
1002	May	Sales	2500
1002	May	Cost of Sales	850
1002	May	Gross Profit	1650
1002	May	Operating Exper	400
1002	May	Net Profit	1250

With Dimension for Publish Selected

Cost Centers	Months	Sales	Cost of Sales	Gross Profit	Operating Expense	Net Profit
1001	May	1000	350	650	300	350
1002	May	2500	850	1650	400	1250

3. Select the e.List items to be published. As a minimum, you must have reconciled all e.List items in an application before you execute the publish job.

4. Select the options to be used when publishing.

5. Click on the **Publish** button. The program will create a publish job. You can monitor the publish job by using the **Monitor Console** branch.

Publishing data changes (incremental publish)

When you publish data using the Table-only Layout structure, the program takes a snapshot of the data entered in the Contributor Web Client, and then publishes and stores this in the published tables. Practically, you select all nodes to publish, even though you can choose to publish selected nodes. Depending on the number of e.List items being published, and the availability of job servers, a publish job can take anywhere from a few minutes to many hours. Because of the batch nature of the publish mechanism, a latency period exists between the time that users input plan numbers in the Web Client, and the time when the program populates the plan numbers in the publish container by using the publish feature. Because of this latency, it was impractical to produce a real time reporting solution in versions prior to 8.2, especially when IBM Cognos reporting studios relied on planning published containers.

The incremental publishing feature, also called trickled publishing, solves this real-time data publish and reporting problem. Instead of publishing all nodes, the incremental publish scans data changes and publishes only the changes.

For example, assume there are five e.List nodes in an application. When you publish the application using the Table-only Layout option, the program publishes all nodes. (We assume that you have selected all nodes to be published.) Now, assume that a user enters revised plan numbers in e.List node 4. Without the incremental publish feature turnedon, you must publish all nodes, as you, as an administrator, cannot tell who has entered or revised planning numbers on the Contributor Web Client , or when they did this. However, when you have incremental publish turnedon, the program would publish only e.List node 4.

It is important to note that a stabilized application will get the most benefit from the incremental publishing feature. If your application requires significant changes, such as e.List updates or model structural changes, you have to republish all nodes before you go back to using the incremental publish feature.

To accomplish real-time publishing and reporting, you have to configure the following items:

- Configure the Table-only Layout publish container
- Publish all nodes by using the Table-only Layout publish
- Configure incremental publish
- Configure macro incremental publish
- Schedule the macro by using the Scheduling feature in the IBM Cognos Connection

Publishing using the View Layout

The View Layout was the only type of publishing available in IBM Cognos Planning version 7.2 and earlier. IBM Cognos kept this layout for its **backward compatibility**, as many applications and models are dependent on this feature. You can also transmit data from the View Layout published tables to external databases, such as data mart or data warehouse. Some differences between both layouts are noted in the following table:

Table Layout	View Layout
Greater flexibility in reporting on planning data	Intended for backward compatibility
Source to other data mart and source systems	Source to other data mart and source systems
Required by Generate Framework Manager Model Admin Extension	Slower publish performance and inefficient data storage
Employs better naming conventions	

Several tables are created when you run the View Layout publish. Three important types of tables are D-List items tables, hierarchy tables, and D-Cube export tables. You can find explanations of these tables in the previous section. You can create BI Reporting models from these tables to report on planning data. The program also creates user-friendly views of the published cubes (ev_cubename).

The following are the steps to publish the View Layout:

1. Select **Your Application | Development | Application Maintenance | Dimensions for Publish**. The selection of dimension for publish is **optional** in the **View Layout** publish.

2. Execute the GTP.

3. Select **Your Application | Production | Publish | View Layout.**

4. Create a new container, if one has not yet been created. Add this new publish container to the Job system by opening the Job Server Cluster branch and selecting a cluster or job server. Note that you cannot use the Table-only Layout publish container for the View Layout publishing. Read the section on *Storing Published Data* earlier in this chapter.

5. Select the cubes to be published.

6. Select the e.List items to be published.

7. Select the options to be used when publishing.

8. Click on the **Publish** button. The program will create a publish job. You can monitor the publish job by using the **Monitor Console** branch.

Automating publishing jobs

You can automate publishing jobs by using the following macros:

- Publish — View Layout
- Publish — Table Only Layout
- Publish — Incremental Publish

Understanding the impact of changes

Changes to e.List, model, and dimension for publish may range from having no impact, to having a significant impact, on the publishing process, tables, and BI reports. Some of these changes, and their impacts, are noted below.

e.List changes

- When you add e.List items, you have to reselect these added e.List items on the Publish screen. The Publish screen tries to select e.List items that were most recently used in situations where e.List items have been removed.
- When you modify an e.List or D-List hierarchy, for example, adding/removing a hierarchical level, you have to adjust the BI (Framework Manager) models so that the reports do not break.

Model changes

Changes in the model structure, for example by changing D-List items, adding or removing a D-List from a cube, or reordering the dimensions in a cube, can range from having no impact, to having a significant impact. For example, when you delete dimensions in a cube, a reconfiguration or restructuring of publishing parameters and published tables is required. The Framework Manager model, if attached to the publish table, needs to be reconfigured so that the reports do not break.

Dimension for publish changes

When you change the dimension for publish, the program needs to restructure the published tables. The Framework Manager model, if attached to the publish table, needs to be reconfigured so that the reports do not break.

Reporting Planning data using BI Tools

This section explains the different methods that can be used to access planning data for BI reporting purposes.

Real-time reporting options

There are two ways that you can access live data:

- Publish the application as a package to IBM Cognos Connection
- Use Planning Contributor as a data source in Framework Manager

Publish the application as a package to IBM Cognos Connection

You can create a planning package of the ABC application in IBM Cognos Connection by running a GTP and selecting the **Create Planning Package** option. You will then be able to report directly off the planning package by using any of the IBM Cognos Studios. You can also determine the name and location of the package in IBM Cognos Connection in the GTP options in the Application Maintenance folder.

Carry out the following steps to create a planning package using GTP:

1. Select the ABC application in the Contributor Administration Console.
2. Click on the Go to Production icon .
3. The Go to Production wizard opens. Click on **Next**.
4. Select the **Create Planning Package** option. Click on **Next**.

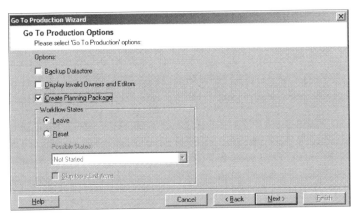

5. Click on **Next** again, and then click on **Finish**.

You can now open one of the IBM Cognos Studios to report directly off of the package. When you open the studio, you will be able to select the planning package for reporting off, as shown:

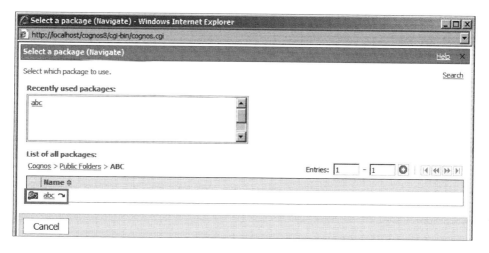

Using IBM Cognos Planning Contributor as a data source in Framework Manager

You can create a Framework Manager model and choose IBM Cognos Planning Contributor as the data source to access the planning data held in the application database. This method is using the PDS server to access the ABC Contributor application database. The following steps show how to access the ABC Contributor application datastore using IBM Cognos Planning Contributor as a data source.

1. Open Framework Manager.
2. Create a new project by clicking on **Create a new project**.
3. Select the language you want to use.
4. The Metadata wizard will appear. Select **Data Source** as shown:

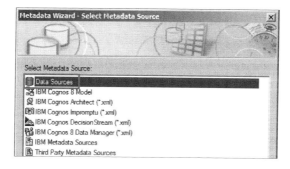

5. Select **Cognos Planning – Contributor** as shown here. Click on **Next**.

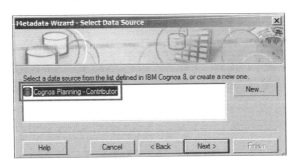

6. The wizard will then show a list of cubes that belong to the ABC application. Select one of the cubes to import and click on **Next**. The cube will be imported.

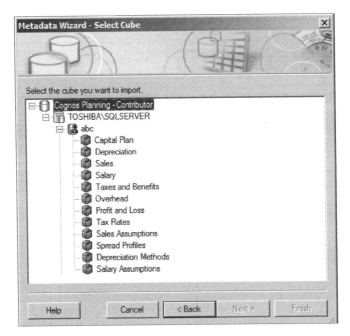

To add additional cubes in Framework Manager, go to the Project View, select the model, click on **Actions**, and then click on **Run Metadata Wizard** to run through the process again and import other cubes into the Framework Manager model.

Reporting from published data

In this section, we explore the option of reporting from Contributor planning data that has been published to a star schema datastore. The publish process essentially collects the planning data stored in XML format in the application datastore and transfers it to a star schema datastore. This planning data is now ready to easily be accessed and reported on by using external reporting tools. There are two ways in which you can report off published planning data:

1. Build a Framework Manager model by running the **Generate Framework Manager Model Admin** extension in the Contributor Administration Console.

2. In Framework Manager, build a Framework Manager model that uses the publish datastore as a data source.

Creating a Framework Manager model using the Framework Manager extension

This method involves creating a Framework Manager model using the Framework Manager model extension in the Contributor Administration Console. When the extension is first run, it will create two models: a base model and a user model. The base model should always be an exact replica of the Contributor model. Whenever changes are made to the planning model, the extension should be run again in the Contributor Administration Console to ensure that the base model is up-to-date. You can synchronize the base and the user model in Framework Manager in order to keep both versions in sync. The user model is where additional adjustments are made in Framework Manager. An example of adjusting the user model may be to add a component to bring the Actuals data into the model.

Before running the extension, there are a number of considerations to address, such as the options to be selected when publishing the application. Additionally, there are considerations to be addressed when selecting the options while running the extension. These considerations are listed in the following section.

Publishing considerations

The Framework Manager extension only works with the Table-only publish Layout. You should consider the following publishing options prior to running the Framework Manager Extension:

- **Dimension for publish**: This is the dimension that forms columns in the publish table that is creating the planning data. Ideally, you can choose a dimension that is static and does not change often. This will ensure that the columns in the publish table are minimally impacted by structural changes in the underlying model.
- **Rollups**: To speed up the publishing process, you can avoid publishing aggregated data, as this data can be aggregated using a reporting tool.
- **e.List items**: Selecting only planner nodes will speed up the process.
- **Zeros**: To speed up the publishing process, zeros should not be published.

The publish process can be automated by using a Publish Table-only Layout contributor macro. The considerations above are all options that can be configured in the publish macro.

Framework Manager considerations

In addition to the publishing options mentioned above, you should also consider the following Framework Manager options that are configured while running the extension:

- **Framework Manager Model location**: This is the location on the server where the model is stored.
- **Package Name**: This is the name of the package in IBM Cognos Connection.
- **Package location**: This is the location of the package in IBM Cognos Connection.
- **Cubes**: The extension allows you to select the cubes that you want to include in the Framework Manager model.
- **Data source query subjects**: This option allows you to select the list types that you want to include in your model. These lists are based on the e.List and D-Lists of the underlying planning model. Selecting the derived or complete hierarchy lists will create a dimensional model. The following list types are available:
  - **Unformatted lists**: These are the unformatted lists stored in the publish table datastore. These tables have an `it_` prefix in the database.
  - **Derived hierarchy lists**: These are simple hierarchy lists stored in the publish table datastore. These lists will contain a simple parent-child relationship. These tables have a `sy_` prefix in the database.
  - **Complete hierarchy lists**: These lists contain more complex calculations, and are stored in the publish table datastore. These tables have a prefix of `cy_` in the database.

Creating the model

To create a Framework Manager model using the extension, perform the following steps:

1. In the Contributor Administration Console, click on the **ABC** application.

2. Navigate to the **Admin Extensions** folder.

3. In the rightmost pane, under **Extensions**, click on **Generate Framework Manager Model**, and click on **Run**, as shown:

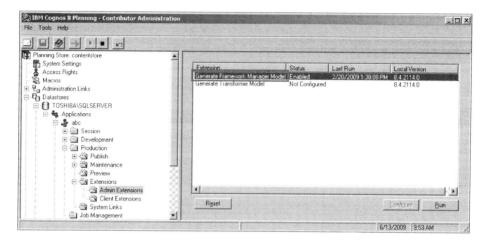

4. The **Generate Framework Manager Model** wizard appears. Click on **Next**.

5. When creating a new model, select the option to **Create a new Framework Manager Model**.

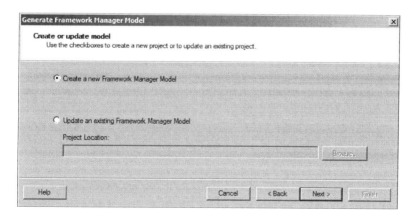

6. On the next screen, enter the location of the Framework Manager model, the package name, and the location of the package in IBM Cognos Connection.

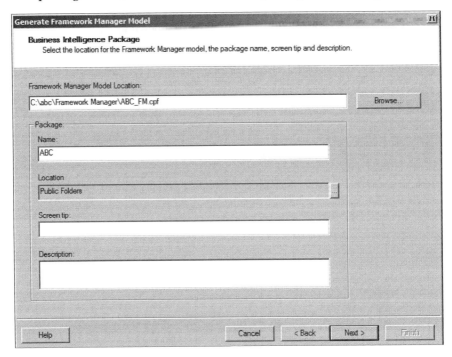

7. On the next screen, select the cubes that you want to report from.

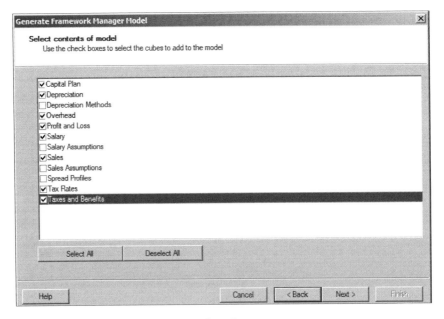

8. On the next screen, select the list types.

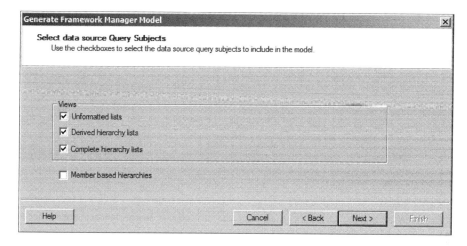

9. Click on **Next** twice, and then click on **Finish** to generate the model.

To generate a report from the package created by running the Framework Manager extension, open one of the reporting studios in IBM Cognos Connection and select the package as the source for reporting.

Exploring the Framework Manager model

Once the Framework Manager model has been created, you can make changes to it in Framework Manager. The changes are made to the user model and not the base model. If any changes are made to the underlying planning model, the base and user models should be synchronized in Framework Manager to keep the user model up-to-date. These changes, and any additional changes made to the model in Framework Manager, can subsequently be published to IBM Cognos Connection.

The Project Viewer in Framework Manager will display two views of the data structure of the model: the Physical view and the Business view. These two views are in the Model folder in the Project Viewer.

The Physical view shows the database query subjects that make up the model, as shown below. The **Cube Tables** folders consist of the query subjects sourced from the dimensions selected for publish. The other folders represent the list types selected for inclusion in the model when the Framework Manager Extension was run.

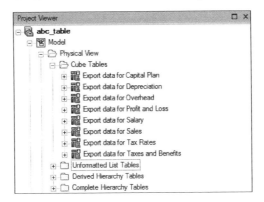

The Business view displays the dimensions and the star shema groupings, as shown:

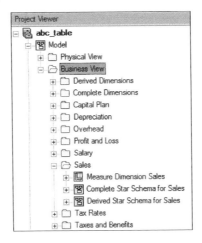

The remaining folders in the Project Viewer show the data sources and packages created when the extension was run, as shown:

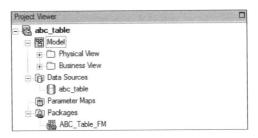

Summary

In this chapter, you have learned how to create publish containers, how the two different publish layouts—the Table-only Layout and the View Layout—work, and the impact on publishing and reporting of changing e.Lists, models, and the dimension for publish. You have also learned how to produce real-time reporting by publishing the application as a package, and by using IBM Cognos Planning Contributor as a data source in Framework Manager. Lastly, you have discovered the process for creating a Framework Manager model by using the Contributor's Framework Manager Extension.

14
Maintaining Analyst Models

In this chapter, we will explain how Analyst macros can be created and used to automate common tasks, such as importing and exporting data. We show how these macros can be scheduled so that the update process can be completely automated. Additionally, we will explain how the Analyst administrator can manage user access to Analyst models by adding users, groups, or roles and assigning them rights to the libraries. Finally, we will briefly explain how to create flowcharts in Manager to illustrate the model data flow, and how to build custom menu screens so that users can easily navigate around the model.

Automating common tasks using Analyst macros and batch jobs

Analyst macros can be used to carry out any repetitive task, and these macros can be executed or scheduled at the click of a button. Typical tasks will usually involve updating data or the structure of the model. Commonly, Analyst macros can be created to import, export, or move D-Cube data around models, and also to update D-Lists. A macro step is added for each step of the process. For instance, imagine that you are required to automate a process where the product dimension of the Revenue D-Cube is updated every morning. Subsequently, some data is loaded into the Revenue D-Cube. At the end of the day, the information from the Revenue cube is exported to a text file. This is a three-step process, as follows:

1. Update the product D-List of the Revenue cube.
2. Load data into the Revenue cube.
3. Export data from the Revenue cube.

A macro can be created for each step of the process, and scheduled to execute when required. We'll revisit this example again later on in the chapter; let's first go through some of the typical Analyst macros that are available to perform these repetitive tasks.

Types of Analyst macros

Analyst macros fall into several different categories. The following is a list of typical macros used to perform some of the more common repetitive tasks and the category that they fall into:

Category	Typical Tasks	Macro Step Name	Description
D-Cube Macros	Open a D-Cube.	@DCubeOpen	This opens a D-Cube or a slice of the D-Cube, depending on the D-List selection in the macro.
	Update a D-Cube.	@DCubeUpdate	This will run all the D-Links going into the D-Cube that are in the Update List of that D-Cube.
	Update a slice of a D-Cube.	@SliceUpdate	This will perform an update to a D-Cube, oneslice at a time. This macro is used for large D-Cubes.
	Zero the contents of a D-Cube. Use this macro with the zero command specification.	@SliceCommand	This will apply a D-Cube command to a D-Cube slice, based on the D-List selection in the macro.
	Export the contents of a D-Cube	@DCubeExport	This will export the contents of a D-Cube or a selection of the D-Cube to a text file or the clip board.
	Publish the contents of a D-Cube	@Publish	This will publish the contents of a D-Cube to a datastore.
D-List Macros	Open a D-List	@DListOpen	This opens a D-List.
	Update a D-List	@DListUpdate	This will update the contents of a D-List based on the Import Link options within that D-List.
	Export a D-List to text file in an e.List file format.	@ExportToe.List	This will export the contents of a D-List to a text file in a format that can be imported as an e.List in the Contributor Administration Console.

Category	Typical Tasks	Macro Step Name	Description
D-Link Macros	Execute a D-Link	@DLinkExecute	This will execute a D-Link specified in the macro.
	Execute a series of D-Links in a specific order.	@DLinkExecute.List	This will execute a series of D-Links in a specific order.
ODBC Macros	Connect to an ODBC source.	@ODBCConnect	This will log on to and open an ODBC source. This macro is typically placed at the beginning of an @ MacroExecute macro that contains a macro that is using this ODBC source.
	Close an ODBC source.	@ODBCClose	This will close an ODBC source. This macro is typically placed at the end of an @MacroExecute macro that contains a macro that using this ODBC source.
Control Macros	Execute a series of macros	@MacroExecute	This will execute a series of macros in a specific order.
	To show a message at macro runtime	@Message	This will show a message at macro run time.
	To add an comment in a macro	@Rem	This will add a comment in a macro but will not be displayed at runtime.

Some D-Cube macro steps require a D-Cube to be open and become the active object in the window before it can be executed. For instance, the D-Cube export macro (@DCubeExport) step will only work if a D-Cube is already open and is the active object. To automate a D-Cube export task, you can create a D-Cube export macro step and precede it with a D-Cube open macro (@DCubeOpen) step. Because the D-Cube needs to be saved and closed, you can add a Close macro step as the final step of the macro, as explained below.

The following is a list of all D-Cube macros that require an active object:

- @DCubeExport
- @DCubeCalculate
- @DCubeClearMask
- @DCubeCommand

- @DCubeDeselect
- @DCubeIncreaseSelect
- @DCubeInput
- @DCubeLoadFormat
- @DCubePage
- @DCubePageId
- @DCubePrint
- @DCubeReselect
- @DCubeTranspose

The Close macro step can be inserted as the final step of the macro to close the D-Cube during runtime without human intervention. Upon closing the D-Cube, the system will automatically prompt for a **yes** or **no** to save the D-Cube before closing it. The macro can be configured to close automatically with a yes (Y) or a no (N) to save the D-Cube. Selecting the **Y** option will ensure that there is no 'Save' prompt at runtime. However, by default, the D-Cube will save and close anyway, so selecting the **N** option will suffice.

Creating and running Analyst macros

Analyst macros can be created in two ways. A macro can be created manually, by using a wizard, or recorded.

Creating a macro using the wizard

Let's manually create a macro that automatically opens the Sales D-Cube:

1. Click on the **New Macro** icon ⊞ on the tool bar. The Macro wizard will appear.

2. Click on **Insert** to add a new macro step. The **Function Selection** box will appear. In the leftmost pane select **D-Cube**, and in the rightmost pane select **DCubeOpen**.

3. Click on **Next**, and the **Edit Parameters** box will appear. Click on the **Edit DCube** button and select the **Sales** D-Cube. Click on **OK**, and then click on **Finish**.

4. Save this macro as **DCubeOpenSales** in the ABC library.

Recording a macro

Macros can be recorded, and then edited if necessary. In this example, we will create a D-Cube export macro that will export the contents of the Sales D-Cube to a comma-delimited file. The exported file will be exported to the export folder of the ABC library, will contain column headings, and will consist of multiple columns, in the following order: Sales Calc, e.List, Stores, Products, and Period. To record the macro:

1. On the menu bar, click on **Tools | Macros | Record.**
2. A box will appear on the screen to notify you that the recording is in process.

3. On the menu bar, click on **File | D-Cube | Open**.
4. Select the ABC library from the libraries list.
5. Select and open the ABC D-Cube.
6. On the menu bar, click on **D-Cube | Export**.
7. A configuration dialog box will be displayed. On the **Export** tab, configure the options as shown in the screenshot below. The selections made will reflect how the format of the exported file appears.

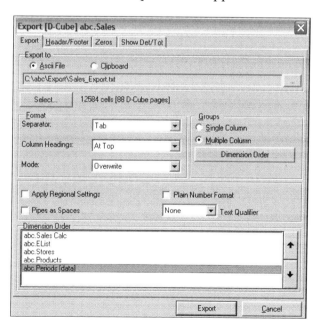

In the export location box, name the file `Sales_Export` and change the format to Comma Delimited (`*csv`).

The dimension order can be changed by clicking on the up and down arrows. This specifies the column order in the exported file.

No other configuration is needed at this point. Click on **Export** to export the Sales D-Cube.

[The process of exporting data from a D-Cube is discussed in more detail in Chapter 6.]

8. Close the Sales D-Cube. Click on **No**, when the **Save** prompt appears.

9. Click on the **Stop Recording** button. A box will appear listing the macro steps recorded for this macro.

10. Let's complete the configuration of this macro. Click on the **@DCubeExport** macro step, and then click on the option **Edit List**. The **List Editor** box will appear. Under **WriteMode=Overwrite**, type **Default=Yes**. This ensures that there is no prompt to override the existing file when the macro is run.

11. Again, click on the **@DCubeExport** step, and then click on the **Edit File** button. Change the path to the following:

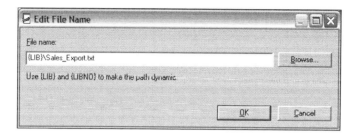

12. This ensures that the macro will export the contents of the D-Cube to the file in the library folder, wherever this folder may exist on the network. This prevents the location from having to be amended, should the library be moved to a new location.

13. Click on the **@Close** macro step, and change the option to **N**. This ensures that a save prompt does not appear when the D-Cube closes during macro run-time.

14. Save the macro as **DCubeExportSales**, in the ABC library.

15. The Macro Steps should appear as follows:

Executing a macro

These macros can be executed by clicking on **Tools | Macro | Run** on the menu bar, and then selecting the macro. Alternatively, click on the macro run icon on the toolbar, and then select the macro to execute.

Automating typical tasks

In this section, we explain how common tasks, such as updating D-Lists and D-Cubes and importing and exporting D-Cube data, can be automated.

Updating a D-Cube structure using macros

Typically, updating the structure of a D-Cube will involve updating the D-Lists of a D-Cube. A DListUpdate macro can be created to run any D-List that is configured as an **Import link**. The **Products** D-List in the ABC library is configured as an Import link, as follows:

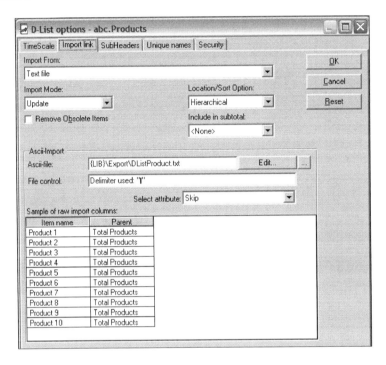

This update can be run manually, or through a DListUpdate macro. This **Import link** will update the Products D-List by importing the hierarchical contents of a text file into the D-List. This macro can be created as follows:

1. Click on the New Macro icon ![icon] on the tool bar. The Macro wizard will appear.

2. Click on **Insert**, to add a new macro step. The **Function Selection** dialog box will appear. In the leftmost pane select **D-List**, and in the rightmost pane select **DListUpdate**.

3. Click on **Next**, and the Edit Parameters dialog box will appear. Click on the **Edit DList** button, and then select the **Products** D-List in the ABC library. Click on **OK**, and then on **Finish**.

4. Save this macro as `DListUpdateProducts` in the ABC library.

Updating D-Cube data using macros

A common way of updating the data contents of a D-Cube from various data sources is to create a DCubeUpdate macro. In this example, we'll create a DCubeUpdate macro to import data from a text file into the Sales Assumption D-Cube, and then move this data into the Sales D-Cube. This macro will contain two D-Cube update macro steps: one to load the data from the text file into the Sales Assumption D-Cube, and the other to move this data to the Sales D-Cube.

This macro will run any D-Links that are in the Update List of the two D-Cubes. Let's look at the update D-Links of the Sales Assumption and the Sales D-Cubes. Open both the Sales Assumption and Sales D-Cubes, on the menu bar, and then click on **D-Cube | D-Links | Update**. An **Update List** box will appear, showing any D-Links targeting this D-Cube that will be run if the DCubeUpdate macro is executed. For example, the Sales D-Cube has one D-Link in the Update List as shown:

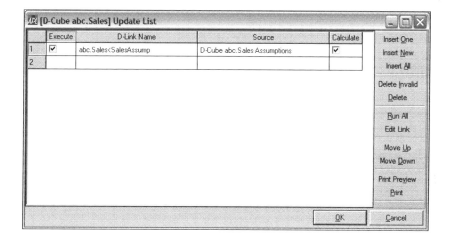

We can use the Macro wizard to create the DCubeUpdate macro, as follows:

1. Click on the **New Macro** icon ![icon] on the toolbar. The Macro wizard will appear.

2. Click on **Insert**, to add a new macro step. The **Function Selection** box will appear. In the leftmost pane select **D-Cube**, and in the rightmost pane, select **DCubeUpdate**.

3. Click on **Next**, and the **Edit Parameters** box will appear. Click on the **Edit DCube** button and select the **Sales Assumption** D-Cube in the ABC library. Click **OK** then click on **Finish**.

4. Repeat steps 2 and 3 for the Sales D-Cube.

5. Save this macro as `DCubeUpdateSales`, in the ABC library.

Importing and exporting data using macros

The process of importing data from or exporting to a D-Cube can be automated by using Analyst macros.

There are numerous methods for importing data into a D-Cube and these were discussed in detail in Chapter 7. Typically, D-Links are used to move data into D-Cubes from various data sources, such as a database, a text file, or another D-Cube. A DLinkExecute macro can be created to automate this import process.

We can use the Macro wizard to create the DLinkExecute macro as follows:

1. Click on the **New Macro** icon ⿻ on the toolbar. The Macro wizard will appear.

2. Click on **Insert** to add a new macro step. The **Function Selection** box will appear. In the leftmost pane select D-Link, and in the rightmost pane select **DLinkExecute**.

3. Click on **Next**, and the Edit Parameters box will appear. Click on the **Edit DLink** button, and then select the **Sales<SalesAssump** D-Link in the ABC library. Click on **OK**, and then **Finish**.

4. Save this macro as DLinkExecute SalesAssumptions, in the ABC library.

Likewise, the DCubeExport macro, created in the 'Record a Macro' example above, can be used to export the data contents of a D-Cube.

Running a series of macros

All the macros created in the above examples automate specific processes. The three processes in the examples being a D-List update, a D-Cube update, and a D-Cube export. We can create a single macro to run all of these processes. This single macro can then be run from a batch file, and scheduled to be executed at any given time. We cover the batch execution and scheduling of Analyst macros in the next section.

In this example, we will create a macro that will perform the following processes:

1. Display a notification that a macro will run and what the automated processes will be.

2. Update the Products D-List by executing the DListUpdateProducts macro.

3. Update the data in the Sales Assumption and Sales D-Cubes by executing the DCubeUpdate macro.

4. Export the data contents of the Sales D-Cube to a text file by executing the DCubeExport macro.

5. Display a notification that the macro has completed successfully.

We can use the Wizard to create this macro, as follows:

1. Click on the **New Macro** icon on the toolbar. The Macro wizard will appear.

2. Click on **Insert** to add a new macro step. The **Function Selection** box will appear. In the leftmost pane select **Control**, and in the rightmost pane select **Message**.

3. The **Edit Parameters** box will appear. In the message box, type: **This macro will update the Products Dimension and the Sales D-cube then export the contents to a text file. Continue?** This message will appear when the macro is first executed.

> The pipe '|' character can be used when you want to continue writing the message on a new line.

4. In the **Buttons** box, select **YN** as shown. This will give the user an option to continue or cancel out from the macro:

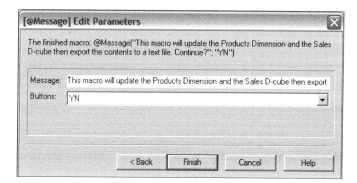

5. Click on **Finish**.

6. This is the first macro step, which runs the first process.

7. Click on **Insert** to add a new macro step. The **Function Selection** box will appear. In the leftmost pane select **Control**, and in the rightmost pane select **MacroExecute**.

8. Click on **Next**, and the **Edit Parameters** box will appear. Click on the **Edit Macro** button and select the DListUpdateProducts macro. Repeat this step for the macros DCubeUpdateSales and DCubeExportSales.

9. Finally, add the last message step by typing in the message **The macro has successfully completed!** In the **Buttons** box, select **O**. This allows the user to close the message when the macro is complete by clicking on **OK**.

10. Save this macro as `UpdateSalesAll`, in the ABC library. The macro steps should appear as they do in the following screenshot:

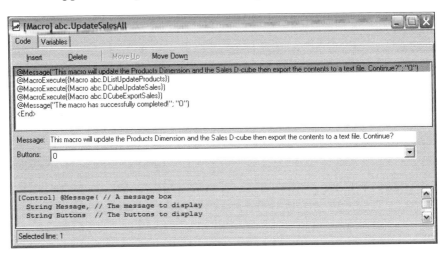

Let's test the macro by clicking the macro run icon  on the toolbar, and then selecting the UpdateSalesAll macro. When the macro is executed, the following message pops up:

11. Click **OK**.

The macro will continue to execute. On completion, a message will pop up saying that the macro has completed, as follows:

Scheduling Analyst macros

Commonly, macros or batch jobs can be scheduled and executed from the command line by using the `CepBatch.exe` batch utility program. A batch job runs an Analyst macro, and is created using the Analyst Batch Utility wizard. Either the macro or the batch job can be executed from the command line and scheduled using a scheduling tool.

Creating a batch job using the Analyst batch utility wizard

Let's create a batch job that can be scheduled to run the UpdateSalesAll macro.

From the menu bar:

1. Click on **Tools | Batch Utility Wizard.**

2. Click on **Next**.

3. On the Create or modify a batch job screen, select the option to **create a new batch job**.

4. Click on **Next**.

5. On the select a macro screen, make the following selections:

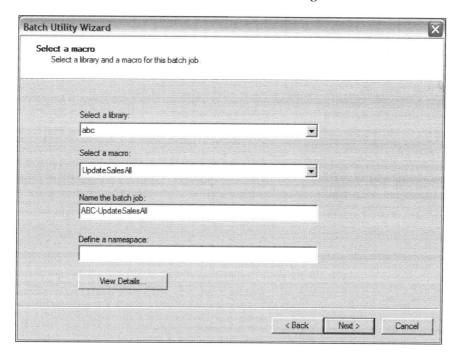

When you log on to IBM Cognos Connection, you may have to select a namespace. This will happen if your environment uses more than one namespace. If this is the case, then in the batch utility wizard, specify the namespace that you log on to, in the **Define a namespace** box, so that the batch jobs can automatically be executed. Alternatively, if your environment has only one namespace, you can leave the **Define a namespace** box blank.

6. Click on **Next** and then select a location for the log files.

7. Click on **Next**.

8. Confirm all of the information on the **Completing the Batch Utility Wizard** screen.

9. Select the **Run the batch job on finish** option, to test the batch job.

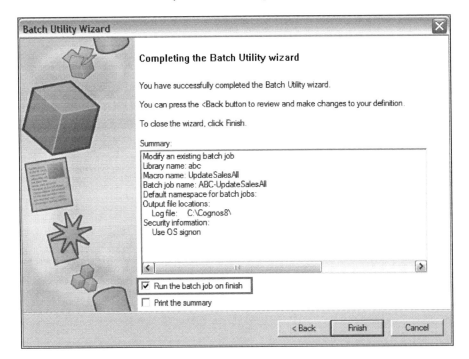

10. Click on **Finish**.

11. The batch job will run, and notify you when it has completed.

When executing Analyst macros from a batch file, always ensure that there are no @Message macro steps that prompt for a response from the user, as this will cause the macro to hang.

Scheduling a batch job

A batch job can be scheduled by creating a batch file that contains the macro parameters of the batch job. Let's create a batch file for the UpdateSalesAll batch job created in the previous example.

1. Click on **Tools | Batch Utility Wizard**.

2. Click on **Next**.

3. On the Modify a batch job screen, select the option to **Modify or delete an existing batch job**.

4. Select the ABC library and the UpdateSalesAll batch job.

5. Click on **Next**, and then **Next** again, until you reach the Completing the batch utility wizard screen. On this screen, ensure that the **Run the batch job on finish** option is unchecked.

6. Click on **Finish**.

7. The command line for this batch job will be copied to the Windows clipboard, as shown:

8. Create a batch file that can be scheduled, by opening Notepad and pasting the clipboard contents into it. The command line for this batch job will be

   ```
   C:\PROGRA~1\cognos\c8\bin\CepBatch.exe -b -l "ABC-UpdateSalesAll"
   ```

9. Save the file as a batch file (*.bat). A scheduling tool, such as Windows Scheduler can be used to execute this batch file.

Analyst macros are generally executed in Analyst or by using a batch file. However, Contributor macros can also be created to execute Analyst macros. This option is explained in more detail in Chapter 15.

Administering libraries and users

In this section, we will explain how System Administrators can assign user access to Analyst libraries.

Managing access to Analyst libraries

System administrators assign access to a library by adding users, groups, or roles, and assigning them rights.

Security is configured in IBM Cognos Connection. The topic of adding users, groups, and roles in IBM Cognos Connection is beyond the scope of this book. In this section, we will explain how to assign the users access to libraries from groups set up in IBM Cognos Connection.

In the following example, there are two users who require access to the ABC Analyst library. The first user, Tom, needs WRITE access to the library so that he can add and make changes to it. Sarah only needs READ access so that she can access and view the D-Cube contents of the library. Tom is a member of a group called ABC Analyst Write. To assign Tom access to the ABC library, we add this group to Analyst and assign this group Write access to the ABC library. Sarah is a member of the group ABC Analyst Read. To assign Sarah access to the ABC library, we add this group to Analyst and assign this group Read access to the library.

The following steps are performed to assign these two users access to the ABC library.

1. From the menu, click on **File | Administration | Maintain Libraries and Users**.
2. Click on the **Users, Groups and Roles** tab.
3. Click on **Add**.

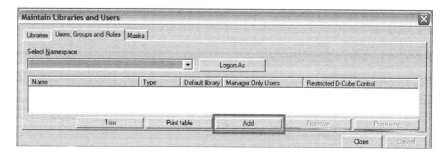

4. In this example, we will use the default IBM Cognos Namespace. The IBM Cognos Namepace will be displayed, as shown:

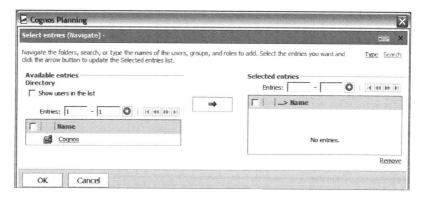

5. Click on the IBM Cognos Namespace to view the groups, roles, and users. Select the two groups, **ABC Analyst Write** and **ABC Analyst Read**. Click on the green arrow to move the two groups to the **Selected entries** box. Click on **OK**.

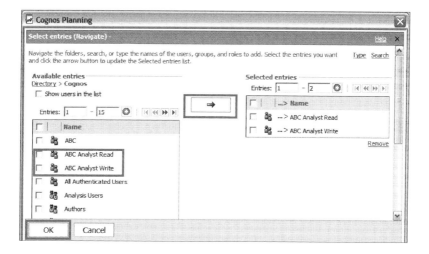

The two groups have now been added to Analyst.

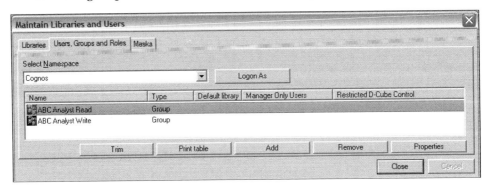

6. Now we will assign the two groups rights to the ABC library. Click on the **Libraries** tab, and then select the ABC library.

7. Click on **Properties**. The properties box for the ABC library will open.

8. Select the **Access** tab, and then click on **Add**, to add the two groups.

9. Select the **ABC Analyst Read** group, and assign it **Read Access** and then click on **OK**, as shown below:

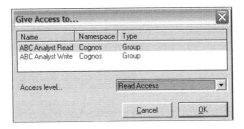

10. In the library properties box, click on the **Access** tab, and then click on **Add**. Select the ABC Analyst Write box, and assign it Write access. Click on **OK**. The ABC library now has two groups assigned to it. The **ABC Analyst Read** group has **Read Access**, and the ABC Analyst Write group has **Write Access**, as shown below:

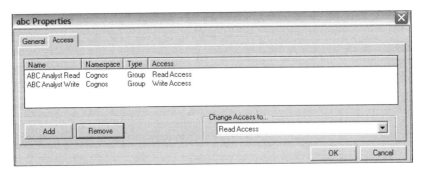

The following access can be assigned to libraries in Analyst.

Access Level	Description
Read	The user can only view and copy Analyst objects. The user can view the data of a D-Cube. The user cannot make or save changes to the original D-Cube. To make changes to the data of the D-Cube, the user must save a copy of the D-Cube.
Write	The user can view and save changes to Analyst objects.
Control	The user has Read and Write access to Analyst objects, and can assign access to Analyst objects to other users.

Managing Analyst objects

In this section, we will explain how you can use the **Library Functions** box to locate, open, run, copy, print, and delete Analyst objects such as D-Lists, D-Cubes, and Macros. To open the **Library Functions** screen, click on **File | Library Functions** from the menu. The following screen will be displayed:

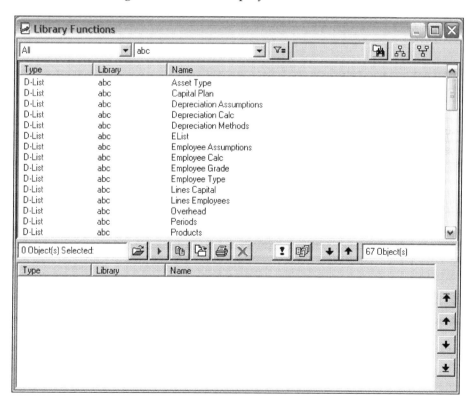

The **Library Functions** screen has two drop-down boxes. The first drop-down box shows a list of object types, such as D-Cube or D-List. The second drop-down box shows a list of libraries. It also contains a series of buttons that can be used to process specific object management tasks. The following is a list of these buttons, and a description of what processes can be performed by clicking them:

Icon	Name	Description
	Filter	This can be used to create a filter when locating or selecting objects. The * symbol can be used as a wildcard. The = sign can be used to find objects that match the exact criteria. Alternatively, use < > to locate objects that do not match the criteria entered.
	Find	This can be used to locate objects in a library. Type in the name of an object and it will be highlighted in the top pane.
	Show Dependents	This will show what objects are being used by the selected object. If a D-Cube is selected, clicking on this icon will display the D-Lists that make up this D-Cube. If a D-List is selected, any saved formats used by this D-List will be highlighted.
	Show Precedents	This will show the objects that use the selected object. If a D-Cube is selected, clicking on this button will display any D-Links that use this D-Cube as a source or target. If a D-list is selected, any D-Cubes or D-links that use this D-List will be highlighted.
	Open	This will open any selected objects. A single object or a selection of objects can be opened at once.
	Run	This will execute selected objects, such as D-Links and macros.
	Copy	This will copy selected objects to the same library, or to a different library, depending on the parameters entered. As library object names are unique, any objects copied to the same library will require a new name.
	Move or rename	This will move objects to a different library, using the same name or a different name. Additionally, this button can be clicked to rename objects.
	Print	This will print miscellaneous information about selected objects and object usage. For instance, if a D-Cube is selected, you can print information about the components of the D-Cube, such as the D-Lists and any usage information such as D-Links that use this D-Cube.

Icon	Name	Description
✕	Delete	This will delete objects if they are not being used anywhere else. For instance, if you want to delete a D-Cube that is part of a D-Cube update macro, the system will not let you. You will first have to remove the D-Cube from the macro, or delete the macro, before deleting the D-Cube.
!	Check Integrity	This will check to see if a library is self-contained or if other objects from other libraries are required for it to work. For instance, a D-Cube may contain a D-List that is stored in another library. Using the Check Integrity feature on a library or a selection of objects will list any external library objects needed for these objects to function. This feature should be used prior to moving or copying libraries to a different server location. For example, consider a library that has a D-Cube that contains a D-List stored in another library. T hen migrate the library that contains the D-Cube from one environment to another, where each environment has a separate Analyst instance. If you attempt to open the D-Cube in the new environment, it will not open because it cannot find the external D-List.
(icon)	Copy Wizard	The Copy Wizard can be used to copy a library, a set of libraries that are linked together, or a selection of library objects. The Copy Wizard section below explains some of the other tasks that can be performed by using the wizard.
↓	Move object into the selection box (the bottom pane)	This will move the highlighted objects in the top pane to the selection box.
↑	Move object out of the selection box	This will move objects out of the selection box.
⤒ ↑ ↓ ⤓	These four arrows are used to move objects to the top of a list, one place up a list, one place down a list or to the bottom of the list	These arrows are used to move highlighted objects up or down in the selection box.

Other maintenance tasks

The following sections describe additional maintenance tasks that can be performed through the **Library Functions** screen.

Highlighting unused objects

You can select any library objects that are not being used by other objects. This functionality is generally used for removing obsolete objects from a library. Although the objects highlighted are not being used by other objects, this does not necessarily mean that they are not needed. Objects such as macros, D-Links, or even D-Cubes that are not being used by other objects will show up, but this does not mean they are obsolete. It is important to check each selected object's role in the model before deleting them. To locate these objects, go to **File | Library Functions**, select a library in the top pane, right-click on it, and select **Highlight unused objects** from the context menu, as shown:

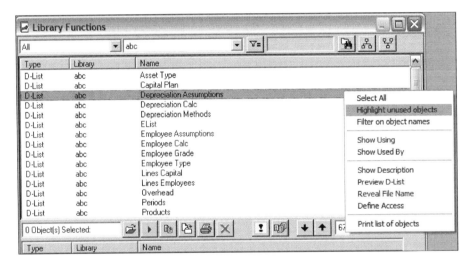

Previewing D-List

You can view the contents of a D-List without opening it. Select the D-List in the **Library Functions** screen, right-click on it, and then select **Preview D-List** from the context menu, to view its contents.

Reveal File Name

You can view the file name of an object, and its location on the server. Select the D-List in the **Library Functions** screen, right–click on it, and then select **Reveal File Name**. A dialog box will appear showing the filename and its location on the server.

Defining Access

You can grant users access to specific library objects, such as D-Cubes. Open the **Library Functions** screen, select an object such as a D-List or a D-Cube, and right-click on it to bring up the list of menu options. Select the **Define Access** option. The **Access to object...** dialog box will appear. Click on **Add** to add a group or role, and use the drop-down box to assign the level of access for this group to the object.

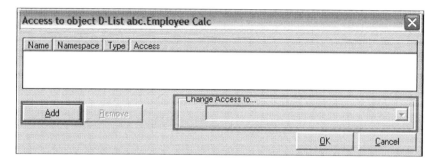

Using the Copy Wizard to Copy Libraries

The following is a list of some of the common tasks that can be performed using the Copy Wizard:

1. Make a copy or multiple copies of a single library.

2. Make a copy or multiple copies of a set of libraries.

3. Make a copy of a set of libraries, maintaining the references between the libraries.

4. Merge two libraries into a single library.

Creating menus and flowcharts using Manager

A detailed explanation of Manager is beyond the scope of this book. In this section, we discuss some of the functionality of this program. Manager is used to visually display the Analyst model workflow and to create simple user menus for easy navigation of the model. You can create flowcharts, menu, tables, and graphs in Manager, based on the underlying model in Analyst.

The following is a flowchart of the ABC Company model. This flowchart is based on the underlying Analyst model, and shows how all of the D-Cubes are connected to each other through the D-Links. The flowchart is also used as a menu and contains a button called **Update All** that runs all of the update processes defined in the model.

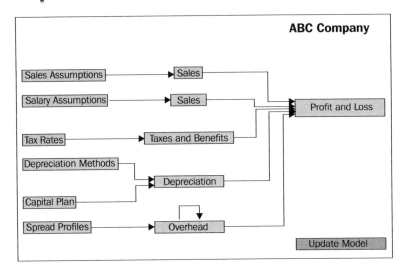

The following is a summarized description of the menu items in Manager:

Menu Item	Description
File	Create new reports. Open, save and close reports. Configure the reports, such as making background changes.
Edit	Copy, edit, delete, and position items such as buttons, text boxes, and arrows on a report.
D-Cube	Open D-Cubes and D-Links. Run macros and open Analyst.
Table	Edit and format tables.
Graph	Edit and format graphs.
Text	Create a text boxe and format text box borders and fonts. Link text boxes to D-Cubes, D-Links, macros, and other reports , in order to create a user menu.
Arrow	Create, format, and position arrows.
Bitmap	Import and format bitmap images. Link bitmap images to Analyst objects such as macros.
FlowChart	Create new buttons, and control the behavior of actions when these buttons are clicked.
Window	Minimize or refresh a window.
Help	Display the help contents.

Summary

In this chapter, you learned how to completely automate common tasks such as importing and exporting data from the model. You also learned how to give users rights to Analyst libraries and also to the objects contained in these libraries. Finally, you were given an introduction to how you can build effective flowcharts in order to visually demonstrate the workflow of a model, and also how you can build menu screens so that users can easily navigate around a model.

15

Maintaining Contributor Applications

This chapter explains how to automate typical administrative tasks in the Contributor Administration Console using macros. The chapter also explains how to grant access to other Contributor administrators to perform administrative tasks. Finally, we explore the nature of Contributor jobs and the role and management of job clusters and job servers. By the end of this chapter, you will have learned the following:

- How to create macros to automate repetitive tasks such as import and publish of data

- How to schedule these macros to run in IBM Cognos Connection or from a batch file

- How to set up rights for specific administrative functions so that Contributor Administrators can perform tasks such as Go to Production

- The nature of jobs and how they can be monitored

- How to create and manage job clusters and servers

Automating tasks using Contributor macros

Contributor macros can be used to automate repetitive tasks such as synchronization and GTP of a model, import of data into a contributor application and publish of data. Contributor macros typically consist of a number of macro steps. For example, consider that we need to update a contributor application on a daily basis. The steps involved may consist of updating the D-Lists of a D-Cube, synchronizing the D-List changes made in Analyst with the contributor application, updating the e.List of the application and finally running a GTP to make these changes available to on the Web.

A macro containing these macro steps can be built to automate this process and may contain the following steps:

Step	Macro step name	Description
1.	Execute Analyst Macro	This macro step may execute an Analyst macro that updates D-Lists within the Analyst model.
2.	Synchronize	This macro step will synchronize the application with the latest D-List changes made in the underlying Analyst model.
3.	Import e.List	Imagine that an e.List text file is generated on a daily basis. This macro step will import this e.List into the application.
4.	Go to Production	This macro step will make the changes available to the users on the Web.

In this section, we will explain how to automate these processes by creating and running macros. We begin by explaining how the creation and execution of macros are controlled using macro security. We will then familiarize ourselves with some of the common macros used and how these macros are created and executed manually. Finally, we describe how these macros can be scheduled using batch files and through IBM Cognos Connection.

Types of Contributor macros

Contributor macros can be categorized according to the nature of the process being automated. The following is a list of typical macros used to perform some of the more common administrative tasks.

Process	Typical tasks	Macro name	Description
Updating a Contributor application	Execute an Analyst Macro	Execute Analyst macro	This macro will execute an Analyst macro. When updating contributor applications, typical analyst macros may consist of D-List updates.
	Synchronize an application	Synchronize	This macro will run a synchronization process for an application.
	Import an access table	Import Access Table	This macro will import an access table into an application from a file.
	Import e.List and Rights to an application from a file	Import e.List	This macro will import e.List into an application from a file.
		Import Rights	This macro will import rights into an application from a file.
	Run a Go to Production	Go to Production	This macro will run a Go to Production for an application.

Process	Typical tasks	Macro name	Description
Working with data	Import data to an application	Upload an Import File	This macro will load data into an import table for a cube from a text file.
		Prepare Import	This macro will run the Prepare Import process.
	Publish data from an application	Publish – View Layout	This macro will publish application data to a view publish container.
		Publish – Table Layout	This macro will publish application data to a publish container in table layout form.
		Publish – Incremental Publish	This macro will publish any e.List nodes that contain changed data for any cubes within an application.
	Move data between or within applications	Execute an Administrator Link	This macro will execute an Administration link.
Other Tasks	Run a Contributor macro	Execute Macro	This macro will execute another Contributor macro.

Macro security

Users have to be granted rights in the Contributor Administration Console to create, edit, delete, transfer, and execute Contributor macros. Users are first granted rights to create macros. Subsequently, users are then granted rights to edit, delete, execute, and transfer macro steps to and from specific macros.

Rights to create macros are granted at the **Planning Administration Domain** (PAD) level and not at the macro level. Access Rights are explained in depth later on in this chapter.

When a macro is first created by a user, this user by default has all the rights associated with this macro. They are able to edit, delete, execute, and transfer macro steps to and from the macro. Other users' rights to this macro are dependent on the rights granted to them by the Planning Rights Administrator. Only members of the Planning Rights Administrator group can grant or revoke Access Rights to macros.

Creating, editing, and running Contributor macros

In this section, we describe how you can create, edit, and run Contributor macros. We also describe how macro steps can be copied be transferring to new or other macros.

Creating, executing, and editing macros

Creating a macro is a two step process. The first step is to create the macro and the second step is to create and add macro steps to the macro. Let's create a Contributor macro to update the Products D-List in the ABC library. To do this, we can create a Contributor macro to run the DListUpdateProducts Analyst macro. As we are running an Analyst macro, we will need to create the Execute Analyst macro step and ask it to run the DListUpdateProducts Analyst macro.

To create the new macro:

1. In the **Contributor Administration** Console, click on **Macros**.

2. Click on **New**.

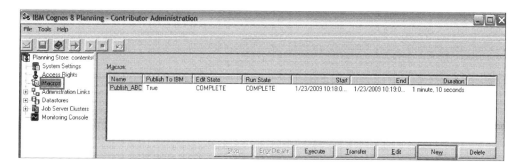

3. Type in the **Macro Name** in the **Macro Properties** box.

4. Select the **Publish to IBM Cognos Connection** checkbox if you want to publish this macro to IBM Cognos Connection. This will allow you to run and schedule macros from IBM Cognos Connection.

5. Click on **OK**. At this point the macro has been created but the edit state for the macro will display **Incomplete**. This means that further configuration to the macro is necessary and that the macro is not ready to be executed.

6. We add the macro step when the **Select new macro step type** box appears. Navigate to and select the **Execute Analyst Macro** step.

7. Click on **OK**.

8. A box appears allowing you to configure the Execute Analyst macro step.

   ° Type in the following name for the macro step: **Execute Analyst Macro Update Products D-List**.

   ° In the **Analyst Macro** section, click on the ellipsis. A box will appear allowing you to select the analyst macro. Select the ABC library and the **DListUpdateProducts** macro.

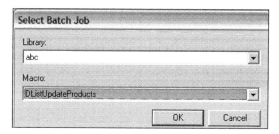

   ° Click on **OK**.

9. In the configuration box, validate the macro and click on **OK**. Validating the macro will ensure the configuration is valid.

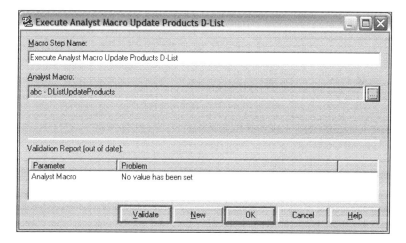

If you highlight the macro in the **Macro** screen, you will see the macro steps that belong to that macro.

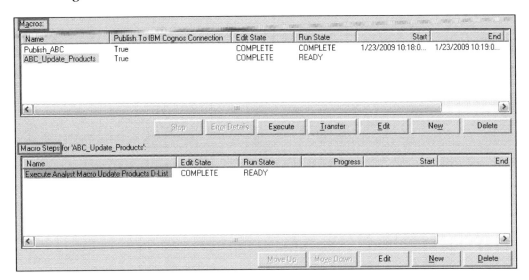

Executing a macro

To run the macro manually in the Contributor Administration Console, highlight the macro and click on **Execute**. A box will appear informing you that the macro is now running.

You can monitor the status of the macro by looking at the **Run State** column for that macro in the top pane. When the macro has finished, the **Run State** will say **COMPLETE**. If the macro fails for some reason, it will say **CANCELLED**. Additionally, this information and macro progress can be viewed for each macro step of the macro in the bottom pane.

Editing a macro

You can change the name of macros or macro steps by highlighting them and clicking on the **Edit** button.

Deleting a macro

Macros and macro steps can be removed by highlighting them and clicking on the **Delete** button.

Transferring macros and macro steps

You can create copies of macros or back up macros by transferring macros or macro steps to new or other macros by performing the following steps:

1. In the **Contributor Administration** Console, click on **Macros**.
2. Highlight the **ABC_Update_Products** macro.
3. Click on **Transfer**.
4. The **Transfer Macro Steps** box will appear for the **ABC_Update_Products** macro.

This box allows the following options:

1. **Direction**: This controls whether you copy macro steps to or from the **ABC_Update_Products** macro:

     ° **From**: Copy macro steps from the **ABC_Update_Products** macro. If this is selected, the options appear as follows:

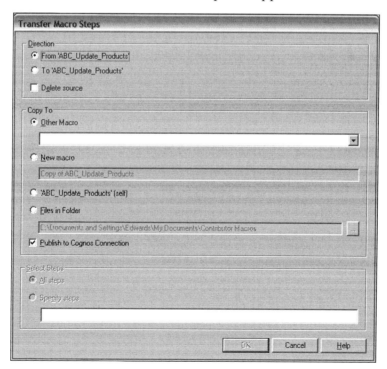

○ **To**: Copy macro steps to the **ABC_Update_Products** macro. If this is selected, the following options are available:

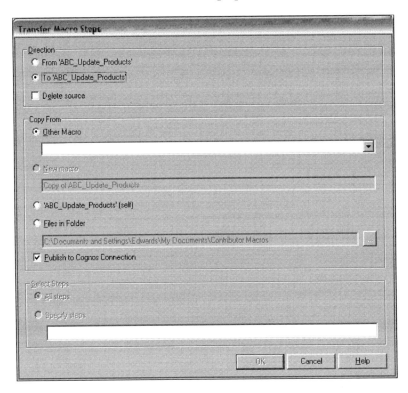

○ **Delete source**: Delete the macro steps from the source macro when the transfer is complete.

2. **Copy From**: Here you specify the location where you copy the macro steps from:

   ○ **Other Macro**: You can select other existing macros.

   ○ **New macro**: You can copy the macro steps to a new macro.

   ○ **Self**: You can copy the steps to the same macro.

   ○ **Files in Folder**: You can export the macro steps to a file that can be imported at a later date. This method is useful for back up individual macros.

3. **Select Steps**: Individual steps can be selected and transferred.

Automating typical tasks

In this section, we will explore macros that are used by companies everyday to automate typical administrative tasks such as updating applications, importing data, and publishing data.

Updating a Contributor application

The following steps are typically carried out to update an application:

1. Update the underlying Analyst model.
2. Update the Contributor application with the changes made in Analyst by synchronizing the application.
3. Import the updated e.List into the application.
4. Import data into the application.
5. Run a GTP on the application to make the changes and updated data available to users through the Web.

All these steps can be automated as macro steps and placed in a single macro. This macro can then be executed from the Contributor Administration Console or even scheduled on a periodic basis.

Let's create a macro that contains all these steps.

To create a new macro:

1. Click on **Macros**.
2. Click on **New**.
3. Give the macro the name **Update ABC Application** and publish it to IBM Cognos Connection so that we can schedule it.
4. When the list of macro steps appears, click on **Cancel**. We will add the steps at a later date.

Now let's add the macro steps to the macro.

1. **Update Analyst Model**: We want to automate the process that updates the ABC Products D-List. We have already created a contributor macro to perform this task, so all we need to do is create a macro step to execute this macro. Let's add this step to the macro:
    ○ Highlight the ABC Update Application macro.
    ○ In the lower pane, click on **New**.
    ○ In the **Select new macro step type** box, select **Execute Macro**.

- ○ Configure this macro step as below, give it the name **Execute Macro ABC Update Products** and select the **ABC_Update_ Products** Contributor macro as displayed here:

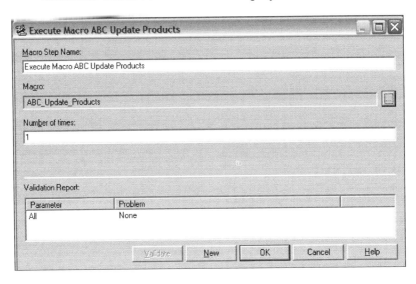

- ○ Click on **OK**.

2. **Synchronize the application**: We now want to update the application with the changes made in the underlying Analyst model by synchronizing the application. We can do this by adding the Synchronize macro step:

- ○ Highlight the ABC Update Application macro.
- ○ In the bottom pane, click on **New**.
- ○ In the **Select new macro step type** box, select **Synchronize**.
- ○ Configure this macro step as shown in the following screenshot; give it the name **Synchronize ABC**. To select the ABC application, click on the ellipsis and navigate to and select the ABC application under the contributor datastore instance.

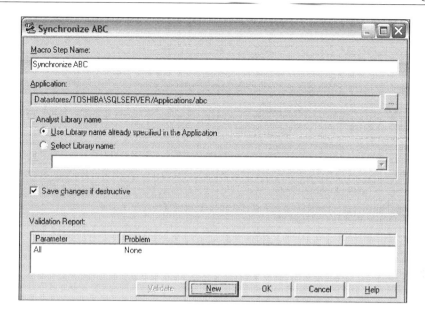

- ° Click on **OK**.

A destructive synchronize occurs when D-Cube dimensions have been added, deleted, substituted, or reordered, and when D-List items have been deleted or changed to a calculation. This kind of model change can result in data loss. During a manual synchronize, you can simply not save the changes and prevent possible data loss during a destructive synchronize. When synchronizing using a macro, you can uncheck the **Save changes if destructive** option if you do not want data loss to occur during a destructive synchronize.

3. **Import the updated e.List**: We now want to update the application with the latest e.List by importing it from a file:

   - ° Highlight the ABC Update Application macro.
   - ° In the bottom pane, click on **New**.
   - ° In the **Select new macro step type** box, select **Import e.List**.
   - ° Configure this macro step as below:
     - i. **Macro Step Name**: Import e.List.
     - ii. **Application**: ABC.
     - iii. **e.List path**: Type in the location of the e.List file.
     - iv. **Trim leading and trailing whitespace**: Leave unchecked. You can check this box if the source data contains leading and trailing whitespace which in good practice should not be the case.

    v.   **First row is heading**: Check this if the file has column names.

    vi.   **Delete undefined items**: Check if you want to delete entries in the existing e.List that are not in the file. Any e.List items that are deleted during the import will result in data loss.

    vii.   **File type**: Select either text file or Excel file. Check the option **Attempt to determine delimiter based on file extension**.

    viii.   **Errors and Warnings**: Check **Stop if warnings or errors returned from import** if you want the macro to fail if there are any import errors.

    ix.   Click on **Validate**.

    x.   Click on **OK**.

4. **Import data into the application**: We now want to load sales data into the application from a text file. We can do this using the two macro steps, Upload an Import File and Prepare Import.

    ○   Upload an Import File:

      i.   Highlight the ABC Update Application macro.

      ii.   In the bottom pane, click on **New**.

      iii.   In the **Select new macro step type** box, select **Upload an Import File**.

      ix.   Configure this macro step as follows:

        1.   **Macro Step Name**: Give it the name **Upload Import Sales File**.

        2.   **Application**: Select the ABC application by clicking on the ellipsis and navigate to and select the ABC application under the contributor datastore instance.

        3.   **File to Upload**: Type in the path location of the Sales import text file.

        4.   **Target Cube Name**: Use the ellipsis to select the Sales cube.

        5.   **Remove existing data in import table**: Check this option if you want to delete existing data preloaded to the Import table. If you leave this option unchecked, data that contains matching dimension items will replace existing preloaded data in the import table. Data with unmatched hierarchies previously loaded to the import table will remain.

        6.   Click on **Validate**.

        7.   Click on **OK**.

- ° Prepare Import:

  i. Highlight the ABC Update Application macro.

  ii. In the bottom pane, click on **New**.

  iii. In the **Select new macro step type** box, select **Prepare Import**.

  iv. Configure this macro step as below; give it the name **Prepare Import Sales**. To select the ABC application, click the ellipsis and navigate to and select the ABC application under the contributor datastore instance.

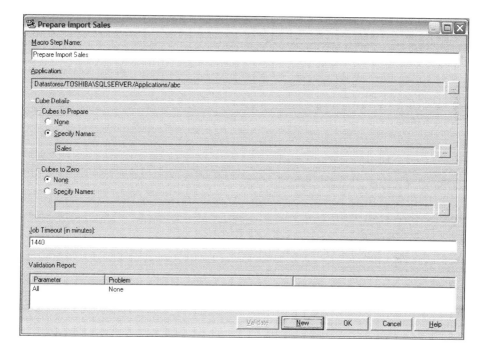

  v. Click on **Validate**.

  vi. Click on **OK**.

5. **Run a Go to Production for the application**: We now want to make these application changes and updated data available to users through the Web by running a Go to Production:

   - ° Highlight the ABC Update Application macro.

   - ° In the bottom pane, click on **New**.

   - ° In the **Select new macro step type** box, select **Go to Production**.

- ° Configure this macro step as below; give it the name **Go to Production**. To select the ABC application, click the ellipsis and navigate to and select the ABC application under the contributor datastore instance.

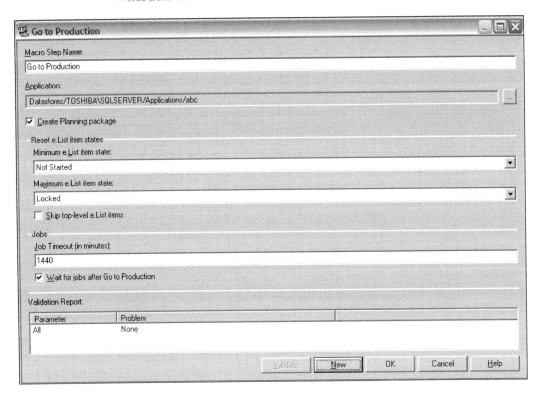

- ° Click on **Validate**.
- ° Click on **OK**.

Now we can update the application by clicking on a single button. Run the **Update ABC Application** macro by highlighting it and clicking on **Execute**.

You can monitor the progress of each macro step by highlighting the macro and watching the lower pane.

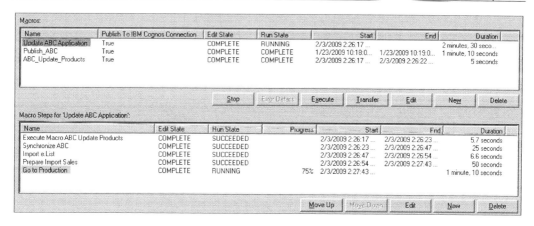

The preceding screenshot displays the run state of all the macro steps and the progress of any steps that are currently running. This tells us that the macro has been running for **2 minutes** and **30 seconds** and that the first four steps have completed successfully. It also tells us that the **Go to Production** step is 75% complete.

Publishing data from a Contributor application

We can automate the process of publishing data from a Contributor application by using one of the publish macro steps available to us in the Contributor Administration Console. Let's create a macro that automates the process of publishing data from a Contributor application to a publish table. We perform the following steps to create the macro:

1. Click on **Macros**.
2. Click on **New**.
3. Check the option to publish to IBM Cognos Connection.
4. Click on **OK.**
5. When the **Select new macro step type** box appears, select the macro step **Publish – Table Only Layout.**
6. The following configuration can be used to publish all the cubes from the ABC model:
    ○ **Macro Step Name**: Enter the name of the macro. In our example, we put **Publish ABC Company**.
    ○ **Select Publish Container**: Select the publish container to publish the data to.

- **Use persisted parameters for all settings**: Checking this ensures that the same parameters for all settings are used each time the macro step is executed.
- **Data Options**.
  i. Create columns with data types based on the **Dimension for publish**: You can ascertain the data types published based on the **Dimension for publish** option selected.
  ii. Only create the following columns: You can restrict the columns being published based on the **Dimension for publish** by selecting specific data types such as numeric, text values, formatted values as text and date values.
- **Include rollups**: You can check this option if you want to include calculated items. Unchecking this option means no calculated items are published to the table.
- **Include zero or blank values**: Check this option if you want to publish zero or blank values. This will increase publishing time.
- **Prefix column names with data type**: Only check this option if you would like to prefix the column name with the data type.
- **Translation to Publish**: You can select a translation to publish.
- **Table Options**: You can publish user annotations, audit annotations, and attached documents.
- **Cubes to Publish**: Select which cubes you want to publish.
- **e.List items to Publish**: Select if you want to publish all e.List items, only planner nodes, or any specific nodes.

Running and scheduling Contributor macros

Some of the more common ways in which the Contributor macros can be executed are as follows:

- They can be run manually from the Contributor Administration Console
- They can be run and scheduled to run in IBM Cognos Connection
- They can be run from IBM Cognos 8 event
- They can be run from a batch file

Some of the more common ways that they can be scheduled are in IBM Cognos Connection and by scheduling the execution of batch files.

Scheduling Contributor macros in IBM Cognos Connection

Before macros can be executed in IBM Cognos Connection, they must be published to IBM Cognos Connection. Macros are published to IBM Cognos Connection when they are created. Once published, they can be run and scheduled in the following way:

1. Open IBM Cognos Connection.

2. On the welcome page under the **Administration** section, click on the IBM Cognos content icon ⚒.

3. Click on the **Configuration** tab.

4. Click on the **Content Administration**.

5. Click on **Planning** and then **Macros** to view the Contributor macros that have been published to IBM Cognos Connection. The following screenshot displays the ABC macros available to run or schedule.

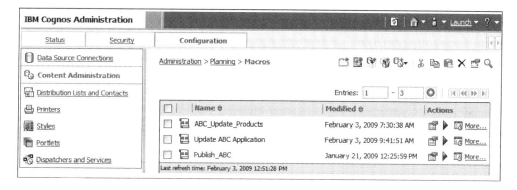

6. To run the macro:

    °   Check the box against the macro that you want to execute and click on the **Run** icon ▶ under **Actions**.

    °   You have the option to run the macro now or at a later date.

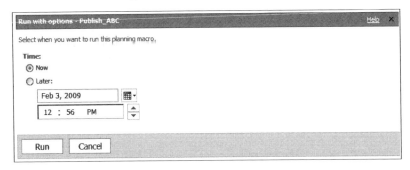

7. To schedule the macro:

    °   Check the box against the macro that you want to execute and click the **Schedule Macro Name** 📇 icon under **Actions**.

    °   A box will appear allowing you to schedule the macro to run using a variety of options.

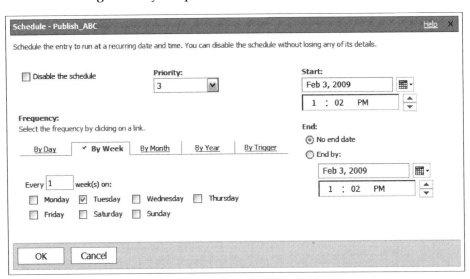

If you would like to schedule a series of macros, it may be easier to create a single job in IBM Cognos Connection to run a series of published contributor macros. We can do this as follows:

1. Open IBM Cognos Connection.

2. On the welcome page under the **Administration** section, click on the **My Home** icon 🏠.

3. Click on the **New Job** icon 🗔 as shown:

4. The **New Job** wizard appears. Type in a name for the job and select **My Folders** for the location of the job (your Contributor Administrator will notify you where to save jobs in IBM Cognos Connection). Click on **Next**.

5. To add Contributor macros, click on **Add** and navigate to the contributor macros located in the location **Cognos | Administration | Planning | Macros** and select the macros to add moving them across using the green arrow. You can modify the sequence of macros, run the macros all at once or sequentially, and allow macros to continue should a predecessor macro fail.

6. Click on **OK** and **Save Only** to save the job. To schedule the job, check the box against the job that you want to execute and click on the **Schedule Job Name** 📋 icon under **Actions**.

7. Use the configuration box to schedule the job.

Scheduling Contributor macros using batch files

Contributor macros can be scheduled using batch files and the epMacroExecutor.exe file.

1. Using Notepad, type in the code used to run a Contributor macro. This code is available in the IBM Cognos help files.

2. Save the file as a batch file (.bat) file.

3. Use the Windows scheduling tool or another third party tool to schedule the execution of the batch file.

Controlling rights to administrative functions

Access to administrative functions in the Contributor Administration Console such as synchronizing an application or publishing data is granted by assigning Access Rights to groups or roles to perform these functions. For example, members of the Planning Rights Administration group may assign rights to other administrators to import data or run Go to Productions for specific contributor applications.

In this section, we will look at some of the typical functions that can be performed in the Contributor Administration Console, and how groups and roles can be added so that they can be assigned rights to perform these functions.

Typical operations that can be assigned rights

In this section, we show some of the typical operations that an administrator can perform in the Contributor Administration Console. Groups and roles can be added and assigned rights to perform these operations.

To facilitate the process of assigning rights, these operations can be filtered at the different levels shown:

- Planning Administration Domain
- Datastore
- Application
- View Publish Container
- Table-only Publish Container
- Application Folder
- Job Cluster
- Job Server
- Macro
- Link

The typical operations are listed below:

- Run Go to Production for an application
- Set an application online or offline
- Set an application as a source or a target for Administration Links
- Remove applications from the PAD
- Assign or remove applications to an application folder
- Link to a publish container
- Create a publish container
- Configure the Web Client for an application
- Maintain an application
- Work with an e.List and rights for an application
- Work with Access Tables and Saved Selections for an application

- Import data to an application

- Synchronize an application with Analyst

- Create Translations for an application

- Publish data from an application

- Delete Annotations from an application

- Add a job cluster

- Add a job server

- Edit a macro

- Execute a macro

As you can see, Access Rights can be assigned to a group or role to perform most administrative tasks in the Contributor Administration Console.

Assigning Access Rights

In this section, we will show how Access Rights can be assigned to groups and roles so that Contributor Administrators can perform administrative tasks in the Contributor Administration Console.

Adding groups and roles

Before rights can be assigned to a group or role, they need to be added in the Contributor Administration Console. Imagine that we want to assign a group of rights to perform a Go to Production on the ABC application. We must first add the group, if it does not already exist, in the Contributor Administration Console then we assign that group rights to perform the Go to Production.

We have created a group called ABC Application Update that we want to assign these rights to. To add the group so we can assign the rights:

1. In the **Contributor Administration** Console, click on **Access Rights.**

2. Click on **Add**, as shown in the screenshot:

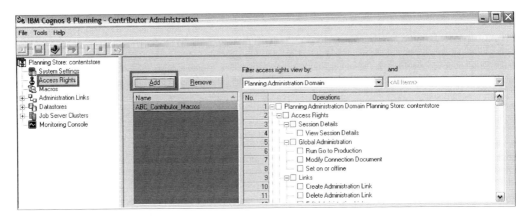

3. A box will appear showing the available namespaces. Click on **Cognos** and navigate to the group ABC Update Application.

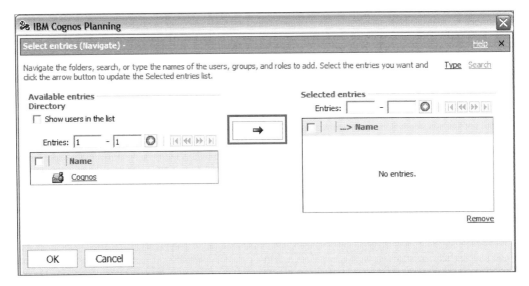

4. Check the box next to the group and click the green arrow to move it to the selected entries box.

5. Click on **OK**. The group has now been added and the right to run a Go to Production can now be assigned.

Assigning Access Rights to the group or role

To assign the Go to Production rights to the group for the ABC Application:

1. Click on **Access Rights** to view the groups available.

2. Select the group **ABC_Update_Application** in the left pane.

3. Click on the down arrow for the **Filter Access Rights view by** and select **Application** as shown:

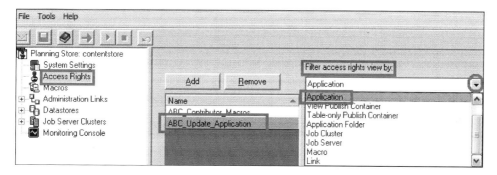

4. A list of applications and the Access Rights available for these applications will be displayed. Under **Application ABC**, place a checkbox against **Run Go to Production** as shown:

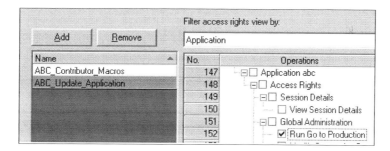

5. Click on the **Save** button on the menu bar.

6. The following box will appear stating the Access Rights have been successfully updated.

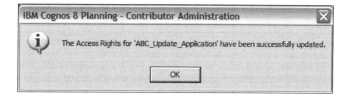

Administrators who are members of this group will now be able to run a Go to Production for the ABC Application.

Cascading rights

You will be prompted to cascade rights down when you assign rights at the higher levels such at the PAD level, the Datastore level, or the Job Cluster level. If you say yes, any objects, such as, applications that sit on the datastore, for example, will be assigned the same rights assigned at the higher level. When you assign rights at the higher levels, groups will automatically be assigned rights to subordinate objects that are added at a later date, whether you cascade them down or not.

Monitoring jobs and managing Job Servers

In this section, we will explore what jobs are, how they can be monitored in the Contributor Administration Console and how they can be managed by the Contributor Administrator.

Administrative activities or tasks such as a prepare import, reconcile, or publish are called jobs and these run on single or multiple job servers. When a prepare import is being executed, a prepare import job runs on the job servers. This job is split into job items for each e.List item. If you run a prepare import job for an application that contains 10 e.List items, there will be 10 job items. To increase the performance of jobs, additional job servers can be added that will pick up the different job items. This will speed up the processing time of the job being executed.

All application and publish datastores must be added to a job server or job cluster, so that any jobs related to these objects can be processed.

Typical jobs

The following table shows some of the different types of jobs that are run when certain administrative tasks are executed.

Job Name	Description
Cut-down models	This job will create Cut-down models.
Cut-down tidy	This job removes any Cut-down models that are no longer needed.
Export queue tidy	This job will remove any items from the export queue that are out of date and obsolete.
Import queue tidy	This job will remove any data blocks from the import queue that are no longer needed.
Inter-app links	This job runs when an administration link is executed and transfers data between applications.
Prepare import	This job will prepare the import data blocks for each e.List item in preparation for the reconciliation process that updates the application with the latest imported data. This job runs when data is imported into the application.
Publish	This job runs when a view only layout publish is executed.
Reconcile	This job will ensure the application is up-to-date.
Reporting publish	This job runs when a table-only layout publish is executed.
Validate users	This job will ensure the current owner or editor of an e.List node has the right to access that node.

Monitoring jobs

When jobs are executed, their progress can be monitored in the **Job Management** screen or the **Monitoring Console**. Both of these can be accessed in the Contributor Administration Console as shown:

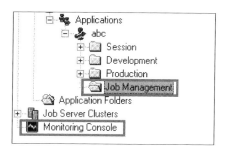

The Job Management screen

The following is a screenshot of the **Job Management** screen:

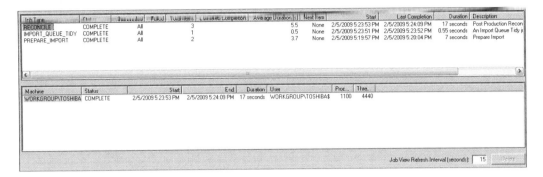

The **Job Management** screen displays the following information:

- **Job Type**: This column shows any jobs that are currently running, queued, or the most recently completed jobs.

- **Status**: This column shows the status of a job. The following are all the possible job statuses:

Job status	Description
CANCELLED	The job was cancelled.
COMPLETE	The job has successfully completed.
CREATING	The job is being created.
QUEUED	The job has been queued and is waiting to be picked up by a job server.
READY	The job has been created and is ready to be executed.
RUNNING	The job is currently running on the job servers.

- **Succeeded** and **Failed**: These columns show whether a job has succeeded or failed.

- **Estimated Completion**: This column shows what the expected completion time is going to be.

- **Start** and **Last Completion**: These columns show when the job last started and the last completion time and date.

- **Duration**: This column shows how long the job took to run.

- **Description**: This column briefly describes what the job does.

Because publish jobs are administrative processes that target the publish containers, you need to click on the drop-down arrow in the **Job Management** screen and select the publish table to monitor publish jobs.

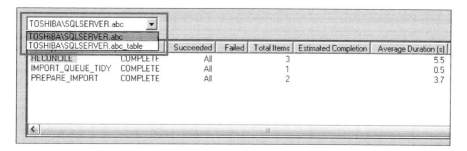

The bottom pane gives you some additional information on the servers that the jobs are executing on.

When in the **Job Management** screen, double-click on the failed job to access more information on the cause of the failure. Additionally, access the `planningerrorlog` file for even more information on the failed job.

The Monitoring Console

The Monitoring Console makes it easier to monitor jobs by splitting the different processes into five categories represented by tabs as shown:

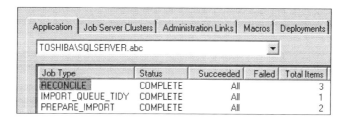

The categories are:

- **Application**: This screen is similar to the **Job Management** screen explained above.

- **Job Server Clusters**: This tab gives you a snapshot of what objects and job tasks are being processed on a job cluster and server. The following screenshot shows **Job Server Clusters**:

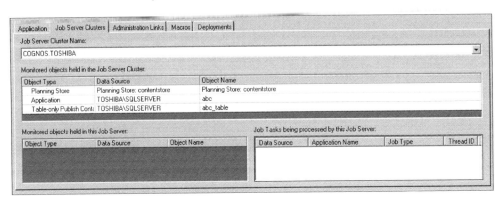

- **Administration Links**: This tab shows you the progress of any jobs running when administration links have been executed.

- **Macros**: This tab will allow you to monitor the status of macros.

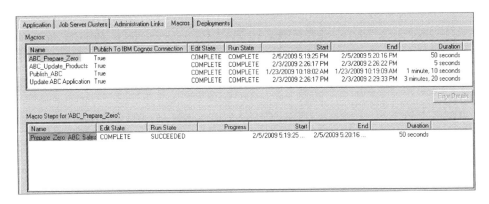

- **Deployments:** This tab will display the run state and progress of the import or exports of deployment packages.

Managing Job Clusters

In this section, we will explain how to add job clusters and job servers. Before you can process any administrative tasks such as reconciliation or publish, you must create a job server cluster and add job servers to it so that jobs can be executed.

You can also add additional job servers to an environment to improve processing power and job performance.

Adding a Job Cluster

To add a job cluster:

1. In the **Contributor Administration** Console, right-click on **Job Server Clusters** and click on **Add Job Server Cluster...** as shown:

2. When the **Add Job Server** box appears, type in a name for the job cluster.
3. Click on **Add**.

Now that the Job Cluster has been added, we add the **Job Server**.

Adding a Job Server

To add a Job Server:

1. Under the **Job Cluster** just added, right-click **Job Server** and click on **Add Job Server** as shown:

2. When the **Add Job Server** box appears, from the drop-down box select the server you want to add to the cluster.
3. Click on **Add**.

Now that the job clusters and job servers have been added, you will need to add to them the Planning Store and any applications and publish datastores that you want to process jobs for. You can either add these objects to the cluster or to individual job servers.

Adding objects to a Job Cluster

To add objects to a Job Cluster:

1. Select the name of the Job Cluster in the tree.
2. In the right pane under **Monitored Objects**, click on **Add**.
3. In the **Monitor Objects** box, highlight any objects that you wish to add.

[💡 Use the *Shift* button to select multiple objects.]

4. Click **Add**.

Adding objects to a Job Server

To add objects to a Job Server:

1. Under the **Job Server**, click on the **Monitored Objects** folder.
2. Click on **Add**.
3. In the **Monitor Objects** box, highlight any objects that you wish to add.
4. Click on **Add**.

Removing Job Servers

To remove a Job Server:

1. Right-click the **Job Server**.
2. Select **Delete Job Server**.

Removing Job Clusters

To remove a Job Cluster:

1. Right-click on the **Job Server Cluster**.
2. Select **Delete Job Server Cluster**.

Removing objects from a Job Cluster or Job Server

1. Click on the **Job Cluster** or **Job Server**.
2. In the right pane, highlight the object you want to remove.
3. Click on **Remove**.

Summary

In this chapter, you learned how to automate repetitive tasks such as import and publish of data by creating macros. You learned how to schedule these macros to run in IBM Cognos Connection or from a batch file.

The second half of the chapter briefly recapped how access to perform operation in the Contributor Administration Console can be configured. We finished with a recap on how a contributor application can be secured.

16
Maintaining Security

This chapter summarizes the area of IBM Cognos Planning security. Much of the subject of Analyst and Contributor security has been covered in depth in Chapters 14 and 15, respectively.

We begin this chapter with an overview of IBM Cognos Planning security explaining the following security concepts and areas:

- Authentication and authorization
- Users, groups, and roles
- IBM Cognos namespace

The second half of this chapter recapitulates how security is configured in Analyst and Contributor.

Overview of security in IBM Cognos Planning

In this section, we will look at how users access IBM Cognos Planning through authentication and gain access to IBM Cognos Planning resources through authorization. We'll also explore how users, groups, and roles fit in with IBM Cognos Planning security. Finally, we will briefly look at the IBM Cognos Planning 8 namespace.

Authentication and authorization

Let's look at how authentication and authorization fits in with IBM Cognos Planning security.

Authentication

By default, when security is not configured in IBM Cognos Planning, anyone can access the system. Alternatively, IBM Cognos Security can be configured to use a third party authentication provider to validate user logins by adding the third party authentication provider as a namespace.

When you log in to a network, you must provide a username and password. Your user name and password, also known as your login credentials, are stored in an authentication provider. The authentication provider will validate the login information you provided when you try to access the system to ensure that you have Access Rights. IBM Cognos 8 security sits on top of this. When you try to access IBM Cognos Planning, the system will first check your login credentials that are stored in the authentication provider. If they are valid, you will have access to the system.

Authorization

Now that you have access to IBM Cognos Planning, the next step is to define what you can and cannot do when you are authenticated in the system. Authorization to the different components and functionality of the IBM Cognos Planning System are defined by granting users, groups or roles access to the different components and functionality of IBM Cognos 8.

Users, groups, and roles

In this section, we explore the concept of users, groups and roles in IBM Cognos Planning security.

Users

Users represent the individuals or system accounts that should have access to the system. These are created and stored in the authentication provider. Users are not created in IBM Cognos 8. To grant Access Rights to users, typically you can add them to a group or a role. You then assign that group or role access to the different components or functionality of IBM Cognos 8.

Groups

Groups are an assembly of users or other groups that have the same access permissions based on the fact that they are a member of the same organizational section or unit. For example: a business unit, cost centre, region, or department.

Roles

Roles are an assembly of users, groups, and other roles that are blended together because they have a common function to perform. For example: Analyst Administrators or Contributor Administrators roles.

IBM Cognos 8 namepace

Groups and roles can be created in the authentication provider and added to IBM Cognos 8 namespace. They can also be created in the IBM Cognos 8 namespace, or you can use the pre-built groups and roles that come with the IBM Cognos 8 namespace.

To view the contents of the IBM Cognos namespace

The IBM Cognos 8 namespace comes with a selection of pre-built groups and roles. You can perform the following steps to view these groups and roles (using IBM Cognos version 8.4):

1. Open IBM Cognos Connection.

2. Click on Administer IBM Cognos Content.

3. Click on the **Security** tab. You will see a list of all the namespaces available to you including the IBM Cognos 8 namespace.

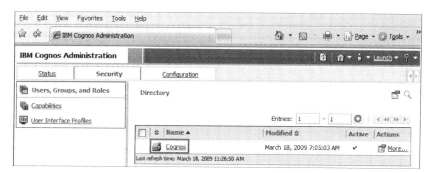

4. Click on the IBM **Cognos** namespace to view its contents.

The creation of groups and roles in the IBM Cognos 8 namespace is beyond the scope of this book.

IBM Cognos 8 namespace planning roles

The IBM Cognos 8 namespace comes with two planning roles—Planning Rights Administrator and Planning Contributor Users. These two roles can be included in your security model or you can delete them and build your own roles.

Planning Rights Administrator

Members of this role can access and perform administration functions and assign security to others in the Contributor and Analyst systems.

Planning Contributor Users

Members of this role can access the Contributor Web Client or Contributor for Excel. For a user to be able to access the Contributor Web Client and enter forecast data, the administrator must add them to a group that is a member of the Planning Contributor Users role.

Capabilities

Capabilities grant access to specific IBM Cognos components. A role should be granted permissions to a capability so that members of that role can access a particular planning component. The Planning Rights Administrator role has permissions to the Planning Administration capability allowing members of the Planning Rights Administrator role access the Analyst and Contributor systems. The Planning Contributor Role has permissions to the Planning Contributor capability allowing members of the Planning Contributor role to access the Contributor Web Client and Contributor for Excel.

The creation of capabilities is beyond the scope of this book.

Managing security profiles

In this section, we will briefly recap how system administrators manage security to Analyst and Contributor. We will look at how administrators can grant access to Analyst users to specific objects such as D-Cubes or D-Lists. We will also explore briefly how system administrators grant access to other administrators to perform various functions in the Contributor Administration Console.

Analyst security

In some cases, the default security settings in Analyst may be sufficient. This may be the case where an environment may consist of a very small number of Analyst users. However, in an environment where there are many users accessing Analyst, it is typical to configure Analyst security to control which libraries these users have access to. Additionally, access to Analyst objects such as D-Cubes and D-Lists and D-List items can also be set.

The system administrator can assign security at library level, object level and D-List item level.

Assigning security at the library level

The process of assigning security at library level is covered in depth in the latter section of Chapter 14. To summarize, a system administrator assigns access to Analyst libraries by performing the following tasks:

1. The system administrator ensures that the user is a member of the group or role that they should have access to the library. He can confirm this in IBM Cognos Connection or the Authentication provider.

2. The group or role is added to Analyst.

    a. Click on **File | Administration | Maintain Libraries and Users**.
    b. Click on the **User | Groups and Roles** tab.
    c. Click on **Add**.
    d. Navigate through the namespace to the groups or roles and add them to Analyst.

3. The group or role is subsequently assigned read, write, or control rights to the library.

    a. On the **Analyst** menu bar, click **File | Administration | Maintain Libraries and Users**.
    b. In the **Libraries** tab, highlight the library that you want to assign Access Rights to.
    c. Click on **Properties**.
    e. Click on the **Access** tab.
    f. Click on **Add**.
    g. In the **Give Access to...** box, add the group or role you want to assign access to.
    h. Set the access level to read, write, or control.
    i. Click on **OK**.

Assigning security at object level

The system administrator can assign access to an object or a selection of objects such as D-Cubes or D-Lists. Carry out the following steps to assign access to the ABC Sales D-Cube.

1. On the **Analyst** menu bar, click on **File | Library | D-Cubes**.

2. Highlight the ABC D-Cube.

3. Right-click and select **Define Access** from the menu.

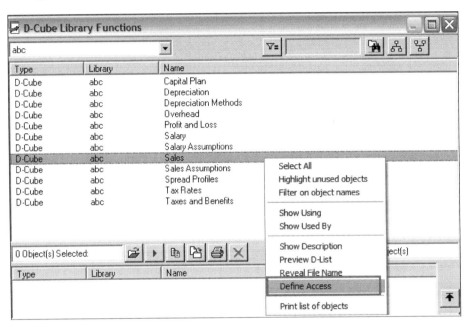

4. The **Add Access to Object** screen pops up. Click on **Add**.

5. Add the group or role and assign them read, write, or control access.

6. Click on **OK**.

Assigning security at item level

The system administrator can also assign access to an item by using masks. For example, imagine that you have a Payroll D-Cube that contains a line for salaries. If you want to conceal these salaries from certain Analysts that have access to this D-Cube, you can use a mask and apply it to the item Salaries in the D-List. This is a two step process. First add the groups or roles to the mask then you apply that mask to the item or group of items in the D-List. Masks can be applied to a single object or a group of objects. The security applied is Read, Write, or Invisible as shown:

Access Level	Description
Read	Items can only be viewed not edited by the user. However, values can be changed through breakback by the user.
Write	Items can be edited by the user.
Invisible	Items are hidden from the user.

You can create and apply a mask to a D-List item using the following steps:

1. Create the Mask

    a. On the **Analyst** menu bar, click on **File | Administration | Maintain | Libraries and Users**.

    b. Click on the **Masks** tab.

    c. Click on **Add**.

    d. In the **Add New Group** screen, move the group or role from the left pane to the right pane. Use one of the three buttons between the two panes to specify the level of access.

    e. Click on **OK**. You will now see the mask in the **Masks** screen.

2. Apply the mask to a D-List Item.

    a. Open the D-List that you want to apply the mask to.

    b. On the **Analyst** menu bar, click on **D-List**, options then select the **Security** tab.

    c. In the **Multiple Assignment** section, use the drop-down to select the mask.

    d. Click on the **Assign** button to assign it to D-List items.

    e. Click on **OK**.

Contributor security

In this section, we will summarize the topic of Contributor security that was explained in depth in Chapter 15.

The configuration of security in Contributor involves the following:

*   Assigning Access Rights to administrators to perform administrative functions within the Contributor Administration Console

*   Managing Macro security

*   Managing access to the Contributor application

Access Rights

Access Rights are assigned by the Contributor system administrator to other Contributor administrators so that they can perform administrative tasks. These tasks may involve configuration of the application such as synchronization or GTP, data imports, and publishing of data.

Any member of the Planning Rights Administration group can assign Access Rights. Access Rights are assigned to members of groups or roles for specific operations. These rights can also be set at various levels, for example, the Planning Administration Domain, datastores, applications, job cluster, or job server.

Please see Chapter 15 for a detailed explanation of the process of assigning Access Rights and for the list operations that rights can be assigned for.

The following steps summarize how you can assign Access Rights to a group or role:

1. Click on **Access Rights** to see the groups available. You can add a group or role if you need to (please see Chapter 15 for the steps for this process).
2. Highlight the group or role you want to assign rights to.
3. Filter on the level that you want to assign rights to such as application or job server.
4. Check the operations that you want to assign the rights for.
5. Click on **Save**, and then click on **OK**.

Macro security

Users can be granted rights to create, edit, delete, transfer, and execute contributor macros. Only members of the Planning Rights Administrator group can grant or revoke Access Rights to macros.

Controlling access to the Contributor application

Access to the contributor application is managed by assigning groups and roles access to an e.List. A detailed explanation on how to secure an application can be found in Chapter 10. In this section, we will summarize the process.

The first step of assigning rights for a user to a contributor application is to place them as a member of a group. This group is then imported into the Contributor Administration Console and assigned rights to an e.List. These rights can be assigned to the entire e.List, a single node or to a portion of an e.List. The available rights that can be assigned are submit, view, edit, and review depending on the role within the forecasting process.

Summary

In this chapter, we have explained the topic of IBM Cognos security explaining the concepts of authentication, authorization, and the IBM Cognos 8 namespace.

The second half of the chapter briefly recapped how to gain access to perform the operation in the Contributor.

Administration console can be configured. We finished with a recap on how a contributor application can be secured.

Index

business users 28

C

CAC 19, 210
calculation D-List 100
CamNamespaceName 218
CamObjectName 217
CamObjectType 218
changes, impact
  e.List, changes 299
  dimension for publish, changes 295
  model, changes 295
client extensions, Contributor extensions
  about 205
  data, importing 207
  Export to Excel extension 207
  Print to Excel extension 205, 206
Cognos
  planning with 7
Cognos Analyst 21
Cognos Business Intelligent (BI) tools
  IBM Cognos Connection Web Portal 18
  IBM Cognos Event Studio 18
  IBM Cognos Framework Manager 18
  IBM CognosMetricDesignerandMetricStudio 18
  IBM CognosReportingStudios 18
Cognos Contributor 21
Cognos Finance <> Analyst D-Link
  creating 158
Cognos package
  data, importing from 157
  using, as source 157, 158
Cognos Planning
  about 7, 13
  access levels 220
  application data, securing 220
  benefits 14
  Corporate Performance Management (CPM) 13
  data validation feature 227, 228
  data validation feature, configuring 228
Cognos Planning Contributor
  using as data source, in Framework Manager 297, 298
Cognos Planning System, Contributor

Administration Console
  Access Rights, Console Tree location 170
  Datastores, Console Tree location 170
  Datastores, menu location
  jobs, Console Tree location 170
  job server cluster, Console Tree location 171
  job servers, Console Tree location 171
  planning store, Console Tree location 169
  settings 168
  system settings, Console Tree location 170
  system settings, Console Tree used 169
  working, steps 168
collaborative
  versus confrontational 9
common library 61
confrontational
  versus collaborative 9
connection web portal, IBM Cognos 25
Console Tree location, Contributor Administration Console
  Access Rights 170
  administration links 175
  application folders 175
  console, montoring 176
  Datastores 170
  Datastores/containers, publishing 175
  job cluster 171
  jobs 170
  job server cluster 171
  job servers 171
  Macros 175
  planning store 169
  system, settings 169, 170
consolidation
  versus version control 11
Contributor
  about 210
  to Analyst D-Link, creating 156
  to Contributor D-Link, creating 157
  using, in Excel 279
Contributor Administration Console. See also CAC
Contributor Administration Console
  about 163
  Access Rights, assigning 355
  Access Rights, assigning to groups 357, 358

X

Y

Z

Thank you for buying
IBM Cognos 8 Planning

About Packt Publishing

Packt, pronounced 'packed', published its first book "*Mastering phpMyAdmin for Effective MySQL Management*" in April 2004 and subsequently continued to specialize in publishing highly focused books on specific technologies and solutions.

Our books and publications share the experiences of your fellow IT professionals in adapting and customizing today's systems, applications, and frameworks. Our solution based books give you the knowledge and power to customize the software and technologies you're using to get the job done. Packt books are more specific and less general than the IT books you have seen in the past. Our unique business model allows us to bring you more focused information, giving you more of what you need to know, and less of what you don't.

Packt is a modern, yet unique publishing company, which focuses on producing quality, cutting-edge books for communities of developers, administrators, and newbies alike. For more information, please visit our web site: www.packtpub.com.

Writing for Packt

We welcome all inquiries from people who are interested in authoring. Book proposals should be sent to author@packtpub.com. If your book idea is still at an early stage and you would like to discuss it first before writing a formal book proposal, contact us; one of our commissioning editors will get in touch with you.

We're not just looking for published authors; if you have strong technical skills but no writing experience, our experienced editors can help you develop a writing career, or simply get some additional reward for your expertise.

SAP Business ONE Implementation

ISBN: 978-1-847196-38-5   Paperback: 320 pages

Bring the power of SAP Enterprise Resource Planning to your small-midsize business

1. Get SAP B1 up and running quickly, optimize your business, inventory, and manage your warehouse

2. Understand how to run reports and take advantage of real-time information

3. Complete an express implementation from start to finish

4. Real-world examples with step-by-step explanations

SOA Patterns with BizTalk Server 2009

ISBN: 978-1-847195-00-5   Paperback: 400 pages

Implement SOA strategies for BizTalk Server solutions

1. Discusses core principles of SOA and shows them applied to BizTalk solutions

2. The most thorough examination of BizTalk and WCF integration in any available book

3. Leading insight into the new WCF SQL Server Adapter, UDDI Services version 3, and ESB Guidance 2.0

Please check **www.PacktPub.com** for information on our titles

Small Business Server 2008
Installation, Migration, and Configuration

Set up and run your small business server making it deliver big business impact

David Overton

PACKT

Small Business Server 2008: Installation, Migration, and Configuration

ISBN: 978-1-847196-30-9   Paperback: 408 pages

Set up and run your small business server making it deliver big business impact

1. Step-by-step guidance through the installation and configuration process with numerous pictures

2. Successfully install SBS 2008 into your business, either as a new installation or by migrating from SBS 2003

3. Configure hosted web sites for public and secure information exchange using Office Live for Small Business and Office Live Workspaces

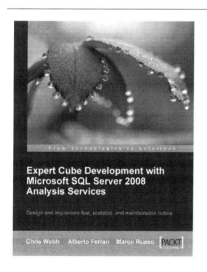

Expert Cube Development with
Microsoft SQL Server 2008
Analysis Services

Design and implement fast, scalable, and maintainable cubes

Chris Webb   Alberto Ferrari   Marco Russo   PACKT

Expert Cube Development with Microsoft SQL Server 2008 Analysis Services

ISBN: 978-1-847197-22-1   Paperback: 360 pages

Design and implement fast, scalable and maintainable cubes

1. A real-world guide to designing cubes with Analysis Services 2008

2. Model dimensions and measure groups in BI Development Studio

3. Implement security, drill-through, and MDX calculations

4. Learn how to deploy, monitor, and performance-tune your cube

Please check **www.PacktPub.com** for information on our titles

7702653R0

Made in the USA
Lexington, KY
11 December 2010